AMERICAN LITERARY NATURALISM AND ITS TWENTIETH-CENTURY TRANSFORMATIONS

AMERICAN LITERARY

Frank Norris,

NATURALISM AND ITS

Ernest Hemingway,

TWENTIETH-CENTURY

Don DeLillo

TRANSFORMATIONS

PAUL CIVELLO

The University of Georgia Press . Athens and London

© 1994 by the University of Georgia Press
Athens, Georgia 30602
All rights reserved
Designed by Betty Palmer McDaniel
Set in ten on fourteen Janson Text
by Tseng Information Systems, Inc.
Printed and bound by Thomson-Shore, Inc.
The paper in this book meets the guidelines for
permanence and durability of the Committee on
Production Guidelines for Book Longevity of the
Council on Library Resources.

Printed in the United States of America
98 97 96 95 94   C   5 4 3 2 1

Library of Congress Cataloging in Publication Data
Civello, Paul.
American literary naturalism and its twentieth-century
transformations : Frank Norris, Ernest Hemingway,
Don DeLillo / Paul Civello.
p. cm.
Includes bibliographical references (p.) and index.
ISBN 0-8203-1649-0 (alk. paper)
1. American fiction—20th century—History and criticism.
2. Hemingway, Ernest, 1899-1961—Criticism and interpretation.
3. Norris, Frank, 1870-1902—Criticism and interpretation.
4. DeLillo, Don—Criticism and interpretation.
5. Naturalism in literature.   I. Title.
PS374.N29C58   1994
813'.520912—dc20   93-41004

British Library Cataloging in Publication Data available

To Wendy and Tony

CONTENTS

EIGHT

Fields, Systems, and DeLillo's
Postmodern Transformation of Literary Naturalism

NINE

End Zone: The End of the Old Order

TEN

Libra: Undoing the Naturalistic Novel

ACKNOWLEDGMENTS

I would like to thank, above all, Richard Lehan for his critical comments, suggestions, and encouragement throughout this project. He is a model of professional decency and dedication. I would also like to thank Robin Gajdusek for his support for my work and, more important, for his enthusiasm for Hemingway and Hemingway scholarship, which could not help but be an influence. Thanks also to Donald Pizer, Don Graham, and Joseph R. McElrath, Jr., for their kindness and inspiration, as well as their criticism, and to Maximillian Novak and Lucia Re, both of whom read and commented on an early draft of the manuscript. I also deeply appreciate the work of Nancy Grayson Holmes, Kim Cretors, Madelaine Cooke, Debbie Winter, and the rest of the editorial staff at the University of Georgia Press.

I must also acknowledge Macmillan Publishing Company for permitting me to quote from Ernest Hemingway's novels *The Sun Also Rises* and *A Farewell to Arms*, as well as the nonfiction work *Death in the Afternoon*, and Viking Penguin Inc. for permitting me to quote from Don DeLillo's novels *End Zone* and *Libra*. An earlier version of Chapter 10 appeared in *Arizona Quarterly* 48.2 (Summer 1992): 33–56.

Finally, I would like to express my gratitude to my wife, Wendy, for her support and love. Books, indeed, are for the scholar's idle times.

AMERICAN LITERARY NATURALISM AND ITS TWENTIETH-CENTURY TRANSFORMATIONS

INTRODUCTION

American literary naturalism is not of a piece. Like most sweeping literary movements (Romanticism and modernism come immediately to mind), naturalism resists any set definition we may try to impose on it. In fact, Charles Child Walcutt begins his seminal work on naturalism, *American Literary Naturalism: A Divided Stream*, by conceding the impossibility of such a definition. He compares the movement to Proteus; naturalism, he says, is "of a Protean slipperiness," changing form before we can grasp it with our critical apparatuses, before we can trap it within our interpretive paradigms.[1] Indeed, we see great divergence among the early works of literary naturalism. The Spencerian universe depicted in Dreiser's *Sister Carrie*, for example, is far different from the LeContean universe in Norris's *Octopus;* so too is the former's urban milieu from the latter's rural setting. And humanity's battles with the capitalist economic forces in both those novels differ markedly from its battles with the forces of nature in London's works, or, for that matter, from its battles with the "red animal" of war in Crane's *Red Badge of Courage.* Even among the works of an individual author, there is divergence. As we shall see, Norris depicts two different responses to Darwinism in *Vandover and the Brute* and *The Octopus.*

As might be expected, this divergence within American literary naturalism extends to the criticism that surrounds it, criticism that has accrued substantially over the past forty years. Literary critics who have dealt with naturalism can, I think, be usefully divided into four broad and often overlapping groups: early theorists, history-of-ideas critics, European-influence critics, and recent theorists. The early theorists, preeminently Charles Child Walcutt and Donald Pizer, tended to view naturalism thematically and in terms of literary technique.[2] The history-of-ideas critics, of whom Pizer is also in the forefront, examined American literary naturalism against the background of the late nineteenth-century scientific, philo-sophical, and literary milieu.[3] They felt, and still feel, that naturalism is best understood as an expression of the central ideas of that era. The European-influence critics, of course, have traced the influence of nineteenth-century European writers—particularly Zola—on their American naturalistic pro-tégés.[4] And recent theorists, who have been responsible for the current burgeoning of criticism on American literary naturalism, have either re-conceptualized naturalism as a narrative form, or denied its existence or usefulness as a category.[5]

This book is an attempt to work the ground left vacant by the early theorists and history-of-ideas critics, on the one hand, and the recent theo-rists—particularly the New Historicists—on the other. For, as I see it, the main shortcoming of the early and recent critics is that, despite their dif-ferent methodologies, both conceive of naturalism either as a static form largely confined to the late nineteenth century, or as a literary anachronism in the twentieth.[6] With one exception, neither view naturalism as a narra-tive mode closely aligned with historical processes, one that is developed and transformed as it moves through time.[7]

My argument, then, is twofold. First, it is based on the assumption that the narrative reality of naturalism is grounded in contemporary construc-tions of "reality"—particularly scientific and philosophical constructions. As such, naturalism concerns itself with a central post-Darwinian crisis: the collapse of humanity's conception of an order in the material world, an order that had formerly imbued that world with meaning. Naturalism, I argue, depicts the rift that opens as a result between the self and the ma-terial world—now perceived as one of meaningless, indifferent force—and points toward a resolution of it. My argument also propounds that as natu-ralism moves forward through time—that is, as it is "re-presented" in mod-ern and postmodern texts—it is transformed markedly. I argue, in effect, that terms such as "naturalism," "modernism," and "postmodernism"—terms usually used to denote separate narrative forms—prove too exclu-sive, that, in fact, there is a "modern" naturalism and a "postmodern" naturalism. These "naturalisms" confront the newer scientific paradigms of the early twentieth-century human sciences and the later constructs of the new physics and systems theory, just as late nineteenth-century natu-ralism had confronted Darwinian and post-Darwinian "reality."

Frank Norris, my example of nineteenth-century naturalism, depicts in his work what I call the post-Darwinian condition: the rift between the self and the material world that Darwinism produced. Here the material world is nature, both humanity's biological nature and its biological environment. Darwinism had effectively destroyed the Enlightenment conception of a divinely created, ordered universe in which human beings—also divinely created—could feel "at home"; in addition, it had destroyed any ordering structure through which they could subsume their "bestial" nature to their moral and spiritual selves. In *Vandover and the Brute*, Norris depicts a man caught in this new world of deterministic force in which the traditional order and ordering structures have collapsed. Vandover becomes a victim of nature, succumbing, à la Zola, to a biologically determined mental illness. In *The Octopus*, however, Norris presents a different response to this post-Darwinian condition; in effect, Norris reinvests meaning into the natural world by reestablishing God in it. While there is initially a rift between the self and nature, it is only a perceived rift, not an actual one. Human beings need only learn to perceive the divine presence that lies immanent within the natural world in order to be reconciled to it.

Ernest Hemingway, a distinctly "modern" writer, nevertheless exhibits several features of literary naturalism in his work: the collapse of the old order that had imbued the material world with meaning, the subsequent rift between the self and that material world, and the struggle to reconcile the two. His work, however, shows a marked departure from the naturalism exhibited in Norris's *Octopus* in that the self no longer *perceives* an order in the material world—for there is none—but *creates* its own. This exemplifies the modernist belief in consciousness as an ordering principle; the Hemingway hero puts forth consciousness in the face of destructive natural force (of which war, as we shall see, is a part). He imbues existence with a personal, rather than divine, meaning. Such a meaning, however, must be firmly grounded in his experience in the material world; it must not be based on an abstraction. In *A Farewell to Arms*, the order that Frederic Henry creates for himself and Catherine, an order that apotheosizes love to an absolute and that therefore possesses an affinity with the collapsed Christian paradigm, fails in this regard. It is an order that attempts to separate them from the natural, biological world—an impossibility—rather than reconciling them to it, and they fall victim to the "biological trap." Yet in *The Sun Also Rises*, Jake Barnes slowly learns to "live in it," to create an order that gives meaning to existence *within* a world of indifferent material force. He learns, in other words, how to create his own personal order that is not belied by experience.

Don DeLillo also depicts a rift between the self and the material world — in this case, the postmodern, "built" environment that has grown in complexity beyond humanity's comprehension. Yet the collapse of the old order is here a collapse of the old cause-and-effect scientific paradigm — precisely that which Zola, Norris, and the other nineteenth-century literary naturalists had embraced. DeLillo's material world is not one of linear causality, but one of interconnecting systems. The self, then, does not stand in relation to a material world in which it must perceive a spiritual order (as in Norris), nor does it create an order that enables it to live in the material world (as in Hemingway), but instead it is itself a part of that systems order, inextricable from it. There is no separation between subject and object, and therefore no "objective" reality. This condition creates a new dilemma for the self: how to find meaning in a world that is ultimately unknowable, a world in which order lies beyond one's rational comprehension. In *End Zone*, Gary Harkness and several other characters try to apply the obsolete linear paradigm to experience, to events in the material world, and as a result remain isolated from that world, trapped within their own paradigm that gives them an inaccurate picture of reality. In *Libra*, Nicholas Branch, Lee Harvey Oswald, and others attempt the same thing with similar results. Yet, more important, *Libra* depicts the end of the Zolaesque "experimental novel" in which the novelist can stand apart from his "experiment" and watch it unfold objectively. DeLillo presents us in *Libra* with what he himself calls "a new map of the world,"[8] one that undermines the scientific foundation of Zola's and Norris's naturalism, and that therefore "undoes" the naturalistic novel.

I have chosen in this study to focus on six novels — two from each of the three authors — rather than attempt to cover each author's entire canon. While there are certain limitations to this approach, there are also certain advantages. By examining closely a few representative texts in light of my conceptual paradigm, I hope to elucidate the complexities and nuances of those works as they pertain to it, and at the same time to avoid reducing them to an undifferentiated mass, and my conceptual paradigm to a Procrustean bed. I have purposely selected two texts from each author that exhibit marked differences in the depiction of the naturalistic dilemma and in the transformation of the naturalistic form. As a rule, the first text focuses on the collapse of the old order and the self's inability to come to terms with it; the second text points toward a successful resolution of the metaphysical crisis. The exception here is DeLillo's *Libra,* which does not attempt to resolve the crisis internally—that is, within the novel's dramatic context—but rather puts forth a new paradigm that helps us to rethink it. I have also begun each of the three parts of this study with a chapter that attempts to ground each author's work—and each author's transformation of literary naturalism—in a broader transformation of humanity's conception of itself and the universe.

CHAPTER ONE

MAN, GOD, AND NATURAL LAW:

DARWINISM AND THE

DARWINIAN DEBATE

Religion is primarily a social phenomenon. Churches may owe their origin to teachers with strong individual convictions, but these teachers have seldom had much influence upon the churches that they founded, whereas churches have had enormous influence upon the communities in which they flourished.

BERTRAND RUSSELL

Charles Darwin was certainly no founder of a church, but he was the founder of a scientific theory that had a profound effect on late nineteenth-century humanity and its conception of itself, of nature, and of God. Yet, as with the church founder, Darwin's direct influence beyond the strictly biological field was overshadowed by the various and often contradictory permutations and interpretations of his theory of evolution—Darwin's "church," to extend the analogy. And as the founding of a church inevitably produces a virulent backlash from the old orthodoxy, a backlash that often helps popularize the new church and extend its influence, so too did the publication of *The Origin of Species* in 1859 spark an outcry and foment a debate that took Darwin's theory beyond the field of biology—where Darwin the founder had intended it to remain—and into such diverse fields as philosophy, sociology, economics, theology, and, of course, literature.

Darwin's theory in itself was not a general theory of evolution at all, but a specific theory of biological evolution. There had been several evolutionary theorists before Darwin, and some, such as the geologist Charles Lyell, had been successful in explaining the dynamics of evolution in the inorganic world.[1] There had even been several proponents of organic evolution, but no one, not even Lamarck, could give a plausible explanation of how such an organic process would work.[2] Darwin provided an explanation and, in so doing, succeeded for the first time in explaining organic phenomena in natural, rather than in supernatural, terms. Darwin was aware of Thomas Malthus's *Essay on the Principle of Population* (1798; rev. ed. 1803),[3] a study that indicated that population growth would outstrip food supply if it were not held in check by various natural factors such as famine and disease, and had himself observed a wide range of morphological variation among individuals within each species. As a result, Darwin reasoned that in the competition for food and subsistence—in the "struggle for existence," as he termed it—those individuals within each species with advantageous variations would be more apt to survive and thus reproduce, passing their traits down to their offspring. Darwin's two major discoveries, the two keys to this dynamic process, were those of randomly occurring variations in offspring and what he called "natural selection."

Darwin knew nothing of genetics—Gregor Mendel's groundbreaking genetic study of pea plants, although begun before the publication of *The Origin of Species*, was not widely known until the turn of the century—and therefore he could not account for the mechanism of variation, only affirm its existence.[4] He suspected, however, that it had something to do with reproduction and that it was haphazard. In this he was amazingly prescient, for our modern knowledge of genetics confirms that morphological variation is genetically and therefore reproductively linked, and that the primary cause is random genetic mutation.[5] It is a process of accident upon accident, and it provides the material on which natural selection operates. In natural selection, nature (i.e., the environment) "selects" which variations are indeed advantageous to survival in that particular environment. Individuals with deleterious traits are destroyed, and those with beneficial ones live to reproduce, preserving the trait within the species. Over time, the interconnected processes of random variation and natural selection will generate new, divergent species from a common stock.

Although Darwin carefully avoided metaphysical speculation in *The Origin of Species*, the metaphysical implications of his theory were clear. Darwinism was implicitly an assault on traditional Christian orthodoxy and on the view of humanity and nature that that orthodoxy maintained, and thus many of Darwin's contemporaries found it completely unacceptable. For one thing, Darwinism seemed to deny teleology, to deny a design and hence to deny a rational "first cause" of natural phenomena. The very nature of randomly occurring variations—in other words, variations via accident— argues against teleology, against design. Design is, by definition, *not* accidental. Moreover, the process of Darwinian evolution is itself "purposiveless"; were evolution synonymous with progress (as many would claim), then evolution would perhaps argue design. Yet it is important to realize that Darwinian evolution is not primarily progressive, but adaptive. It is progressive only in so far as it moves a species toward greater adaptability to a particular environment, not—as would often be claimed—toward an idealistic higher form. When Darwin speaks of "improvement" of a species, it is this adaptability to which he is referring; in Darwinian evolution, the highest form of life in a tropical swamp could very well be a frog.

Of course, arguing against design and disproving design are two different things, a distinction that would not be lost on many religiously minded supporters of Darwin. But, as Cynthia Eagle Russett points out, while Darwinism could not disprove design, it did render it an "unnecessary hypothesis."[6] Natural phenomena could now be explained solely in naturalistic terms with no need to appeal to the supernatural or religious. In fact, this refutation of the argument by design, of teleology in natural process, attacked the foundation of religious orthodoxy; it attacked God Himself. Without design there need be no designer. The clergyman Charles Hodge enunciated this realization and the fear it produced in his essay "What Is Darwinism?" when he claimed that the essence of Darwin's theory was the rejection of "teleology, or the doctrine of final causes. . . . the denial of design in nature is virtually the denial of God."[7] Darwinism, logically considered, effectively banished God from nature, banished the "Creator" from His own "creation."

Thus Darwinism presented a very different world than that of orthodox Christianity. The Darwinian universe was an indifferent universe; it was *not* an ordered, providential universe created and guided by a beneficent, if sometimes wrathful, personal deity. It was a universe propelled solely by impersonal, natural forces, forces "silently and insensibly working"[8] without need of a "sensible" first cause. Moreover, humans were no longer privileged, no longer the only organisms created in God's own image. Instead, they were just animals—albeit highly developed and successful ones. The individual, too, was no longer preeminent; only the preservation of the species was important in the overall scheme.

Darwinism had ramifications beyond the cataclysmic effect on the spiritual self such a philosophical realignment inevitably produced; it affected the moral self as well. By presenting a universe indifferent to human suffering and fate, Darwinism stripped the natural world of the comforting moral order with which traditional Christianity and even more recent religious sects had imbued it. Nature was no longer God's one true revelation, as the eighteenth-century Deists believed, nor was it a symbol of spirit, a spirit that was inherently good and virtuous, as Emerson and the Transcendentalists would have it. Rather, nature was amoral, a world in which individuals were neither rewarded nor punished for their moral conduct, but succeeded solely because of their physical "fitness" and their ability to adapt to environmental change. Thus nature no longer provided a model on which human beings could base their personal moral conduct or construct a moral order for society. Such a situation, if not rejected outright, could produce only two antipodal responses.

The first, and predominant, response was to subscribe to a strict determinism. According to this view, a human being was just one material phenomenon in a universe of material phenomena, and therefore his behavior was determined much like the behavior of chemicals in a chemical reaction: according to strict physical laws of cause and effect. Despite his protestations to the contrary, a human being had no free will, no moral freedom; he was a slave to natural forces. Thus humanity's relationship with nature split into paradox: on one hand, the individual as a physical, natural being was an intricate part of the natural world; on the other hand, the individual as a moral, rational, and spiritual being was torn and alienated from that world. Nature was no longer his friend, his mentor, his home; it was his slave-master who sought to undermine his human dignity and against whom he therefore had to struggle.

The second response, which while nascent in the nineteenth century would come to the fore in the twentieth, was to shift emphasis away from nature as a moral guide and toward the individual consciousness. Morality thus does not disappear; it becomes something self-created, something improvised as the self moves through experience in a morally alien world. Again, there is paradox: the individual as body is natural, at home in nature; the individual as mind, however, is a separate entity, self-consciously existing in a moral wasteland.

Since what makes one human—that is, what makes one unique from all other phenomena—is the mind, the rational, moral, and spiritual self (what from this point on I will refer to simply as the "self"), it is no wonder that the divorce between the mind and nature that Darwinism produced should have had a far more profound psychological impact on humanity than the intricate biological links between human beings and nature that Darwinism also established. The latter provided little solace, and therefore Darwinism spawned a need for reconciliation, a psychological need to reestablish humanity's rational, moral, and spiritual links with nature. Darwin himself was not immune to the psychological upheaval his own theory produced, and, as if presaging several interpreters of his theory that would follow him, Darwin at times in *The Origin of Species* seems to foist on nature and the natural process of evolution the mysticism that was formerly attributed solely to God. It is as if, having once and for all banished God from nature—God who, as creator of both humanity and nature, provided a link between the two—Darwin felt some impulse to reinstall Him within it. He calls the origin of species "that mystery of mysteries,"[9] and, in comparing natural selection to the artificial selection of animal breeders, he poses the rhetorical question:

> can we wonder, then, that nature's productions should be far "truer" in character than man's productions; that they should be infinitely better adapted to the most complex conditions of life, and should plainly bear the stamp of *far higher workmanship?* (my emphasis)[10]

Moreover, in addition to the mysticism, Darwin grants nature the beneficence of the Christian deity:

> When we reflect on this struggle [for existence], we may console ourselves with the full belief, that the war of nature is not incessant, that no fear is felt, that death is generally prompt, and that the vigorous, the healthy, and the happy survive and multiply.[11]

This impulse to deify nature, to reinstall the creator within the creation, would become the overriding concern of several of Darwin's interpreters, particularly in America during the latter half of the nineteenth century. It would be, in effect, an attempt at bridging the gap between the self and nature by reconciling evolution with Christianity, by assimilating Darwin's new theory of the natural world to the entrenched dogma of the Western mind. The various theories thus derived from Darwinism constitute in part what Morse Peckham has called "Darwinisticism."[12] It is this, as distinct from "Darwinism," that would have such profound effects in fields beyond the biological, including the literary.

Perhaps the most characteristic feature of Darwinisticism in all its permutations was the maintenance, at almost any philosophical cost, of an order external to the self, an order that the self does not create, but only perceives. It was, after all, order—rational, moral, and spiritual—that Darwinism had stripped from the natural world, and therefore it was perhaps inevitable that the initial response would be to reestablish that order in much the same form as it had formerly existed. The ordered cosmos had reflected the ordered self in the pre-Darwinian conception of the universe, providing a safe and comfortable "home" in which that self could exist; moreover, the conception of God as creator of both cosmos and self had reinforced the bond between the two and imbued it with a high moral and spiritual significance. Nature was a manifestation of the divine mind, and the human mind, created in the image of the divine, could perceive God through the study of His work, nature. Thus science became not only a rational but also a spiritual endeavor. This was true both for the eighteenth-century Deists and rationalists, for whom science revealed God's handiwork, His providential design, as well as for the mid nineteenth-century Transcendentalists, for whom science revealed God's presence informing physical phenomena. The belief in an absolute that lay behind an ordered cosmos had provided the self with much solace, integrating the self with its world as well as integrating its various facets. Thus Darwin's new vision of nature, a vision of a cosmos purposiveless and indifferent, had to be made to incorporate the old vision, one of a cosmos ordered, purposeful, and beneficent. This was, of course, logically impossible, but with a few deft philosophical leaps several scientists, philosophers, and theologians managed to succeed, at least to the popular mind.

The most influential of these reconcilers was Herbert Spencer, although, unlike many others, he did not set out specifically to reconcile evolution with Christianity.[13] Rather, Spencer was interested in constructing a "synthetic philosophy," a cosmic system whose cornerstone was evolution. Yet Spencer's evolution was not Darwin's, and those with orthodox proclivities found it much more palatable. For one thing, Spencer preserved the notion of an ordered universe. He viewed evolution not as an essentially chaotic and random process, but as an ordered process of change. Organisms did not simply adapt to a specific environment, but *all* phenomena moved from lower forms to higher, from simple "homogeneity" to complex "heterogeneity." As Donald Pizer has noted, Spencer "shifted the idea of order from that of static similarity to that of interrelated change."[14]

Implicit in Spencerian order was progress, the movement of phenomena toward perfection. Such a view was made feasible by Spencer's adoption of other "factors" of evolution in addition to natural selection. It was, after all, primarily natural selection that posited a self-generating, purposiveless universe. By demoting natural selection from its preeminence as an evolutionary factor, Spencer took the philosophical sting out of evolution. If evolution was in fact progressive, then it could also be teleological. If one were willing to take the leap, one could claim that evolution itself argued design. Many would.

Of course, any notion of progress toward perfection, even if couched within natural law, suggests ultimate beneficence. The Spencerian universe was not an indifferent universe despite being a deterministic one. The individual horrors produced by the struggle for existence and the subsequent survival of the fittest were recompensed by the eventual perfection of the species—that is, by the greatest good rendered to the greatest number. And although Spencer denied the possibility of knowledge of a "first cause," he did not deny the possibility of its existence. He referred to an "inscrutible Power" that lay behind phenomena, and came to equate this Power with natural force. Thus, in addition to establishing evolution as an ordered, progressive, and beneficent process—a process that could be more easily assimilated to Christian orthodoxy than could Darwinian evolution—Spencer also paved the way for the reintroduction of God into nature. Many subsequent reconcilers of evolution and Christianity would equate God with force, freely interchanging the two terms. God would be moved from His throne on high overlooking nature to nature itself, to an immanence within nature. But He would not be banished.

If Spencer provided the most popular, influential, and philosophical interpretation of Darwinian evolution, the Harvard biologist Asa Gray provided the most significant interpretation issued from the contemporary scientific community. Gray was the first American reviewer of Darwin's *Origin of Species*, publishing his first essay in early 1860 and then subsequently publishing several other essays later collected in his book *Darwiniana*.[15] Gray immediately perceived that the acceptance of Darwin's theory rested not so much on its scientific veracity as on its possible assimilation to orthodox Christian doctrine, particularly on its compatibility with the idea of design or teleology. Therefore in his first essay—simply entitled "The Origin of Species by Means of Natural Selection" (1860)—he only perfunctorily addressed the scientific aspects of Darwinism, and more thoroughly defended Darwin on theological grounds. He even went so far as to claim that it was "far easier to vindicate a theistic character for the derivative theory [i.e., Darwin's theory], than to establish the theory itself upon adequate scientific evidence."[16] The gist of his argument was that Darwin's theory did not *necessarily* preclude or disprove design, that it left, as he wrote in a subsequent essay, "the doctrines of final causes, utility, and special design, just where they were before."[17] To Gray, Darwinism merely demonstrated that design manifested itself in a different form. He argued that natural selection was not an independent natural force, but the agent through which God's design was carried out: "the order or mode in which this Creator, in his own perfect wisdom, sees fit to act."[18] Although stopping short of establishing God's immanence in nature (Gray echoed the Deists in his belief that God created the universe, and then let natural law [for Gray, evolutionary process] effect His design) Gray took a great step in that direction. Natural law, to Gray, was "the human conception of continued and orderly Divine action."[19]

All this is, of course, quite beyond the purview of Darwin's own theory as expressed in *The Origin of Species*, and the "procrustean fate" (*sic*) that Gray later said Darwin avoided by refusing to establish a nexus between divine causation and natural law may have been Gray's own.[20] Yet it once again indicates the profound impact Darwinism had on the contemporary mind, and the extent to which Darwin's contemporaries were willing to twist his theory to fit their own theological and philosophical biases. In addition, Gray's interpretation sheds a different light on two important features of the post-Darwinian reconciliations of the self and nature: the insistence on an order external to the self, and the intellectual connection between the self and that order. It also reveals that this preoccupation with the metaphysical implications of Darwinism was uniquely American.

Whereas Spencer adduced evolution itself as evidence of an ordered universe, Gray, interestingly enough, grounded his argument for an external order within the human mind. In his essay "Evolutionary Teleology" (1876), he claimed that human beings had a "seemingly inborn conception of Nature as an ordered system," and therefore, he suggested, since they conceived of it as such, it was so.[21] "Habitual," rather than "inborn," would perhaps be a more appropriate term, for such a conception had been a fundamental feature of the Western mind for centuries. Nevertheless, Gray's argument and word choice reveal that he believed there was an intellectual connection between the self and nature, that the human mind and the natural world, as creations of the divine mind, reflected both that divine mind as well as each other. After all, the "conception" of an external order was an intellectual conception from a like-ordered mind. Moreover, if it was "inborn," then, according to Christian doctrine, it was divinely instilled. Once again, we see God functioning as the link between the self and nature. Once again, we see that such a link, such a reconciliation, provided much comfort and solace to the self. When Gray cites "our profound conviction that there is order in the universe; that order presupposes mind; design, will; and mind or will, personality," the "profound conviction" rings more of wishful thinking than of fact.[22] Yet that wish is for reconciliation, for the solace that a divine "mind" and "personality" informing nature provides for the human mind and personality.

Gray also highlighted an important distinction between the European and American responses to Darwinism, a distinction that would manifest itself in the literary naturalism produced by the two continents. He noted in his essay "Darwin and His Reviewers" (1860) that most of the theological objections to Darwin's theory were voiced by Americans, thus indicating that this confrontation between science and religion was a uniquely American debate. He claimed that the English mind—although he could just as easily have cited the French or, in particular, Zola's—is "prone to positivism and kindred forms of materialistic philosophy, and we must expect the derivative theory [i.e., evolution] to be taken up in that interest. We [i.e., Americans] have no predilection for that school, but the contrary."[23] Yet despite this disclaimer, Gray himself took the middle road: on one hand, he defended Darwin for being "strictly scientific,"[24] and, on the other hand, he tried to establish, as we have seen, a link between divine causation and natural law. Regarding the former, Gray adumbrated the positivist method when he asserted that Darwin's theory involved "studying the facts and phenomena in reference to *proximate causes*, and endeavoring to trace back the series of *cause and effect* as far as possible" (my emphasis).[25] This is, as we shall see in the next chapter, precisely what Zola advocated for his naturalistic "experimental novel." The only interest, because the only truth, lay in deterministic cause and effect; metaphysics was irrelevant. Furthermore, Gray presaged Zola in drawing a distinction between the "how" (scientific) and the "why" (metaphysical). He accused Louis Agassiz, his colleague at Harvard and a staunch opponent of Darwinism, of "considering only the ultimate *why*, not the proximate why or *how*."[26]

However, Gray insisted that Darwin's focus on the "how" did not preclude the "why." He claimed that the materialistic and atheistic view of "an eternal sequence of cause and effect, for which there is no first cause," was a view that "few sane persons can long rest in."[27] (Note the choice of the words "rest in" rather than "believe in," suggesting that the main problem Gray and others had with Darwinism was not with its logic, but with its frightening ramifications for the self.) Gray further argued that the idea of a "material connection" between life forms did not preclude an "intellectual connection"—"i.e., as products of one mind, as indicating and realizing a preconceived plan."[28] (Again, note the appeal to the mind as both first cause and connecting force.) Finally, Gray even unabashedly put words in Darwin's mouth:

Mr. Darwin, in proposing a theory which suggests a *how* that harmonizes these facts into a system, we trust implies that all was done wisely, in the largest sense designedly, and by an intelligent first cause. The contemplation of the subject on the intellectual side . . . leads to no other conclusion.[29]

Of course, Darwin himself implied no such thing. The "trust" here is mere hope. Gray's interpretation of Darwinism is not Darwinism, but another example of Darwinisticism. There were to be, in response to Darwin's theory, several "other" conclusions.

Of the many more late nineteenth-century reconcilers of evolution and Christianity, the final one whom I will discuss here, and the most important to this study, is Frank Norris's teacher at the University of California, Joseph LeConte. Like Gray, LeConte was a scientist who denied that evolution equaled materialism, that it precluded a metaphysical first cause. He too believed that natural process was a manifestation of divine agency, and that nature was ordered, rationally designed, and intellectually comprehensible. Yet LeConte went further. In his book *Evolution: Its Nature, Its Evidences, and Its Relation to Religious Thought* (1888), he argued that evolutionary process was not divine agency which had been set in motion at the moment of spontaneous creation, but that it was a process in which God Himself was immanent. LeConte was thus one of those reconcilers who directly equated natural force or process with God, with a God "resident *in* Nature, at all times and in all places directing every event and determining every phenomena" (*sic*; LeConte's emphasis).[30] Clearly, LeConte wanted it both ways: determinism, but not materialistic determinism. He therefore posited a divine, intellectual determinism with God as the determining or causal force. He claimed that there was a "complete *identification* of first and second causes" (354, LeConte's emphasis), that "all is natural—i.e., according to law, but all is supernatural—i.e., above Nature, as we usually regard Nature, for all is permeated with the immediate Divine presence" (356). LeConte was quick to point out that this view constituted neither idealism nor pantheism, for he maintained that this God was quite personal, though "less anthropomorphic" (300). Thus, through various philosophical twists and leaps, LeConte established a one-to-one correspondence between impersonal natural process and a personal divine will and, in so doing, took the intellectual connection between the self and nature even further than Gray. Science, once again, became a spiritual endeavor; in an echo of the Transcendentalist credo, LeConte claimed that in observing nature, humanity was reading the "mind of God" (302).

This intellectual connection was further augmented by LeConte's introduction of yet another evolutionary factor—namely, the "rational" factor. LeConte's evolutionary paradigm involved a vertical progression (much like Spencer's) in which a species passed through distinct evolutionary stages toward an ever higher form. At each stage a certain factor dominated, from the Lamarckian factors of environmental pressure and the use and disuse of organs that dominated lower life forms, to the Darwinian factors of natural and sexual selection that dominated the animal kingdom, on up to the rational factor that dominated the human species. LeConte defined this last factor as "the conscious, voluntary co-operation of the thing evolving—the spirit of man—in the work of its own evolution" (79). It was a "conscious, voluntary striving to *attain an ideal*" (86, LeConte's emphasis). Such a factor suggests two important things: first, that the rational self (or one's "spirit," as LeConte alternately called it) was itself natural, an intricate part of the natural process, and, secondly, that one had moral freedom within a deterministic (although not a materially deterministic) universe.

By making the rational or spiritual self natural, LeConte forged an absolute reconciliation between that self and nature. The self was no longer alienated from an indifferent, material universe but was at home in a universe that was, like the self, rational and spiritual. In fact, the purpose that LeConte ascribed to the long process of evolution was the eventual birth and immortality of the human spirit out of the anima of animals, a birth that was primarily the awareness by the self of the essential spirituality of both self and nature. The severing of the "physical, umbilical connection with Nature" (319) engendered this spiritual connection. (Throughout, LeConte used loving, maternal metaphors to describe the relationship between nature and the self. Nature, to the nascent self, was "gestative" mother; to the newborn self, it was "nursing" mother, thus implying consanguinity and, ultimately, reconciliation.) In addition, the individual also had to use his rational self—that is, the rational factor—to "break away from physical and material connection with the forces of Nature . . . in order to enter into higher relations of filial love to God and brotherly love to man" (321). In other words, the ideal that humanity had to strive to attain was that of spiritual reconciliation between the self and, as they were one and the same, God or nature.

One of the key words in LeConte's vocabulary is "co-operation," a word he used to describe the relationship between the self and nature. The birth of the human spirit was an example of such co-operation, for while "mother" nature cut the umbilical connection with her "child," that "child" then had to use voluntarily his newborn spirit to wean himself further from maternal and material nature. As Donald Pizer has pointed out, such a relationship between physical necessity and free will recapitulated within a contemporary evolutionary context the orthodox Christian paradox of free will and predestination.[31] According to Christian doctrine, in a preordained world that is a manifestation of God's will, the individual must align himself with and his conduct to that divine will, or suffer the consequences. To LeConte, the individual had to align himself with and his conduct to natural law, a law in which God was immanent. This was perhaps LeConte's most important contribution to the contemporary conception of humanity and nature, and would have a major impact on the literary naturalism of Frank Norris. What LeConte essentially did was reintroduce a moral order into nature—a moral order that, as we have seen, Darwinism removed—as well as bestow once again on the individual free will and moral choice.

Following the traditional if philosophically groundless assumption that God is good and that all morality emanates from Him, LeConte reasoned that since God was immanent in nature (another of his rather untenable assumptions), then nature and the process of evolution, despite the individual horrors of natural selection, were also good and moral. In an argument reminiscent of Alexander Pope's "whatever is, is right," LeConte claimed that the "evil" of natural selection was only evil from a lower perspective; it was a "necessary condition" (367) for the elevation of a species, including man, to a higher form. LeConte asked rhetorically:

> shall that be called evil which was obviously the necessary condition for attaining our then elevated position? Evil it doubtless seemed to the individuals who fell, and still seems to us who now suffer, by the way in the conflict; but is physical discomfort or even physical death of the individual to be weighed in comparison with the psychical ele-

vation of the individual, and especially of the race? Evidently, then, physical evil even in the case of man is only *seeming* evil, but *real* good. (367, LeConte's emphasis)

Just as the traditional Christian believed that every act of God, even His scourge, was ultimately beneficent, so too did LeConte believe regarding natural law. He claimed that it was only human "ignorance" which prevented one from seeing that "every law of Nature is beneficent" (367).

However, despite human ignorance, LeConte believed that it was still in the individual's power to lead a moral life, if only the person would, to use another phrase from Alexander Pope, "follow nature." The rational factor that LeConte claimed for humanity gave one this power, a power that was essentially free will: the power to make a moral choice. He distinguished between the *"free,* self-determined evolution of the race" brought about by human reason, and the *"necessary* evolution of the organic kingdom" brought about by natural law (86, LeConte's emphasis). LeConte thus constructed a deterministic universe (determined, as mentioned before, by God's will, not by "uncaused" physical force) in which the individual exercised free will. Again, one's moral duty was to "co-operate" voluntarily with God's will, to align one's human will to God's natural law. The philosophical problems such a paradigm presents were perhaps not beyond LeConte's tether, for at one point he seemed to hedge, arguing that while "organic evolution is by *necessary* law, human progress is by *free* or at least by freer law" (88, LeConte's emphasis). The philosophical question, of course, is, what *is* "freer" law?

Sin, then, to LeConte, was anything that went against natural law. For the individual, this included willfully subordinating the rational, moral, and spiritual self to the animal self. According to LeConte's paradigm of distinct evolutionary stages each dominated by a certain evolutionary factor, previous dominant factors did not disappear from a species as it progressed to a higher stage, but were only subordinated to the new factor. Therefore, while the dominant evolutionary factor in humans was the rational, the lesser factor of natural selection also operated. This idea implies that humanity's lower nature, on which natural selection could operate, was also never eradicated, but only subordinated. Donald Pizer has pointed out that this was essentially a reformulation of the traditional Christian concept of the dualism of the spirit and the flesh. A human being was part animal (as manifest by the body and its functions) and part "beyond animal" (as manifest by the reason and spirit). The natural, and therefore moral, state in a human being was to have the spirit subjugate the flesh, the rational subjugate the animal. According to LeConte, "all evil consists in the dominance of the lower over the higher; all good in the rational use of the lower by the higher" (374). It is important to note that LeConte believed that the individual's "lower" nature should not be eradicated, even if that were possible. He argued:

> True virtue consists, not in the extirpation of the lower, but in its subjection to the higher. The stronger the lower is, the better, *if only* it be held in subjection. For the higher is nourished and strengthened by its connection with the more robust lower, and the lower is purified, refined, and glorified by its connection with the divine higher, and by this mutual action the whole plane of being is elevated. (375)

This would become an important concept in the work of Frank Norris.

Spencer, Gray, LeConte, and the plethora of other reconcilers of evolution and Christianity were all trying to fit a new, compelling vision of humanity and nature into the Procrustean bed of an old vision. Such attempts, in addition to mangling Darwin's theory itself, served only to highlight the inadequacy of the old vision, its inability to explain and solve the new problems confronting humanity as it moved into the twentieth century. The American pragmatic philosopher John Dewey perceived this and advocated moving philosophy forward—away from a preoccupation with absolutes and final causes, and toward the knowable and its practical applications. In a lecture at Columbia University in 1909, Dewey called *The Origin of Species* "the greatest dissolvent in contemporary thought of old questions"[32] and accused those who tried to reconcile evolution and Christianity of "intellectual atavism" (399). Specifically, he called Spencer's equating of God with natural force a "faded piece of metaphysical goods" (400), and disparagingly referred to Gray's interpretation of Darwinism as "design on the installment plan" (398). Dewey thus represents a transition from late nineteenth-century philosophy—which had yet to free itself from the "habits, predispositions, and deeply engrained attitudes" (402) produced by centuries of Western theological and philosophical dogma—

to twentieth-century philosophy, which would unapologetically confront a universe devoid of absolutes.

To Dewey, the theological debate that arose over Darwinism was ancillary to the main debate that occurred within science and philosophy themselves. Dewey noted that the goal of ancient philosophy was "to relate all special forms to their one single end and good: pure contemplative intelligence" (395). Therefore, teleology itself was emblematic of intelligence, and we can see from this why the reconcilers' insistence on teleology or design went hand in hand with their belief in an intelligent first cause, a cosmic intelligence that enabled rational human beings to comprehend the natural world around them, and that therefore connected them to that world. Dewey concluded:

> The design argument thus operated in two directions. Purposefulness accounted for *the intelligibility of nature* and the possibility of science, while the absolute or cosmic character of this purposefulness gave sanction and worth to *the moral and religious endeavors of man.* (397, my emphasis)

In other words, the belief in an absolute and in a cosmic design provided solace to pre-Darwinian humanity; it integrated the individual with his world and integrated the several facets—rational, moral, and spiritual—of his self.

Dewey, however, wanted the new philosophy to move away from absolutes, for to him the solace such absolutes provided was neither useful nor responsible. In an argument that undermines LeConte's notion that "every law of Nature is beneficent," Dewey claimed that even if it were "a thousand times dialectically demonstrated that life as a whole is regulated by a transcendent principle to a final inclusive goal, none the less truth and error, health and disease, good and evil, hope and fear in the concrete, would remain just what and where they now are" (400–401). And Dewey went on to argue, since belief in an absolute solves no immediate problems, that the solace humans take in such a belief involves the shirking of the responsibility to try to solve them, involves the shifting of this responsibility "to the more competent shoulders of the transcendent cause" (401). Dewey advocated a new, pragmatic philosophy, one that did not concern itself with fixities but with change or process, and therefore one capable of dealing with the immediate problems confronting humanity. We hear an echo of John Dewey when Jake Barnes declares in *The Sun Also Rises:* "I did not care what it was all about. All I wanted to know was how to live in it."[33]

Dewey claimed that "we do not solve [philosophical questions], we get over them" (402). Darwinism got humanity "over" the old questions of absolutes and final causes, shifting philosophy toward those questions whose answers lay within the realm of the knowable. Moreover, Darwinism helped human beings get over their belief in the certainty of their own knowledge. It was, after all, the belief in an absolute that had made humans feel the universe was knowable in the first place. This epistemological shift from certainty to uncertainty would be augmented by the mathematical and scientific discoveries of men such as Gödel, Einstein, and Heisenberg in the early twentieth century, discoveries that would illustrate the limits of human knowledge as well as the distorting power of the subjective consciousness. The belief in an order external to the self—so important to such men as Spencer, Gray, and LeConte—would be replaced by a belief that a knowable order was imposed on the external world only by the human mind itself. From a twentieth-century perspective, then, the order that the various nineteenth-century reconcilers of evolution and Christianity claimed to have found inherent in the natural, evolving world was in fact only a construct of their own minds. They themselves were an example of that which they sought to deny: of human beings living in a chaotic, purposiveless, and indifferent universe. If there is a post-Darwinian "condition," this is it; and this is what Norris and the other literary naturalists would have to confront each in his own way.

CHAPTER TWO
ZOLA AND DETERMINISM

Charles Walcutt has called Emile Zola the "fountainhead" of literary naturalism, and such an appellation is certainly warranted.[1] Zola was not only the chief originator, theorist, proponent, and practitioner of this new literary form, but he was also the single most influential novelist on the American literary naturalists—Frank Norris, the self-proclaimed "Boy Zola," among them. Yet Zola's naturalism was derived in part from an entirely different interpretation of Darwinism than that being promulgated by Gray, LeConte, and other theistically minded American interpreters, and thus his interpretation often created a conflict within the minds and works of those American writers whom he influenced. Unlike Gray, LeConte, and others, Zola had no interest in metaphysics and was therefore immune to the metaphysical implications of Darwinism that tormented his contemporaries. He felt no need to reconcile evolution with Christianity, nor the self with nature. In fact, Zola saw no division between the self and nature that needed reconciliation. Zola was a strict determinist, believing that everything, including the self, was determined by physical, material forces.

Asa Gray's claim regarding the English mind—that it is "prone to positivism and kindred forms of materialistic philosophy"—was equally true with regard to the Frenchman Zola's. In his essay "The Experimental Novel" (1880), the first major treatise of literary naturalism, Zola embraced the positivist method formulated by his countryman Auguste Comte and advocated its use by the novelist.[2] Comte had wanted to establish science on a more "positive" ground, and therefore proposed a scientific method that went beyond empiricism, beyond the passive and detached observation of phenomena. His method called on a scientist to conduct controlled experiments that would either prove or disprove hypotheses regarding those phenomena. Adapting Comte's method as applied to medicine by the physician Claude Bernard, Zola argued that the novelist should assume the role of the scientist or physician, that his novel should be a controlled experiment in which the characters function as physical phenomena. As the scientist could deduce from his experiment physical laws governing the behavior of chemicals under certain conditions, or as the physician could deduce physiological laws governing the function of the human body, so too could the novelist discover "laws" governing human behavior in society. The discovery of such laws, like the discovery of physical and physiological laws, could then be used to benefit humanity. Human beings would be able to manipulate their environment in accordance with these laws, thus producing a better society.

The application of such a strict scientific method to the novel is, among other things, a means of anchoring literature in the realm of the known. It restrains literature from metaphysical speculation, from dabbling in the uncertainties of philosophy and religion. Zola wanted the novel to deal with the truth, and to Zola the truth resided solely in "things," in physical phenomena, and not in the self and its conceits. He virulently attacked the Romantics for such metaphysical dilettantism, calling romanticism a "disease" and "the ravings of a group of men" who were under the delusion that "the truth is in themselves and not in the things" (36, 37, 44). Science, Zola believed, would move literature away from such "folly," would furnish the writer with a "solid ground" on which he could "lean for support" (52).

Zola thus advocated that literature deal solely with the "how" of things (i.e., material causes) and not with the "why" (i.e., first causes)—a distinction that Gray had made in defense of Darwin's "strictly scientific" theory of evolution. While Zola conceded the strong attraction that metaphysical questions had for humanity, he felt that such questions were best left to the philosophers, that the novelist, as a man of science, "despairs of determining" (38) their answers. Yet, in confining the novelist to the "how," to materialism and deterministic cause and effect, Zola would appear to be locking him out of his traditional demesne: the self or, more specifically, the psychological self. Zola, however, managed to obviate this problem, at least theoretically, by presuming everything, including the self, accountable to and determined by physical law. "Determinism dominates everything" (18), he wrote. As Claude Bernard had applied scientific determinism to physiology, Zola sought to apply it to psychology and to the literary "study" of the psychological self. As if announcing the establishment of a new order, Zola declared that "the metaphysical man is dead; our whole territory is transformed by the advent of the physiological man" (54).

What is implied by "physiological man," among other things, is that Zola saw no division between the self and nature, no rift that needed bridging. The self was natural, a part of the material universe, not set apart from it. Zola's universe was thus the inverse of LeConte's; both were monistic, yet LeConte's embodied a spiritual monism, while Zola's embodied what Walcutt has called a "materialistic monism."[3] LeConte had argued that the human spirit was both separated by and separated itself from material nature, that it awoke into an awareness of the essential spirituality of the universe, a universe in which God was immanent. To LeConte, then, all was a manifestation of spirit. In contrast, to Zola, all was either matter or force. He denied the human spirit was distinct from material nature; it too was ruled by a strict, physical determinism. Zola went to great lengths — and took several logical leaps — to argue that both thought and passion operated "according to the fixed laws of nature" (12). Psychology was, in effect, physiology. He referred to the passions as "complicated machinery" (9) and boldly declared that "a like determinism will govern the stones of the roadway and the brain of man" (17). He even applied, however tenuously, this belief to his *Rougon-Macquart* series of novels, claiming that all the physical and mental dysfunctions of the characters were traceable to a single organic lesion in one of their ancestors.

While LeConte had constructed a spiritually monistic universe primarily as a means of reconciling humanity to it, he also did so to give human beings free will, the ability to make a moral choice within the parameters established by natural law. Such freedom gave humanity hope — the hope to control its own destiny and to build a better society. Zola, however, in constructing a materialistic, deterministic universe, denied human beings free will — at least theoretically. Yet such a denial was not intended to produce the nihilistic gloom that LeConte sought to avoid by granting that free will. On the contrary, Zola also intended to give humanity hope. By demonstrating the inefficacy of the human will in controlling the self, particularly the "animal" self (precisely what LeConte insisted human beings could control through the exercise of free will), Zola attempted to shift humanity's efforts toward controlling the determining factors, primarily the social environment. Herein lay humanity's moral freedom, the opportunity to correct evil and promote good. The role of the experimental novelist, then, was to discover social ills and, as does the physician, in discovering them, ameliorate them. The social purpose of the experimental novel, as proclaimed by Zola, was "to regulate life, to regulate society, to solve in time all the problems of socialism [i.e., sociology]" (26).

Of course this "social engineering," as it would be termed today, is itself an expression of free will; it is the conscious decision and subsequent voluntary action of human beings to change their social environment. The only difference is that this will is directed outside the self rather than toward it. Moreover, as Walcutt has cogently argued, in denying free will, Zola and other naturalistic writers assert their own, for art is itself an expression of the human will. As Walcutt writes:

> No matter how ardently he [the naturalistic writer] appears to be denying the worth or importance of man, the autonomy of the will, the permanence of life, the value of man's spirit, or the power of his knowledge, he is always in some fashion affirming these very things, for art is exercise and proof of them.[4]

This is one of several contradictions between Zola's theory and practice regarding the experimental novel. Walcutt has also demonstrated that Zola's belief in mechanistic psychology—in a psychology that is physiologically determined—does not translate into his novels, that despite his theoretical arguments to the contrary, such a view would necessarily take the novel out of "the domain of personality, where the novel lives."[5] Likewise, the determining factor of heredity is downplayed in practice, for in Zola's novels only environmental factors are integral to the action; the hereditary ones, such as the ancestral lesion, are extraneous. Thus we can understand the downfall of Gervaise and Coupeau in *L'Assommoir* (1877) more in terms of their milieu—the "polluted atmosphere of our urban areas,"[6] as Zola writes in the novel's preface—than in terms of any family history of alcoholism that Zola often alludes to in the course of the novel.

One other contradiction exists within Zola's theory itself, a contradiction that was inherent in the positivist scientific method Zola tried to emulate in the novel. For while the positivists were strict determinists, their method presumed a division between subject and object, between scientist and experiment, which undermined that determinism. They believed that somehow a scientist could step outside the bounds of a controlled experiment, outside deterministic cause and effect. They embraced a view that modern scientists would call naive—namely, that a scientist could conduct an experiment and have no effect on it beyond any effect that the scientist may have originally intended. Such a view presumes a world of division, a world of closed systems in which the system of the experiment has no interaction (again, beyond what the scientist may intend) with that of the experimenter. The scientist is thus not so much a participant in the experiment as an objective observer of an entirely separate system. To put it another way—since nineteenth-century determinists spoke in terms of linear cause and effect and not in terms of systems—the "line" of the observing subject never bisects that of the observed object. This division between subject and object, between scientist and experiment, is analogous to and in fact recapitulates the division between the self and nature we have been discussing. Thus the division between that self and nature which Zola's deterministic materialism denies is manifest by his method. The problem, once again, remains unresolved.

The several contradictions in Zola's work—between his theory and practice, as well as within his theory itself—can perhaps be adduced as evidence of Zola's influence on the American literary naturalists whose work is also rife with contradictions. Yet we may find it more fruitful to regard Zola in ideological opposition to such men as LeConte: the one positing the physiological self at home in a materially monistic universe, the other reconciling the spiritual self to a spiritually monistic universe. A writer such as Frank Norris, clearly and avowedly influenced by both men, could then be seen as fluctuating between these two ideological poles, his own work embodying the contradictions of his mentors. And like these mentors, Norris would depict a monistic universe (alternately materialistic or spiritual or both, depending on the force of each ideology) in which humanity was, or at least *could be*, reconciled. And again, as in the work of his mentors, Norris's work would ultimately unhinge on the logical and philosophical leaps inherent in its contradictions, and its monistic vision would fail to translate to the next century—when a new relationship between the self and nature would have to be formulated.

CHAPTER THREE
VANDOVER AND THE BRUTE
AND THE POST-DARWINIAN
CONDITION

Vandover and the Brute is a work of literary naturalism that reflects the new Darwinian reading of humanity and nature. As such, it embodies several aspects of the metaphysical crisis with which we saw Spencer, Gray, and LeConte grapple: the conflict between Christianity and evolution, the subsequent alienation of the self from nature, and the problem of free will in a deterministic universe. *Vandover* is a literary expression of this post-Darwinian condition, yet in this early work Norris leans more toward a Zolaesque response to it than toward those of his American scientific and philosophical contemporaries. Vandover succumbs to a deterministic fate in a material universe suddenly stripped of a comforting rational, moral, and spiritual order. There is no reconciling vision, no satisfactory resolution to his predicament. Neither, however, is there any of the social optimism that Zola claimed for his experimental novel, and as a result we can begin to see why Norris would move away from materialistic determinism and toward a LeContean vision in his later work.

At the beginning of *Vandover*, Norris presents a scene that suggests all of the conflicts which will be developed throughout the novel. Moreover, he establishes Vandover the character as a representative of post-Darwinian humanity. This is the scene in which Vandover discovers "good and evil," a discovery that really amounts to his learning the "facts of life."[1] Vandover's natural adolescent curiosity is stirred first by reading certain passages in the Bible and by hearing his minister refer to "all women in the perils of child-birth" (7). It is further augmented by the vulgar talk of his high school friends, and then confirmed by reading an article in the *Encyclopaedia Britannica* under the heading "Obstetrics." We can see from this the contemporary movement of authority away from the Bible and religion and toward its new place in the field of science. Vandover's reading of the Bible, something he does only because "his father gave him a quarter for doing so," merely fills him with "vague and strange ideas" (7). It confirms nothing, and Vandover is not satisfied with such uncertainty. Likewise, Vandover only senses "a mystery beneath the words" of the minister's sermon, only feels "the presence of something hidden" (7). Again, the word of God does not suffice; it does not reveal meaning—or, perhaps we should say, it *no longer* reveals meaning or, better still, it no longer reveals a meaning that contemporary humanity seeks. Rather, it conceals that meaning. Vandover, although not consciously rejecting Christian teaching, is deaf to the metaphor and allegory used by Christianity to explain phenomena. Such tropes reveal supernatural rather than natural meaning, and Vandover, unlike his Christian forebears, is simply not interested in the supernatural. The post-Darwinian Vandover craves a different kind of meaning: that which concerns only "natural" facts.

For this, Vandover must turn to a different authority, science. The encyclopedia article on "Obstetrics" provides Vandover with a scientific explanation of a natural phenomenon and confirms for him what the minister's mutterings about "the perils of child-birth" only obliquely suggested. Whereas the metaphorical word of God had left Vandover confused, unsatisfied, and ultimately uninterested, the new word of science enthralls him, and he reads the encyclopedia article "from beginning to end" (8). In addition, the "cold, scientific definitions" he finds in the dictionary give Vandover "some strange sort of satisfaction" (8). Yet there is a price to be paid for this new knowledge. Vandover's "discovery," which is a discovery of science as well as humanity's biological origins, signals "the end of all his childish ideals, the destruction of all his first illusions" (8). We may infer that these ideals and illusions were fostered by his Christian upbringing, that they were in part the ideals and illusions of Christianity itself—namely, those of an ordered, divinely created universe in which human beings felt at home. Certainly the moral order that Christianity attributed to the natural world, and on which humanity based its own morality, crumbles as a result. We are told that Vandover's "rude little standard of morality was lowered immediately" (8), and it is from this point onward that the brute within him begins to assert itself, no longer restrained by Christian morality. Moreover, Vandover's almost unconscious, innate conception of a spiritual order—we remember Asa Gray's notion of humanity's "inborn conception" of such an order in nature—is destroyed:

> Even his mother, whom he had always believed to be some kind of an angel, fell at once in his estimation. She could never be the same to him after this, never so sweet, so good and so pure as he had hitherto imagined her. (8)

Vandover had viewed his mother in terms of the Christian spiritual paradigm, both as "angel" and as that icon of immaculate motherhood, the Virgin. His mother now falls along with the spiritual paradigm that had supported her. They were only illusions Vandover had "believed," only something he had "imagined."

Early on, then, Norris establishes Vandover as a representative of post-Darwinian humanity, of human beings who suddenly find that the comforting yet "childish" illusions of their species' infancy are now threatened by a new, compelling, "factual" conception of the universe and of humanity's place in it. Vandover too feels the anxiety, fear, and horror that many in the late nineteenth century felt. This new knowledge was "very cruel, the whole thing was a grief to him, a blow, a great shock" (8). Human carnality, humanity's biological affinity with the brute, was one of the most frightening aspects of Darwinism to those in the late nineteenth century. Many felt that if this theory were true, then there really was nothing to restrain humans from behaving like brutes, that in fact they would succumb to their basest desires, with dire and unimaginable consequences. This, of course, is exactly what happens to Vandover in the course of the novel. With the acquisition of this new knowledge, Vandover begins his long journey toward self-destruction and, ultimately, insanity.

As we saw in chapter 1, another one of the main consequences of Darwinism was the alienation of the self from nature. The rational, moral, and spiritual self had no affinity with a natural world devoid of such qualities, with a universe stripped of the order that had reflected that of the mind. This split often manifested itself internally—that is, as a split between the self and the physical, "natural" body. This is the primary form it takes in *Vandover*, and we can see it in this early scene. Vandover's discovery of evil is a discovery of human carnality, of humanity's biological origins; the good he associates with the more ethereal self, with the "better self." Vandover thus establishes the natural, biological being as the enemy of the good self, the enemy who seeks to destroy that self. It is, after all, the discovery of his mother's carnality that brings about her fall, that undermines her pure, angelic self in his eyes. And Vandover himself is a man divided: Vandover the artist (his "better self") and Vandover the brute (his natural, biological being).[2]

One can see from this a revision of the age-old Christian drama between the spirit and the flesh, and indeed Norris is, among other things, rewriting the Christian narrative of spiritual crisis in *Vandover*. He places it within a new evolutionary context, and herein lies an important distinction. For while the protagonist in the Christian narrative had recourse to a moral structure through which he could subsume the flesh to the spirit and, through this subsuming, integrate the two into an ordered hierarchy, Vandover has no such recourse. The battle is lost before it is even begun, and so we see foreshadowed in this early scene Vandover's inevitable destruction by the brute within him. Such inevitability must necessarily involve a movement away from free will and toward determinism that, as we shall see later, will be the case.

The shift of authority away from religion and the Church and toward science is only one manifestation in *Vandover* of the weakening and ultimate destruction of a traditional ordering principle. There are several such principles in the novel, each connected in one way or another with spirituality and morality, and each exerting, until its demise, a beneficent influence on Vandover.[3] They are not symbols, in the allegorical sense, of orthodox Christianity, but taken both individually and as a whole they suggest the spiritual and moral order that Christianity provided, and their loss reflects the loss of that order in the wake of Darwin's new conception of humanity and the universe. We can see, of course, the consequences of such loss for post-Darwinian humanity in Vandover and his fate.[4]

But before we look at these various principles of order, we need to examine further a few more instances in *Vandover* where the Church and Christianity are shown to be ineffectual and obsolete. The Church that could not

provide a satisfactory explanation of sexuality and human biological origins soon becomes irrelevant in Vandover's life. When Turner Ravis—one
of the principles of order—invites him to church one Sunday, Vandover
shows up with a hangover. His sickly presence is a parody of piousness, and
when he must grab ahold of the pew in front of him to "steady himself" (52)
we sense a parody of the Church's "steadying" influence, an influence that
is no longer moral and spiritual, but absurdly practical. Later in the novel
Norris tells us explicitly that "religion had never affected [Vandover] very
deeply" (190). He had performed all the rituals—baptism, confirmation,
Sunday services, nightly prayer—yet these had become hollow rituals to
him, empty forms devoid of spiritual significance. "As a rule," we are told,
"Vandover thought very little about religious matters and when he did, told
himself that he was too intelligent to believe in a literal heaven, a literal hell,
and a personal god personally interfering in human affairs like any Jove or
Odin" (191). Once again, Vandover fails to grasp the metaphorical dimen-
sions of Christianity, perceiving only the absurdity of its "literal" truth. His
intelligence is confined only to empirical, natural facts—a scientific intelligence, as it were. He cannot even conceive of a mythical intelligence that
could comprehend the spiritual "truth" revealed by religious metaphor and
allegory. His comparison of the Christian God to pagan gods is pejorative;
he fails, as would many of his late nineteenth-century contemporaries and
twentieth-century followers, to appreciate the insight such an easy comparison reveals about the unity and constancy of the human spirit and its
relationship to the natural world, something that mythologists (e.g., Sir
James George Frazer) and the literary modernists (e.g., T. S. Eliot) would
later discover. Vandover evinces here not only contemporary humanity's
loss of that unifying myth that Eliot would later lament, but, more important, the loss of the intelligence that could appreciate such a myth, its destruction at the hands of a scientific intelligence that had arrogated all truth
to itself. Mythology, including Christian mythology, had lost its meaning.

    Vandover's father is perhaps the most salient ordering principle in the
novel, and of all the individuals who represent order, he has the most influence over Vandover.[5] In itself, his role as father associates him with "Our
Father," the beneficent Christian God. Yet so too do his nicknames: the
"Governor" and the "Old Gentleman." The first connotes a beneficent authority—again, much like the Christian deity—who exercises power only

in the best interest of the governed, only to guide and to keep them on the right path. The latter suggests that this authority is the embodiment of a traditional moral standard, of an old morality that once produced "gentle" men. Vandover's father certainly behaves like such a paragon of morality. He had been a good husband, having closed out his business in Boston and moved to San Francisco in order to alleviate his wife's illness, treating her with dignity, respect, and love until the end. He had also been an honest businessman, making a fortune in capitalist investment yet without abrogating either his personal or his business ethics. And when Vandover confesses to him his role in Ida Wade's suicide—much as a sinner would confess to his priest, or to his God—the Old Gentleman's response epitomizes equable wisdom and virtue: "We will start in again and try to forget all this, not as much as we *can*, but as much as we *ought*, and live it down, and from now on we'll try to do the thing that is right and brave and good" (97).

At his death, the housekeeper unconsciously identifies Vandover's father with God in an hysterical exclamation: "Oh, oh, the good God. . . . Oh, the good, kind master" (133). Vandover laments the loss of his "dear old governor" (133) and only then realizes "how large a place he [his father] had filled in his life" (138). Vandover now finds himself all alone, stripped of a guiding, ordering principle he had taken for granted. Again, the figure of post-Darwinian humanity, Vandover finds that he must "decide questions which until now his father had answered" (138). We soon see how ill-equipped he is in this regard. His first decision involves a choice between apartments, a choice between one conducive to work and one conducive to comfort and pleasure. Vandover chooses the latter. In fact, without the moral guidance of his father, Vandover's fall accelerates. Without a moral icon to emulate and to follow, Vandover lacks a moral structure through which he could subsume the brute to his "better self."

Vandover's "better self"—his rational, moral, and spiritual self—is identified early on with his artistic sensibility. It is this side of his character that prevents him from being "totally corrupted while in his earliest teens" (8), from immediately succumbing to the brute. During the numerous crises in his life—Ida Wade's suicide, his father's death, Turner Ravis's rejection—Vandover "instinctively" turns to his art for salvation. We are told that it is "the one thing that could save him" from the rapaciousness of the brute, that it would be "the last to go" (192).

Art thus functions in the novel as another ordering principle. Its role in Vandover's life is similar to the role Christianity played in former times; it provides the means through which Vandover can achieve salvation, through which his "better self" can subdue the brute. Vandover himself becomes aware of this power and freely associates his art with the Christian spiritual order for which it is a trope. In his greatest moment of spiritual crisis, Vandover's art enters his consciousness as "a manifestation, a writing on the wall" (192). He conceives of it as "a miracle," as "divine" (193); he is thankful for his apparent "deliverance" (194). When he attends the opera during this same crisis, he experiences both a revelation and spiritual transcendence. The music, another art form, moves him such that

> there came over him a vague sense of those things which are too beautiful to be comprehended, of a nobility, a self-oblivion, an immortal eternal love and kindness, all goodness, all benignity, all pity for sin, all sorrow for grief, all joy for the true, the right, and the pure. (187)

These "things" are all Christian virtues and had all been embodied by Vandover's father. Clearly "the true, the right, and the pure" echoes the Old Gentleman's admonition to Vandover to "do the thing that is right and brave and good" (97). And during the opera Vandover transcends his present self, becoming "a little child again, . . . still believing in all his illusions" (187), those same illusions that science and the *Encyclopaedia Britannica* had destroyed.

If art, then, provides Vandover with a means of subduing the brute, of establishing the proper balance between the spirit and the flesh, his early "ideal head" of the pagan goddess Flora is emblematic of such a harmony. Moreover, as a work of art with a religious, albeit pagan, theme, this painting again illustrates the connection between art and religion as ordering principles. The painting depicts the head of Flora, the Roman goddess of flowers, entwined with honeysuckle. The image is one of perfect integration on two levels. First, the human form of the goddess as a symbol of natural fertility suggests the interconnection between the two realms: humanity and nature reflect each other in a harmonious union. Secondly, the ideal head of the goddess, with its connotations of the divinity of the rational, moral, and spiritual self, is embellished and thus its beauty enhanced by the crown of honeysuckle, a product and symbol of nature's fecundity. As in the Christian, Neoplatonic adaptation of pagan mythology in which physical form is a lower emanation than and therefore subordinated to the spirit, nature here is relegated to a subordinate and supporting position, the natural fertility of the goddess subsumed to and in the service of her mind and its spirituality. Flora, presented here at the beginning of the novel, is thus the antithesis of the image of Vandover at the end of the novel: a man devoid of a religious ordering principle and stripped of his artistic ability whose mind has been overwhelmed by a natural disease, his divine self subsumed to the brute. Likewise, this early painting of Flora is the antithesis of Vandover's later, unfinished painting *The Last Enemy*, an example of the naturalist school that, like Vandover himself, is devoid of a spiritual vision and thus of a spiritual ordering principle. In that work, humanity and nature are out of order, the human at the mercy of the beast. And as in Vandover himself, the natural brute (in this case, the lion) poises to devour the lone self.

Two minor characters, Turner Ravis and Dolly Haight, also represent ordering principles whose influence Vandover will lose. Turner Ravis is an example of Norris's "man's woman," a woman who can lead a man away from vice and toward virtue.[6] As such, she is a type of saving grace; she embodies Christian faith and represents the moral order and restraint that that faith provides. We are told that she "influenced [Vandover] upon his best side," that she appealed to "all that was cleanest, finest, and most delicate" (44) in him. She is contrasted with "the girls of the Imperial," those such as Flossie and Ida Wade who appeal only to Vandover's physical desires, to the brute within him. These "chippies" lure Vandover away from Turner, and his indulgence of vice with them eventually kills his "capacity" for the "calm, pure feeling" (190) Turner had fostered. Vandover is thus a man seduced by the easy vice of the city, a figure not uncommon in the late nineteenth century with the mass influx of people into urban areas. Such a demographic shift engendered many problems, not the least of which was weakening the influence of the already weakened Church. Turner's orthodox morality is thus somewhat of an anachronism, a throwback to an earlier, more rural society. It seems out of place in the city, and Vandover, like many of his real-life contemporaries, willfully abandons it. Turner's final rejection of him is only an acknowledgment that their relationship ended long ago.

Dolly Haight is the best of Vandover's friends, a throwback himself to an earlier morality. In fact, Dolly is much like Vandover's father: honest, virtuous, and kind. Yet Vandover's father "passes away" and, we sense, so too does the moral standard that he embodied. It no longer works in the post-Darwinian world, can no longer survive. Dolly, as a representative of an old moral order in this new world, cannot survive either. In fact, it is Dolly's moral naiveté that betrays and ultimately destroys him. Dolly is the only one among his peers who believes that women are virtuous and that a "man's duty" is to protect that virtue. More important, Dolly believes such virtue is "natural," an "instinct":

> I believe that a girl is born with a natural intuitive purity that will lead her to protect her virtue just as instinctively as she would dodge a blow; if she wants to go wrong she will have to make an effort herself to overcome that instinct. (87)

Such a view of the natural and of instinct is clearly antiquated, harking back to a pre-Darwinian era when morality reflected the moral order humanity perceived in nature.[7] However, in *Vandover*, nearly all the natural, instinctual forces we see are associated with evil: lust, greed, and self-interest. Moreover, it is Flossie's natural lust and wantonness that transmits, through no moral fault of Dolly, the natural disease that destroys him. In essence, the old moral order is annihilated by nature itself, by a natural world that is no longer the basis of that order, but which, in the new Darwinian view, denies order.

The loss of all these ordering principles—each indicative of the contemporary loss of the traditional, Christian view of an ordered universe—leaves Vandover confronting a world devoid of rationality, morality, and spirituality. Vandover finds himself ill-equipped, as was late nineteenth-century humanity in general, to face this new Darwinian universe, for his ordered mind can now find no parallel and therefore no affinity with the natural world in which he lives. He feels himself alienated from that world, that same feeling of alienation which we saw in Chapter 1 was one of the most profound and devastating ramifications of Darwinism for mankind. Unable to reconcile himself to nature, to reestablish the rational, moral, and spiritual links that Darwinism had severed, Vandover becomes what many in the late nineteenth century feared all humanity would become:

a victim of an indifferent, deterministic universe. The ordered self would be destroyed by natural force in the world outside and by that same force operating within one's own natural, biological being.

Vandover experiences the irrationality of the Darwinian universe—that is, its incomprehensibility by the rational self—in the irrationality of his own natural instincts. He finds himself alienated from those instincts, unable to comprehend or control them. Dolly Haight had placed the seat of instinct within the rational and moral self. Vandover discovers that instinct in fact exists apart from the self. It is not the self's agent, guiding and protecting its virtue as Dolly would have it, but the self's antagonist. After all, it is an "unreasoned instinct" (20) that leads Vandover while at Harvard to seek out a young woman that his moral self had earlier rejected. That moral self—no doubt a product of his Christian upbringing under the guardianship of his father—felt disgust and repulsion at the young woman's wantonness. But, away from his father's influence, Vandover lacks both the Christian moral vision that could conceive of instinct as beneficent (as does Dolly) and that therefore could sublimate the sexual drive, as well as a moral structure that could check its natural rapacity. His instinctual sexual drive overpowers his moral and rational self, leaving Vandover bewildered. After this first sexual experience, Vandover "could not tell why he had acted as he did, and he certainly would not have believed himself capable of it" (20). It was an irrational, natural force; indeed, it was an "unreasoned instinct" that made him do it.

The power and irrationality of Vandover's sexual instinct lead him to go continually against his best interests. We are told that he knew his "desire of vice" involved the "wilful and deliberate corruption of part of that which was best in him" (24), and yet he persists in vice. He knows that Turner Ravis "influenced him upon his best side" and that Flossie "appealed only to the animal and the beast in him" (44), and yet he pursues Flossie at the expense of Turner. And it is Vandover's sexual license that ultimately destroys him, leading him to contract a debilitating, sexually transmitted disease. Interestingly enough, that disease attacks his mind—the seat of the reason, of the rational self that is so ineffectual against the impetuosity of his libido. The alienation of the self from nature leads to the death of the self; without an integrating structure or a reconciling vision, Vandover is, quite literally, embruted.

Nature in *Vandover*, then, is clearly amoral; it neither rewards nor punishes, but remains indifferent.[8] Moreover, to the moral self whose foundation in the Christian conception of a morally ordered universe had only recently been shaken, this amorality appears malevolent and immoral. Thus the individual once again feels alienated from the natural world in which he lives, his moral self finding no parallel within that world. And once again, that world destroys him.

The embodiment of this new "natural" amorality is Charlie Geary, the new man of business who replaces the old man and the old ways—namely, Vandover's father and all he represented. In fact, Geary is the negative image of the Old Gentleman, similar in that his moral code reflects his conception of nature, yet markedly different in that conception. The Old Gentleman embraced a traditional Christian moral code based on a divinely created and morally ordered universe. He conducted his life accordingly: devoted to his wife and family, ethical in business. Geary, on the other hand, derives his moral code from a Darwinian conception of nature, and he continually defends his conduct by appealing to what, according to Darwinism, is natural. He is avaricious and selfish, yet claims that that is "human nature," that in this world it is "every man for himself" (82). "The weakest to the wall," he says, "the strongest to the front" (288). He tries to "crowd out" a legal assistant suffering from consumption in the firm where he works (an echo of the Darwinian, actually Spencerian, notion of the "survival of the fittest"), and he uses "the instinct of the keen man of business" (222) to cozen his "friend" Vandover out of his valuable property. Such attitudes and actions would not be considered natural by Christian standards; on the contrary, they would be considered unnatural and therefore immoral, and certainly the ironic light in which Norris presents them leads us to believe that that is in fact how they should be viewed. We get the sense that Geary merely uses Darwinism to rationalize his unscrupulous behavior, as did many late nineteenth-century Social Darwinists, and as would the robber baron Shelgrim in *The Octopus* and the speculator Jadwin in *The Pit*. And we sympathize with Vandover when he voices Christian moral indignation and calls Geary a swindler. Nature may be amoral, and Geary may indeed be only following nature in his behavior, yet the moral self is repulsed by the spectacle. Nature, no longer a moral paradigm or mentor, becomes what both Vandover and Geary envision it to be: an engine, amoral and indifferent, crushing humanity:

> It was Life, the murmur of the great, mysterious force that spun the wheels of Nature and that sent it onward like some enormous engine, resistless, relentless; an engine that sped straight forward, driving before it the infinite herd of humanity, driving it on at breathless speed through all eternity, driving it no one knew whither, crushing out inexorably all those who lagged behind the herd and who fell from exhaustion, grinding them to dust beneath its myriad iron wheels, riding over them, still driving on the herd that yet remained, driving it recklessly, blindly on and on toward some far-distant goal, some vague unknown end, some mysterious, fearful bourne forever hidden in thick darkness. (202)

It is a vision of unmitigated horror from any perspective, and not because of nature's sheer destructive force, but primarily because of the moral indifference of that force. To Vandover, who feels himself falling beneath the "iron wheels," the horror is personal and imminent. To Geary, who has this same vision while fantasizing about becoming the president of the United States, it is horror that he can exploit to his own advantage, that he can use to justify his own ruthless ambition, his own scrambling to the front of the herd. Either way, nature is now a moral ogre; and while Vandover may be mentally and physically destroyed by it, Geary, by adopting nature's amorality, is likewise embruted.

Closely linked to this new perception of nature as amoral is the contemporaneous view of it as a spiritual wasteland. After all, it was a divinely created and guided natural world that had embodied moral order. Now that nature seemed to be devoid of that order, so too did it appear to be stripped of that order's creator—this perception is a manifestation of the prevalent fear that by denying design, Darwinism denied a designer. We have already seen how several ordering principles within the novel are taken away from Vandover and how all of them—Vandover's father, Dolly Haight, Turner Ravis, the Church, Vandover's art—are linked with spirituality; yet we need to look closely at how Vandover reacts to this spiritual bereavement, how he responds to a world suddenly stripped of the comfort of an absolute. In doing so, we will again see Vandover as representative of post-Darwinian humanity, of human beings alienated from the natural world with which they had so recently felt integrated.

During the capsizing of the *Mazatlán*, Vandover encounters a Salvationist, a young woman working for the Salvation Army, who is certain of her deliverance from harm: "I'm going to be saved anyhow; I ain't going to drown; Jesus is watching over me. . . . Jesus is going to save me. I *know* I'm going to be saved. I feel it" (115–16). Shortly thereafter she is killed by a blow from the loosened beam of the foremast. Jesus, evidently, was not watching; the Salvationist is not saved. For the first time in the novel Norris explicitly posits a godless, Darwinian universe in which faith is a mere illusion, a human belief with no factual correlative in nature. Yet the earnestness of the Salvationist's belief and the solace it provides her in such a crisis—"What a comfort," she declares, "what a support" (116)—is so compelling that even Vandover, the one whom "religion had never affected . . . very deeply," is moved. "I wish *I* could have such a confidence" (116), he says, "sincerely envying" the woman and her faith. Vandover's emphasis on the "I" indicates his awareness of his own isolation, of his banishment from the consolation of religious belief. As we have already seen, this spiritual exile had been brought about to a large extent by his scientific intelligence and his scientific knowledge—in effect, by his condition as a post-Darwinian man. Yet this new knowledge, while it may have stripped the universe of a deity, did not strip humanity of its need to believe in a deity. In other words, it did not eradicate the spiritual self. Even Vandover the skeptic wishes for such a belief and envies it in another.

During Vandover's first great spiritual crisis, shortly after being bereft of all ordering principles save his art, he once again experiences the effect of his spiritual banishment. It is at this point that we are told that Vandover never thought very much about religious matters, that he considered himself "too intelligent" to be a believer. Yet we are also told that "the moment he rejected a concrete religion Vandover was almost helpless" (191). He now finds himself not in the Christian universe of an ordered hierarchy, but in the labyrinth: a universe without discernible structure, a universe in which he cannot locate himself. There is no apparent means of subsuming the brute to his better self, no "clues" that could lead him safely away from that "fatal central place where the brute had its lair" (192). These "clues" Norris identifies with the religion and the other ordering principles that Vandover had abandoned—again, partly due to his new scientific knowledge. He now discovers that that knowledge has betrayed him, that in disposing of the deity and the divinely conceived universe, it has failed to provide an adequate substitute—that is, a substitute that could provide humanity with the same solace that Christianity had. Force, that amorphous and abstract power which Spencer and other evolutionists had elevated to the level of the deity, fails; it lacks a spiritual essence that could connect the individual's spiritual self to it, that could guide and direct him in times of crisis. "Forces," we are told, "could not help him [Vandover] withstand temptation, could not strengthen him against the brute" (191). Desperate, Vandover begins "searching with frantic haste and eagerness for any one of those clues he had so carelessly cast from him" (192). As in his response to the Salvationist, Vandover once again evinces a nostalgic yearning for the spiritual guidance and consolation that his own "intelligence" had stripped from him.

This yearning culminates during the first onslaught of Vandover's disease. Again he finds himself isolated in an unfamiliar, godless universe where "all the *existing order* of things . . . appeared to draw off like a refluent tide, leaving him alone, abandoned, cast upon some fearful, mysterious shore" (211–12, my emphasis). Yet on this godless—we may say Darwinian—shore, Vandover's spiritual self still remains intact, still craves a correlative in the natural world. No longer merely wishing for such a correlative, Vandover in his desperation cries out for one: "Oh, help me. Why don't you *help* me? You can if you only will" (213). We are told that this exclamation was "an impulse, a blind, resistless instinct" (213). At first, we may feel that in this description Norris's love of melodrama is getting the better of him, for he appears to be aligning instinct—up to this point in the novel associated with the individual's bestial, libidinal being—with Vandover's "better self." Yet such a description highlights the rift within Vandover between his spiritual self and his natural body, two separate entities for which "instinct" conveys two separate meanings. While the body's instinct craves physical satisfaction and strives to dominate and ultimately destroy the self, the self's instinct seeks an ordered correlative in the natural world with which it can identify and through which it can subsume its physical being, thus preserving both in a harmonious whole. Vandover's cry is his self's (or, as Norris calls it, his "soul's") response "to an *intuition* of a force outside of itself" (214, my emphasis). We are reminded of Asa Gray's notion of man's "inborn conception" and "profound conviction that there is order in the universe," an order that to Gray was conceived by a divine creator. Yet there is no divinity here, only force, and at the same time that Vandover expresses hope, we sense his own awareness of its futility. "He gave no name to this mysterious 'You,'" we are told, "this strange supernatural being" (213), and the most salient reason that he does not is that he cannot: such force has no identifiable self. It is not personal, does not reflect the individual's own ordered self. As such, it provides no solace to him. Vandover's predicament was the same that impelled men such as Spencer, Gray, and LeConte to deify natural force—in the case of LeConte, to make force a personal god. If Vandover lacks the intelligence or understanding to reconcile himself to nature, he at least expresses the same yearning that led Gray, LeConte, and others, including Norris himself in *The Octopus*, to attempt such a reconciliation. Vandover, of course, receives no response to his plea. His desperate invocation is met by "nothing, nothing but the vast silence, the unbroken blackness of the night, a night that was to last forever" (214). Norris ironically uses the Christian symbols of "blackness" and "night" to indicate godlessness—not of the individual soul, but of the entire universe. And since it is not the soul but the universe that is reprobate, it is the universe that must be changed. Again we can understand the contemporary efforts to transform the godless Darwinian universe into a divine Darwinistic universe by assimilating evolution to Christianity. For Vandover, however, who must face the unreconciled blackness alone, there is only one possible result: insanity. Unable to find a correlative order outside his own ordered mind, and unable to impose a new order on that external, natural world, Vandover's internal order disintegrates. His disease and the resulting insanity become figures for this final loss of order and, as Vandover is representative of post-Darwinian humanity, figures for the post-Darwinian condition. It was not uncommon in the late nineteenth century to believe that the contemporary "malaise" of Darwinism would result in something akin to insanity. We remember Gray's claim that the materialistic and atheistic view of the universe as "an eternal sequence of cause and effect, for which there is no first cause" (i.e., the Darwinian view) was a view that "few sane persons can long rest in." Clearly, Vandover's fate illustrates Gray's claim.

The loss of Vandover's artistic ability is of course the final blow, the thing that seals his collapse. We have already seen that art functions as an ordering principle and is linked with the spiritual, that it provides the means through which Vandover could be saved. The fact that it falls victim to Vandover's disease—a natural, sexually transmitted disease—suggests the dissociation of the natural from a governing moral and spiritual order. The divine afflatus, as it were, perishes along with the Divinity in the Darwinian universe. And, interestingly enough, the way in which this loss of artistic ability manifests itself is emblematic of the alienation between humanity and nature that resulted from Darwinism. Vandover experiences dysfunction between his mind (his rational, moral, and spiritual self) and his hand (part of his natural, physical being). We are told that Vandover "could not make his hand interpret what was in his head" (196), could not connect the idea with the physical. This disconnection suggests that which exists between the ordered mind and the Darwinian natural world which no longer reflects it—indeed, which no longer "interprets" that mind's conception of an ordered universe, but defies and denies it. "Some third medium," we discover, "through which the one used to act upon the other . . . seemed to be absent" (196). In the pre-Darwinian conception of the universe, God had been that "third medium," had provided the link between the self and nature. As creator of both, He had ordered each alike, had made one the reflection of the other, and thus the self and nature enjoyed an integrated, mutually dependent relationship. Now, however, Vandover's mind and hand, the self and the natural, "seemed to act independently of each other" (196). The result is a disconnected mass of lines on canvas that had "no meaning." Again, we are told that "the very thing that would have made them intelligible, interpretive . . . was absent" (197), and we remember how God's rational, purposive design in nature had given the universe meaning, had made it "intelligible" and "interpretive" to the rational mind. God the "artist" had imbued the forms of nature with life; Vandover the artist, without God, cannot do the same for his "grotesque and meaningless shapes" (197).

There are several other manifestations of this rift between the self and nature in *Vandover*, most notably the recurrent contrasts between the spiritual and the carnal (e.g., Turner and Flossie; the Church and the Imperial), but these function mostly to reinforce those manifestations of the rift that we have already observed, and therefore I will omit discussion of them here. More important is how Norris deals with the problem of free will in *Vandover*, for this too was one of the disquieting philosophical dilemmas posed by Darwinism, many in the late nineteenth century believing that Darwin's theory posited a deterministic universe that denied free will and therefore moral choice. Norris seems to want it both ways in the novel. At the beginning, Vandover exercises free will and is morally responsible for contracting his debilitating disease: "the punishment," we are told, "that he had brought upon himself" (213). Yet once the disease overtakes him, there is a discernible shift away from free will and toward determinism. Vandover is no longer able to make a moral choice, his behavior determined by the physiological effects of the disease. We can understand this shift and the philosophical waffling that produced it if we remember that Norris characteristically waffled between those two ideological poles that were his mentors: Emile Zola and Joseph LeConte. And while there are certainly some aspects of LeConte's philosophy embodied in *Vandover*—in particular, LeConte's view of human beings' dualism (i.e., their dual nature of rationality/animality)—the predominant philosophy evinced throughout the novel, and especially at the end, is Zola's.[9]

As we saw earlier, nature in *Vandover* is not deified as it will be in the LeContean world of *The Octopus;* it is not beneficent, neither in the short nor the long run. Never does an authorial voice, as does Presley's in *The Octopus*, explain to us the LeContean notion that the apparent evil of natural force is working toward a greater good. Never are we told, for example, that Vandover's demise, his destruction beneath the spinning wheels of nature's engine, is for the ultimate benefit of the human herd. And since nature and natural law are not embodiments of God and His will, they provide no moral structure through which Vandover can subsume his animality to his rationality, the brute to his better self. Nature does not and cannot replace those ordering principles that Vandover has lost. Moreover, were Vandover to align himself with nature, he would not be saved; on the contrary, he would be like Geary. For in the context of *Vandover*, Geary is the "natural" man: self-interested, rapacious, amoral. The LeContean notion that it is natural for human beings to subsume their animal aggression to their human spirit is simply not evinced in the natural world of *Vandover*.

Thus it is not so much a personal moral failing on Vandover's part that brings about his fall, but a failing of ordering structures through which Vandover could subsume his bestial nature to his rational and spiritual self. With the collapse of the old order, and with no new order to replace it, Vandover's fall becomes inevitable. True enough, Vandover is to a large extent responsible for the loss of this old order, the loss of the ordering principles often the result of his moral license. During his first great spiritual crisis, he realizes that "one by one *he had wrenched himself free* from all those influences that had tended to foster and to cultivate all the better part of him" (188, my emphasis). He had forsaken religion, neglected Turner, and even hastened, through his dissolute conduct, his father's death. Yet once these ordering principles have all vanished, Vandover is no longer a free moral agent; he can no longer control the brute within him, is no longer its master. We now do not see Vandover *and* the Brute, but Vandover *the* brute: "the brute in him had now grown so large, so insatiable, that it had taken everything, even to his very self, his own identity—that he had literally *become the brute*" (278, Norris's emphasis). The LeContean ethical dualism has collapsed into a Zolaesque materialistic monism in which the individual is a physically determined being in a deterministic universe.[10]

Vandover's disease of lycanthropy, a disease that literally transforms Vandover into the brute, is emblematic of this philosophical shift within the novel from free will to determinism. It is an acquired disease, acquired through Vandover's profligacy. Yet once contracted, it physiologically determines Vandover's behavior. In the same paragraph in which we are told that Vandover's disease was "the punishment that he had brought upon himself" (implying free will), we are also told that "it was Nature inexorably exacting" (implying determinism [213]). We soon see that Vandover is unable to prevent voluntarily a lycanthropic attack; he tries, but his will is ineffectual. "It was evident that now he could not stop himself," we are told during one such attack; "it was like hysterical laughter, a thing *beyond his control*" (264, my emphasis). We remember here Zola's belief in mechanistic psychology, his credo that "determinism dominates everything," including the "brain of man." Vandover, through his disease, becomes the image of Zola's "physiological man." Yet this physiological determinism, this biological control of the self, is not only indicative of Zola's philosophy of man but also of insanity—the final loss of free will, of the ability to be morally responsible for one's actions. We remember again Asa Gray who had argued that the materialistic, deterministic view of humanity and the universe was one that "few sane persons can long rest in." Vandover, who by the end of the novel exemplifies Zola's view, also illustrates Gray's; he is both physiologically determined and insane.

Norris thus dramatizes in *Vandover* the post-Darwinian condition: the sudden loss of the traditional Christian order, the replacement of that order with Darwinian determinism, and the catastrophic result of that determinism on humanity. Yet Norris in *Vandover* does not point toward a reconciliation between the self and nature, as he would in *The Octopus*, by appropriating the reconciling vision of LeConte. Rather, in this early work he turns toward his literary mentor, Zola. As Norris's brother Charles G. Norris wrote in his foreword to *Vandover*, "the influence of Emile Zola is evident throughout the story. The great Frenchman was the inspiration that led Frank Norris to attempt the role of novelist" (vii). And like Zola, who tried to move narrative form into the realm of the new science in his experimental novel, Norris in *Vandover* attempts to rewrite the Christian narrative of spiritual crisis by placing it within a new evolutionary context. We can only speculate, but such a powerful literary influence as Zola must also have been something of a philosophical influence, especially on a young writer writing his first major novel, a young writer who by all accounts had no predilection for abstract philosophy. It appears that it is for this reason that *Vandover* moves toward and concludes with a Zolaesque response to the post-Darwinian condition: not a reconciling vision, but a vision of humanity and nature that needs no reconciliation. As we saw in chapter 2, Zola perceived no division between the two; a human being, including the self, was a material part of a materialistic, deterministic universe. He had no free will, but to Zola, this was no reason for alarm; rather, the inefficacy of the human will meant that once the experimental novel exposed the cause of a problem, the effect could be ameliorated by extirpating that determining cause. In this way, the social purpose of the experimental novel to "solve in time all the problems of socialism [i.e., sociology]" would come to pass.

Norris, who in his essays "The Novel with a 'Purpose'" and "The Responsibilities of the Novelist" also advocated a social purpose for the novel, must have been at least slightly disappointed with the conclusion of *Vandover*.[11] As Charles Child Walcutt has observed, "there is . . . nothing that might contribute to the science of sociology in the events by which he

[Vandover] is destroyed." [12] There are no redeeming social discoveries, no possibilities of a better world. And if Norris, as Donald Pizer has argued, "knows that the Vandovers fall and that the Gearys rise, but his sympathies are all with the Vandovers," [13] then such a world would not be one that, to take Asa Gray slightly out of context, he could "long rest in." [14] By his subsequent work, Norris would also seem to corroborate Gray's claim that Americans have "no predilection" for "positivism and kindred forms of materialistic philosophy," something for which Zola certainly did have a predilection. We can again only speculate, but it appears that it is for these reasons that Norris would exchange Zola "for other gods" — as H. L. Mencken observed in his introduction to *Vandover*—in his later novels. [15] And chief among those gods would be Norris's other mentor, Joseph LeConte.

CHAPTER FOUR
THE OCTOPUS:
NORRIS'S RESPONSE TO THE
POST-DARWINIAN CONDITION

While *Vandover* is a dramatization of a contemporary philosophical problem—what I have called the post-Darwinian condition—*The Octopus* is a literary response to that problem, a dramatization of its resolution. The novel is in this way akin to the plethora of scientific, theological, and philosophical treatises of Norris's day that sought to reconcile humanity and nature by assimilating Darwinian evolution to Christian belief. In fact, as Donald Pizer has cogently demonstrated, Norris appropriated LeConte's evolutionary Christianity as his philosophical framework for *The Octopus.*[1] The novel's dramatic conflicts take place within a LeContean universe, and it is not until the main characters learn to perceive the "truth" of that universe and of their relationship to it that these conflicts are resolved. The fact that such resolutions—indicative of the larger resolution between the self and nature—are philosophical and not dramatic left *The Octopus* open to much critical attack on aesthetic grounds. Yet the aesthetic dissatisfaction with the novel parallels John Dewey's pragmatic disagreement with LeConte and the other Christian evolutionists, a disagreement that would signal the move away from such conceptions and presentations of humanity and the universe in the twentieth century.

We do not witness the demise of traditional ordering principles in *The Octopus* as we do throughout *Vandover*; rather, in *The Octopus*, those principles have already been destroyed before the action in the novel begins. The world of *The Octopus* at the outset is *apparently* one of Darwinian determinism—as it is *in fact* at the conclusion of *Vandover*—a universe of force devoid of either deity or design. The old order is depicted only in retrospect through the nostalgic reflections of a few characters. A centenarian Spaniard recounts to Presley that bygone era in the San Joaquin valley as if it had been a prelapsarian paradise. "Ah, those were days," he says. "That was a gay life."[2] There was little money, yet everyone had plenty of food, clothing, and even wine. De La Cuesta, the owner of Los Muertos, was an omnipotent ruler much like the Christian deity, a figure who "had the power of life and death over his people" (21), yet who only exercised that power for beneficent ends. Moreover, like the Christian deity, he too was the moral center of his people, and at Los Muertos "there was no law but *his word*" (21, my emphasis). Through his guidance and that of the Mission Fathers who also helped settle the valley, the people enjoyed a pastoral existence characterized by a unity of religion and agriculture. They worked the land for spiritual rather than commercial ends, planting wheat, olives, and grapes "to provide the elements of the Holy Sacrament—bread, oil, and wine" (21). The old Spaniard tells Presley that "those industries began in California—from the Church" (21). The settlers of the San Joaquin, through their belief in a deity and through the reinforcement of that belief by the Church, were thus spiritually linked to the land, in harmony with the natural world in which they lived.

Mrs. Derrick also reflects nostalgically about her rural upbringing in eastern Ohio. It too had been a place in which humanity was united with nature, a place "where the farmers loved their land, caressing it, coaxing it, nourishing it as though it were a thing almost conscious" (59). We can assume that, as with the settlers of the San Joaquin, these farmers were bound to the land by their spiritual beliefs, the "conscious" land a manifestation of the divine consciousness that had created the cosmos. Once again, God, as the creator of both human beings and nature, provided the link between the two.

Yet in the late nineteenth-century world in which the old Spaniard and Mrs. Derrick now find themselves, this unifying vision has passed, the Christian deity that provided it a victim of Darwinism and of other scientific and economic advances that have made the "New Agriculture" (633) possible. The Spaniard calls this new agriculture "stupid" (22), while Mrs. Derrick finds "something almost unnatural" about "this *new order* of things"

(60, my emphasis), an order characterized not by unity but by division. There is nothing spiritual about the contemporary relationship between farmer and land. The new farmers of the San Joaquin, we are told, "had no love for their land. They were not attached to the soil" (298). They farm it solely for commercial ends, to make a quick profit, and thus view it as a blind force they must subdue and control—an attitude that precludes unity. In contrast to the farmers of Mrs. Derrick's youth who "caressed" and "nourished" their land, these farmers "squeeze it dry, . . . exhaust it" (298).

Magnus Derrick is the epitome of these new farmers, and as the new owner of Los Muertos he is ironically contrasted with De La Cuesta. Magnus, although considering himself the "exponent of principles" (74) he believes worthy and just, is nevertheless corrupted by his own greed. He embodies the "true California spirit . . . the spirit of the West" (298), that of the pursuit of quick wealth. Such a "spirit" is indeed "spirit-less" in the traditional sense—as formerly embodied by De La Cuesta—and as the moral center of his community Magnus also falls far short of his predecessor. In fact, Magnus fails to provide a moral center at all; he himself is a victim of the natural, economic, and political forces he attempts to control.

The Church that had encouraged and reinforced the spiritual bonds between the farmers and the land in De La Cuesta's day has also been corrupted before the outset of the novel. The Mission's physical appearance is indicative of the Church itself as a spiritual force; it is now "decaying," a ruin of "crumbling plaster" decorated with "naive crudity of ornament and picture" (151). As in *Vandover*, it is no longer relevant to modern humanity. Its chief icon, Christ in agony on the cross, is "but a lamentable vision of tormented anatomy" (151), devoid of spiritual significance. The Mission's priest, Father Sarria, also represents the corruption of the Church. As Magnus Derrick is to De La Cuesta, Father Sarria is to his predecessors, the Mission Fathers. He is a corrupt man of the world posing as a man of God; Annixter catches him with game cocks—an abuse of nature for mercenary rather than spiritual ends, an abuse that parallels the farmers' own abuse of the land for profit. Moreover, Norris strongly suggests, as Stuart L. Burns has demonstrated, that Father Sarria is the mysterious rapist, the "Other," who was responsible for defiling and ultimately killing Angéle and, in consequence, haunting Vanamee.[3] In light of this, Father Sarria's religious counseling of Vanamee becomes the apogee of religious hypocrisy.

The early scene of the sheep slaughter by the railroad illustrates the destruction of the old order and, more important, through Presley's perception before, during, and after, points out the obsolescence of the traditional conception of humanity and nature on which that order had rested. At this point in the novel Presley is a self-proclaimed poet with an antiquated, romantic vision of the West, the West as it had been in De La Cuesta's day.[4] He climbs to the top of a hill from which he can survey the entire valley and projects this vision of the old order onto the present scene which no longer reflects it. He is described, appropriately enough, as "dizzied, stunned, stupified, . . . drunk" at viewing this "whole order of things" (47), this order that is a construct of his own mind. He deludes himself into perceiving the prelapsarian harmony between humanity and nature that the old Spaniard had described, paraphrasing the Spaniard's words regarding the "trinity of great industries, taking their rise in a religious rite" (48)— words that, given the state of the new agriculture, must be taken as ironic. He hears the Mission bells ring out the *de Profundis*—"a note of the Old World; of the ancient regime, . . . sounding there in this new land, unfamiliar and strange at this end-of-the-century time" (48)—yet fails to comprehend why it sounds so strange. Rather, he thinks the *de Profundis* rings "as if in confirmation" of his vision of the West; in fact, it only confirms his own delusion. When the railroad train crashes through the sheep—as Donald Pizer has noted, an image of the new monopoly crushing the old agrarian order—Presley's vision of that order, and the conception of humanity and nature that supported it, are shattered.[5] A universe of natural forces apparently replaces that of the traditional Christian order.[6] The *de Profundis*, we are told, "ceased to ring" (50).

This scene also introduces us to a central concern of the novel and of the "end-of-the-century time" in general—that of perception. Presley believes he perceives a "whole order of things," but he is shocked into realizing that this is not the case. Such a shock parallels that of Darwinism on late nineteenth-century humanity: the divinely ordered, teleological universe now seemed to be a delusion, a construct of the mind that human beings projected onto a deterministic universe. Christian evolutionists such as LeConte responded to this shock and the fear it produced by insisting on an order external to the self, by arguing that evolution was not indicative of materialistic determinism, but that it was itself an example of design.

One need only learn to *perceive* this "fact." In other words, if the traditional Christian conception of humanity and the universe was faulty, so too to LeConte was the Darwinian conception of materialistic determinism. The "truth," as LeConte went to great lengths to explain, lay in between. Evolution was a natural force, but it was not a deterministic force—at least not materially. LeConte, we remember, posited a divine, "spiritual" determinism in which God, not "uncaused" physical force, was the determining factor. Therefore, to LeConte, evolution did not sever the links between the self and nature by denying design and therefore denying the existence of God, but only obfuscated the self's perception of them by reorienting God and His design within natural process itself. LeConte's work, then, was an attempt to make human beings perceive the divine presence informing apparently random evolutionary process and, in so doing, to make humans reperceive those links between themselves and nature, to show them those links in a new, though essentially unchanged, form.

Norris, in incorporating many of LeConte's ideas into *The Octopus*, also incorporated LeConte's awareness of the pitfalls of human perception. For unlike in *Vandover*, where the new order is essentially no order (i.e., materialistic determinism), the new order in *The Octopus* is deterministic in appearance only. *The Octopus* is written upon the premise—derived from LeConte and not fully revealed until the novel's conclusion—that there is an order external to the self. And like his mentor, Norris the "responsible" novelist set out to reveal this order to his audience, to reveal the "true" perception of humanity and the universe behind the deterministic appearance; as a novelist, Norris accomplished this by having a few central characters slowly discover, or rediscover, their moral and spiritual affinity with the natural world. Each character's growth, in other words, is a growth in perception, culminating in that character's awareness of his place within an essentially LeContean universe.

Vanamee is one of the characters who achieves such an awareness, and his awakening is important as it most clearly represents a transition away from the defunct old order and toward the new LeContean order. Vanamee is a type of aboriginal mystic. Presley sees him as an "ascetic," a "seer." Looking at Vanamee, Presley ruminates:

> So must have appeared the half-inspired shepherds of the Hebraic legends, the younger prophets of Israel, dwellers in the wilderness, be-

holders of visions, having their existence in a continual dream, talkers with God, gifted with strange powers. (32–33)

Like the early prophets to whom he is compared, the original "beholders" of the Judeo-Christian vision, Vanamee will behold the "new" vision. He will reject the corrupt teachings of Father Sarria and the Church and will eventually see through the apparent determinism of his post-Darwinian age. As a prophet, he will later reveal the "truth" of this new vision to Presley, thereby spreading the "word."[7]

Yet there is a more profound reason for comparing Vanamee to the early Hebrew prophets. LeConte's evolutionary Christianity, while it was certainly meant to move the Christian religion forward (taking into account, as it did, modern evolutionary theory), was also a movement backward. By arguing that God was immanent in nature, LeConte in many ways was pushing Christianity back to its pagan origins, back to its closeness with nature and natural cycles. The pagans believed that the gods were not only immanent in natural phenomena but *were* those phenomena. Sir James George Frazer pointed out the affinity between the pagan corn-god and Christ in *The Golden Bough*, intimating that the corn-god was perhaps the prefigurement of Christ.[8] After all, both had to die so that their people could live (the pagans physically, the Christians spiritually), both were eaten by their people (the corn-god physically, Christ symbolically in the Eucharist), and both were resurrected (the corn-god each spring, Christ on Easter). LeConte himself was aware of the affinity his version of Christianity had with pagan religions, for he went to great lengths to deny that his version constituted pantheism, insisting that his God was not "diffused" through nature but remained "personal."[9] Yet, in appropriating LeConte's theories to *The Octopus*, Norris did not choose Christ as his controlling symbol—that "lamentable vision of tormented anatomy"—but the wheat; and it is not difficult to discern the consanguinity the wheat as a spiritual force has with the pagan corn-god. Vanamee, then, as a shepherd—a modern instance of the original prophets and "pastors"—will perceive and reveal a version of Christian spiritualism that goes back to the origins, back to Christianity's birth out of pagan myths and natural cycles.

In moving away from nature as a spiritual source, Christianity necessarily relegated nature to a symbolic role. While the pagans believed that the springtime rebirth of the corn was *in fact* the resurrection of the corn-

god, Christians could only see that annual rebirth as a *symbol* of the resurrection of Christ and, by extension, of their own possible resurrection
after death. Father Sarria demonstrates this when he tells Vanamee that
"your grain of wheat is your *symbol* of immortality" (144, my emphasis) as
a means of alleviating Vanamee's suffering over the physical loss of Angéle.
In addition, Christianity itself became highly symbolic, relying on allegory and metaphor, rather than on natural phenomena, to reveal spiritual
truths. And the predominant argument Vanamee has with orthodox Christianity is this symbolism. Much like Vandover, Vanamee has no patience
with religious symbols. Yet Vandover, who was not a spiritual man, simply
could not comprehend them, nor did he have much interest in spiritual
meaning however it may have been revealed. He, like many of his real-life
contemporaries, was interested solely in "natural" facts. Vanamee, on the
other hand, is a very spiritual man, and we can assume that he can comprehend Christian symbolism, and we can be certain that he is interested in
spiritual meaning. He demands, however, as Darwinism forced religiously
minded scientists such as LeConte to demand, that spiritual meaning be
grounded in natural fact. "All is natural," LeConte wrote; "but all is supernatural." [10] The one embodied the other. Thus Vanamee, even before experiencing his revelation, tells Father Sarria that he does not want Angéle
in heaven, in "this vague place of yours," but wants her "material, earthly"
(143). To him, the spiritual must be manifest in the natural, in what he himself calls "reality" (152). At one point, desperate and hysterical, Vanamee
implores Father Sarria: "help me, you and your God; create the delusion,
do the miracle" (148). The ironic juxtaposition of "delusion" and "miracle"
reveals Vanamee's own despair at the possibility of an abstract God performing a miracle that was not simultaneously a delusion. He will have to
wait until nature "does the miracle"—which it will in the form of Angéle's
daughter—a miracle that will indeed be real.

   After voicing his argument with orthodox Christianity to Father Sarria,
Vanamee concludes that "the Answer was not in the Church" (151). This is
the beginning of his awakening, the beginning of a process of perceiving
the spiritual in the natural, and ultimately of perceiving the spiritual connection between himself and nature. He moves out of the Church into the
Mission garden—a midway point between the old orthodoxy and the new
natural spiritualism, a place of both "illusions" and "reality" (151)—and

now appeals "directly to Angéle herself" (153). Vanamee's direct appeal to his deceased lover after his rejection of the Christian God is an appeal to nature, for Angéle is suggestive of a natural goddess—specifically, Flora:

> She came to him from out of the flowers, the smell of the roses in her hair of gold, that hung in two straight plaits on either side of her face; the reflection of the violets in the profound dark blue of her eyes, perplexing, heavy-lidded, almond-shaped, oriental; the aroma and the imperial red of the carnations in her lips, with their almost Egyptian fulness; the whiteness of the lilies, the perfume of the lilies, and the lilies' slender balancing grace in her neck. Her hands disengaged the odour of the heliotropes. The folds of her dress gave off the enervating scent of poppies. Her feet were redolent of hyacinths. (142)

Flora has always been associated with rebirth—Botticelli, for one, exploited this association by portraying Flora strewing flowers in his painting of springtime, *La Primavera*—and certainly Norris was aware of this when he drew the unmistakable comparison between Angéle and Flora. After all, Angéle will eventually be reborn in the form of her daughter. Yet the identification with Flora has added significance. We remember in *Vandover* that before his collapse Vandover had painted an "ideal head" of Flora, and that that painting illustrated the interconnection between humanity and nature: the human form of the goddess as a symbol of nature's fecundity. Moreover, it was Flora's spirituality that connected the two in a harmonious union (the human form as goddess, nature as goddess). In *The Octopus*, of course, Angéle is not a painting; she was at one time a living human being, and because of this her association with Flora indicates the very real connection between humanity and nature that a natural spiritualism—that is, a God immanent in nature—provides. Angéle, as a spiritual human being, had been an intricate part of nature, not separated from it, for nature is also spiritual. The one reflected the other. Such a conception reestablishes humanity's link to nature that the Darwinian conception of a world of material force had apparently severed.

LeConte believed that the human spirit—or the rational factor as he alternately called it—was the culmination of the evolutionary process, that it was "born" from the anima of animals. It had, therefore, a "natural" birth; yet this newborn human spirit manifested itself through an awareness of the essential spirituality of both self and nature. Vanamee's final awakening involves the awareness of this "truth" not only with regard to Angéle but also with regard to all humanity and the natural world. In addition, while this new awareness is a spiritual birth for Vanamee, a revelation, it is a revelation that is also "natural"; nature, acting as a spiritual mentor, reveals the "truth" to Vanamee in the form of the wheat and the natural child of Angéle. At one point just before the revelation, Vanamee compares his mystical feeling of Angéle's presence to the nascent wheat. He tells Presley:

> The grain is there now under the earth buried in the dark, in the black stillness, under the clods. Can you imagine the first—the very first little quiver of life that the grain of wheat must feel after it is sown, when it answers to the call of the sun, down there in the dark of the earth, blind, deaf; the very first stir from the inert, long, long before any physical change has occurred,—long before the microscope could discover the slightest change,—when the shell first tightens with the first faint premonition of life? Well it [his feeling of Angéle's presence] is something as illusive as that. (216)

Such an analogy between a natural, physical sensation and a spiritual feeling is not merely a trope; it is indicative of the spiritual connection between the self and nature, for what actuates Vanamee's spiritual feeling is the same thing that actuates the growth of the wheat: love. The wheat is a physical manifestation of the divine spirit—the spirit that is immanent within the wheat itself—and its growth is a physical expression of the divine will, invariably identified with love. We remember LeConte's claim that there is a "complete *identification* of first and second causes" (i.e., metaphysical and physical causes), that natural force, such as growth, is an expression of a God "resident *in* Nature, at all times and in all places directing every event and determining every phenomena" (*sic*).[11]

The simultaneous appearance of Angéle's daughter and the new wheat, then, is the ultimate revelation for Vanamee; it fulfills his desire for a natural spiritualism that he had voiced to Father Sarria, and it awakens his consciousness to the spiritual ties between himself and nature. Norris deliberately describes the event as if it were a religious experience, which, of course, it is. Vanamee awaits the "Vision," the "Manifestation" (383). He sends his mind out over the field of sown wheat, which Norris calls "the enchanted sea of the Supernatural" (382). (Again, we hear an echo of LeConte's "all is natural . . . but all is supernatural.")[12] "A cathedral hush overlay the land," we are told. "A sense of benediction brooded low,— a divine kindliness manifesting itself in beauty, in peace, in absolute repose" (390). When Angéle finally appears, she is "a Vision realised" (391); indeed, as the fulfillment of Vanamee's spiritual yearning and as a spiritual being in her own right, she is realized—that is, made real—by her physical presence. Moreover, this spiritual being is the biological product of the natural cycle of life, death, and regeneration. Norris seems to ignore the rather obvious fact that while Angéle's daughter may represent a biological continuum, she would necessarily be an independent spiritual entity. That Vanamee and the "new" Angéle fall so instantaneously in love—as if Vanamee's and the original Angéle's love had only been on an eighteen-year hiatus—is ludicrous. Nevertheless, the philosophical basis for Norris's dramatization, however tenuous, is understood; the spiritual must find expression through the natural, must be "realised" in the natural. Vanamee perceives that Angéle is not the "symbol" of immortality, as Father Sarria had told him regarding the wheat, but is "the *proof* of immortality" (393, Norris's emphasis). The sudden emergence of the wheat confirms this "truth," as it too is a realization and proof of an immortal spirit—of God who is immanent within it. This parallel, then, between Angéle's "rebirth" and the wheat's "rebirth" highlights the affinity between humanity and the natural world: both are natural expressions of the spiritual, and as such each reflects the other. Angéle, we are later told, "was realised in the wheat" (638). Vanamee and nature are reconciled.

Annixter experiences a similar revelation—in fact, it occurs during the same night, at a nearby location—yet as Annixter is a very different character than Vanamee, his revelation emphasizes a different aspect of the LeContean universe—namely, the moral. But before Annixter can undergo a moral regeneration, he must, like Vanamee, be spiritually "born"—that is, become aware of the essential spirituality of both himself and nature. As with Vanamee, this comes about through the realization of his love for a woman and the perceived connection between that realization and the "realization" of the wheat.

Annixter's lover, Hilma, is, like Angéle, both a real person and a representative of the harmony between humanity and nature. We are told that

she possessed "the original, intended, and natural delicacy of an elemental existence, close to nature, close to life, close to the great, kindly earth"
(85). And like Angéle, Hilma too is suggestive of a fertility goddess: a goddess of milk and motherhood. While Angéle had been redolent of flowers,
Hilma is "redolent and fragrant with milk" (166). Later, when she is pregnant, she is the image of fecundity: "the radiance of the unseen crown of
motherhood glowing from her forehead, the beauty of the perfect woman
surrounding her like a glory" (504). This connection between her spiritual
self and the spirituality of the natural life force that operates through her
makes her an ideal catalyst for Annixter's awakening, for his "salvation"
(380). She is a reflection of the earth itself, the earth that is described as the
"loyal mother" who gives birth to the wheat.

While Vanamee's realization of his love is a physical realization—that
is, his spiritual feeling finds its physical object in Angéle's daughter—
Annixter's is a spiritual realization. After all, he already has the physical
object in Hilma, but he must be made aware of love itself, which can, and
eventually does, connect him to her. Human love is once again reflected in
the divine love that actuates natural process, and Norris draws a parallel
between them by describing the emergence of both in similar naturalistic
terms. The feeling of love in Annixter, "the little seed, long since planted,
gathering strength quietly, had at last germinated" (368) within him. Likewise, at the same moment the wheat, "the little seed long planted, germi-
nating in the deep, dark furrows of the soil, straining, swelling, suddenly in
one night had burst upward to the light" (369). As in Vanamee's revelation,
this simultaneity confirms Annixter's spiritual birth, his awareness of a
spiritual universe with which his own newly awakened spirit is in harmony.

As suggested earlier, this spiritual awakening manifests itself in Annixter
primarily as a moral regeneration. His new perception of the spirituality of
nature brings about a reevaluation of what it means to be a "natural" man.
His previous life had been one of selfishness. He tells Presley, "I was a machine before, and if another man, or woman, or child got in my way, I rode
'em down, and I never *dreamed* of anybody else but myself" (467). This
comparison of his former self with a machine reminds us of the "engine" of
nature in *Vandover* "crushing out" and "riding over" humanity, an engine
that was indicative of a deterministic universe. And in that novel the most
successful exploiter of that engine, the character who emulated it in his own
behavior toward others, was Geary—the natural man within the context

of such a deterministic universe. But, as we have seen, the universe in *The Octopus* is not that of *Vandover*; it is not deterministic but is a LeContean universe informed by a spiritual presence, impelled by a first cause, and is therefore moral. In conceiving of God as immanent within the natural world—God the moral center and source of all good—LeConte succeeded in reintroducing a moral order into that world. Nature once again provided a moral paradigm that human beings could emulate, for natural law was now God's will, not indifferent force. A natural man, then, was a moral man, one who chose—for such a paradigm endowed him with free will—to follow natural law, to co-operate (to use LeConte's own term) with it. And for the individual this involved subsuming his animal self (characterized by such qualities as selfishness, greed, and lust) to his rational self (character-ized by love, compassion, and virtue). To choose not to follow natural law was to sin. Thus the preenlightened Annixter, who is very much like Geary, cannot be considered a natural man within the LeContean universe of *The Octopus*; on the contrary, he is the antithesis of one. His moral self is not aligned with the moral order of nature but instead goes against it.

Annixter's comparison of his former self to a machine also reminds us of the Railroad, the predominant engine image in *The Octopus*. This "iron-hearted" monster, this "soulless Force" (51), is in stark contrast to the beneficent spiritual force that lies immanent within all natural phenomena. As such, the Railroad is clearly immoral; it does not "follow nature," does not follow beneficent natural law—including the economic law of supply and demand—for the benefit of humanity, but instead abuses and exploits that law for its own selfish ends. Shelgrim, the president of the Pacific and Southwestern Railroad, tries to rationalize his company's behavior by tell-ing Presley that the Railroad is only an agent of uncontrollable forces— that is, deterministic forces. He compares the Railroad to the wheat, claim-ing that "Railroads build themselves" just as "the Wheat grows itself" (576). His rationalization echoes Geary's rationalization of his "natural" behavior, yet again, since we know that the universe of *The Octopus* is not deterministic, we also know that Shelgrim's rationalization is specious.[13] The self-engendering wheat is an expression of beneficent, divine will, not blind, deterministic force. The Railroad, on the other hand, is an expres-sion of Shelgrim's selfish will. The wheat feeds the people, but the Railroad, rather than expediting that end, hinders it.

S. Behrman, the representative of the Railroad in Tulare County, is also representative of its immoral force. He too tries to rationalize the Railroad's behavior by arguing that freight rates are determined by economic law, by "all the traffic will bear" (350). Yet economic law cannot be so coldly deterministic since, to Norris, economic law is an aspect of beneficent natural law. The freight rates are in reality determined by S. Behrman's and the Railroad's greed. However, unlike Geary—S. Behrman's moral counterpart in *Vandover*—S. Behrman does not rise, but falls. Vice is not rewarded in the moral universe of *The Octopus* as it is in the deterministic universe of *Vandover*, and the moral force in the novel, nature, metes out the punishment. In a heavy-handed and rather ludicrous *deus ex machina*, S. Behrman is destroyed by the wheat.

Annixter, then, who by his own comparison had been very similar to Geary, Shelgrim, and S. Behrman, learns from his spiritual awakening that the universe is not a deterministic machine. He perceives that it is in fact impelled by a moral and spiritual presence and therefore provides a moral paradigm on which he can base his life and conduct. He learns to "follow nature," to "co-operate" with it, and in so doing redefines himself as a "natural" man. His love for Hilma begins to grow into a general compassion for humanity, recapitulating the burgeoning beneficence of nature itself:

> Where once Annixter had thought only of himself, he now thought only of Hilma. The time when this thought of another should broaden and widen into thought of *Others*, was yet to come; but already it had expanded to include the unborn child—already, as in the case of Mrs. Dyke, it had broadened to enfold another child and another mother bound to him by no ties other than those of humanity and pity. In time, starting from this point it would reach out more and more till it should take in all men and all women, and the intolerant selfish man, while retaining all of his native strength, should become tolerant and generous, kind and forgiving. (498)

The parallel between this description of Annixter's expanding benevolence and the oft-repeated descriptions of the "expanding" fields of wheat, the beneficent harvest rolling "like a flood from the Sierras to the Himalayas to feed thousands of starving scarecrows on the barren plains of India" (651), is unmistakable. Annixter, his newborn human spirit following and co-operating with nature, becomes, like his moral mentor, a beneficent force.

Presley, the only other character in the novel to experience an awakening, gradually learns to perceive the spirituality of the universe while at the same time discovering a new aesthetic through which to depict it. His spiritual awakening, in other words, goes hand in hand with an artistic re-vision. He is in many ways the alter ego of Norris himself, the writer who must find the "romance" in the "real," who must redefine the romantic to include the mundane.[14] In a development reminiscent of the *Künstlerroman*, Presley by the end of the novel has gained the perceptual and artistic maturity necessary to write the true naturalistic epic — the "Epic of the Wheat" that Norris himself has just written.[15]

Presley had come to the San Joaquin valley to write an epic romance, an antiquated literary genre that befit the old pastoral order of De La Cuesta's day. This traditional romance demanded the "great scheme of harmony" (12) between humanity and nature that had then existed — in fact, could only represent such an idyllic world. The contemporary strife between the ranchers and the Railroad, as well as between the ranchers and the land, would need a new form of artistic expression.[16] Yet at first, Presley can only view this strife as "the one note of harsh colour" (12) in his romantic vision. To him, "the romance seemed complete up to that point. There it broke, there it failed, there it became realism, grim, unlovely, unyielding" (12). This distinction between romance and realism Norris himself would attack. In his essay "A Plea for Romantic Fiction," Norris argued that romance need not confine itself to "the drama of a bygone age," that it was not "inappropriate" on "Fifth avenue, or Beacon street, or Michigan avenue." [17] He insisted that the romantic could be found in the commonplace, if a writer would only learn to perceive it there. Realism, to Norris, noted "only the surface of things," and it was up to romanticism to reveal the "truth" that lay beneath that surface.[18] Norris's emphasis on perception, on the writer's need to perceive the "romance" in the "real," obviously correlates to the theme of perception in *The Octopus*. Presley, as a writer, must learn to perceive his "True Romance" not outside the conflict between the ranchers and the Railroad, but within that banal strife over "grain rates and unjust freight tariffs" (13). And this need for perceiving the "truth" of romance within the banality of the "real" certainly parallels Vanamee's desire for a spiritual "truth" grounded in "Reality." Artistic perception, then, is both the result of and a metaphor for spiritual perception, for seeing the spiritual "truth" beneath natural force.

On first surveying the expanse of the San Joaquin valley, Presley had projected an obsolete romantic vision onto the scene. The railroad train's subsequent slaughter of the sheep destroyed that vision and Presley's traditional Christian conception of humanity and nature that had supported it, leaving him confronting an apparently deterministic universe. For most of the novel Presley conceives of the universe as such; he calls the wheat a "colossal power . . . indifferent, gigantic, resistless" (448). Human beings, to Presley, are only "Liliputians, gnats in the sunshine" (448), fighting to control this insuperable force with which they have no spiritual affinity. And after Presley's confrontation with Shelgrim, during which Shelgrim tells him that the Railroad is only an agent of indifferent forces, Presley conceives of nature in the now-familiar image of the engine:

> Nature was, then, a gigantic engine, a vast cyclopean power, huge, terrible, a leviathan with a heart of steel, knowing no compunction, no forgiveness, no tolerance; crushing out the human atom standing in its way, with nirvanic calm, the agony of destruction sending never a jar, never the faintest tremour through all that prodigious mechanism of wheels and cogs. (577)

Not only does this description equate nature with the destructive force of the Railroad, but it also equates Presley's unenlightened conception of nature with that of Mrs. Derrick. She conceives of it in the same terms, almost verbatim:

> nature . . . became relentless, a gigantic engine, a vast power, huge, terrible; a leviathan with a heart of steel, knowing no compunction, no forgiveness, no tolerance; crushing out the human atom with soundless calm, the agony of destruction sending never a jar, never the faintest tremour through all that prodigious mechanism of wheels and cogs. (180–81)

Yet Mrs. Derrick is a woman who lacks perspicacity, both natural and aesthetic. Her vision cannot penetrate below the surface, cannot perceive the spiritual force behind nature's fecundity. In fact, she does not even want to look, willfully blinding herself to it:

> She did not want to look at so much wheat. There was something vaguely indecent in the sight, this food of the people, this elemental

force, this basic energy, weltering here under the sun in all the unconscious nakedness of a sprawling, primordial Titan. (60)

Her timidity, her fear of confronting "this elemental force," prevents her
from perceiving the connection between that force and a spiritual presence
which her own metaphor intimates exists. The Titan, to Mrs. Derrick, is
not a spiritual god manifest in physical form, but a purely physical, sexual
force. The wheat as Titan, then, is not divine, but "indecent." And as a result of this perception, Mrs. Derrick remains alienated from the natural
world, feels "that certain uncongeniality which, when all is said, forever
remains between humanity and the earth which supports it" (180).

Mrs. Derrick's perceptual limitations also carry over into aesthetics. She
reveres the effete, gentile poetry of the "little magazines," anathema to
both Norris and Presley. She cannot see "any romance, any poetry in the
life around her" (61), but looks to "bygone eras" and foreign lands for it.
Her idea of romance is thus divorced from the "real"; just as she cannot
perceive the spiritual in the natural, she cannot perceive the romance in
the mundane.

Presley, who for much of the novel shares Mrs. Derrick's view of nature
as a deterministic engine, concomitantly lacks an astute aesthetic perception. Even though he abandons his "Song of the West"—a romantic epic
that, in its exaltation of a bygone era, has much in common with Mrs. Derrick's romances—he nevertheless begins writing in a genre that is equally
limited: that of social realism. His poem "The Toilers" is little more than
socialist propaganda that reflects his current vision of a deterministic world
of conflicting forces—in this case, the economic forces embodied by the
ranchers and the Railroad. It is realism devoid of romance, a literature that,
to repeat Norris's own words, notes "only the surface of things." In fact,
we find out from Shelgrim that Presley took his inspiration not from his
experience at the Los Muertos ranch, but from a painting called "The Toilers" he had seen in his friend Cedarquist's house. Presley's poem is thus
detached from life itself, provides no insight into it. It is merely a copy of
another work of art, a surface of a surface. As Shelgrim tells Presley, "you
might just as well have kept quiet" (574).

It is not until Presley's enlightenment, not until he can perceive the spiritual "truth" behind natural force, that he is capable of discovering a new
aesthetic through which to depict that truth. After the massacre at the irri-

gation ditch, Presley once again stands on the hill overlooking the entire San Joaquin valley, the same hill from which he had earlier projected his antiquated romantic vision. Now, however, he projects his new deterministic vision of a universe of force onto the scene:

> FORCE only existed—FORCE that brought men into the world, FORCE that crowded them out of it to make way for the succeeding generation, FORCE that made the wheat grow, FORCE that garnered it from the soil to give place to the succeeding crop. (634)

Soon after this, however, he encounters Vanamee, who, playing the role of prophet, reveals to Presley the "truth" that he himself had learned from nature. Vanamee paraphrases LeConte, telling Presley that regardless of appearances, the universe is teleological, the design beneficent. After all, the "seeming evil" (to use LeConte's term) of Angéle's rape and death was in fact "real good," for it resulted in Angéle's daughter, in an Angéle "more beautiful than ever" (636). Likewise, Vanamee intimates that the evil of the massacre and of the Railroad's victory is also only "seeming," for it is transient and will, in the end, produce good. He tells Presley that he must view the world from a higher perspective. "Never judge of the whole round of life by the mere segment that you can see," he tells him, again paraphrasing LeConte. "The whole is, in the end, perfect" (636).

Presley, however, is not fully convinced until later when, on the ship bound for India, he thinks of the wheat. Once again, as in the revelations of Vanamee and Annixter, the wheat acts as a spiritual catalyst—in this case, confirming to Presley the teleological beneficence of the universe. It is the wheat that remains, the wheat that is the "good" that endures after the "evil" has passed. "Yes," Presley ruminates, "good issued from this crisis, untouched, unassailable, undefiled" (651). The ship's cargo of San Joaquin wheat will feed the "starving scarecrows" of India. Echoing Vanamee, and through Vanamee LeConte, Presley reasons that

> the individual suffers, but the race goes on. Annixter dies, but in a far distant corner of the world a thousand lives are saved. The larger view always and through all shams, all wickednesses, discovers the Truth that will, in the end, prevail, and all things, surely, inevitably, resistlessly work together for good. (651–52)

Yet the unrestricted flow of the wheat to India is not the only good to issue from the conflict between the ranchers and the Railroad; Presley's attainment of the "larger view" is also an auspicious effect. For one thing, the "larger view" reconciles him to the natural world, for now he perceives that this world is not indifferent but is in fact beneficent, a manifestation of divine design. But perhaps more important, the "larger view" will also enable Presley as an artist to depict this world in its true light. The "responsibilities" of the novelist, by Norris's own definition, include penetrating "through all shams" in order to discover and reveal the "Truth" in the real world. Presley, by means of his enlightened perspective, is now able to do that. He has reached the level from which he can write the "True Romance": not the antiquated romance of his "Song of the West" or the social realism of "The Toilers," but a work of art that will reveal the romance in the real, a work akin to Norris's own "Epic of the Wheat."

As we have seen, the awakenings of Vanamee, Annixter, and Presley all amount to an awakening of perception; each learns to perceive the essential spirituality of nature and, in consequence, his own moral and spiritual links to the natural world. This new perception not only reconciles each character to that world but also helps resolve the dramatic conflicts in the novel. For example, at the end of the novel, Presley's awareness of the teleological beneficence of the universe brings about a philosophical resolution to the central conflict between the ranchers and the Railroad. In Presley's mind, that conflict is no longer "the world-old war between Freedom and Tyranny" (307) he once thought it was, but becomes a necessary stage in a progress toward "good." In other words, it becomes no conflict at all. Much criticism has been heaped on *The Octopus* for what seems to be a tacked-on philosophical panacea that resolves the novel's dramatic conflicts by denying them. Yet, for the purposes of my own argument, what is most interesting about this criticism is its resemblance to John Dewey's philosophical refutation of LeConte and the other Christian evolutionists. For while the literary critics attacked Norris for offering a philosophical resolution to dramatic conflicts, Dewey attacked the Christian evolutionists for propounding *abstract* philosophical solutions, predicated on the existence of an absolute, to practical, worldly problems for which the question of an absolute was irrelevant. And by dramatizing LeConte's philosophy in *The Octopus*, Norris consequently dramatized the flaws in that philosophy that

Dewey would refute, and unwittingly wrote the swan song of such a depiction of humanity and the universe in American literature.[19]

Dewey rejected the "larger view" that constitutes the perceptual awakening of each of the main characters in *The Octopus*, as well as the solace that that view brings with it. To him this view of an evolutionary yet divinely guided, teleological universe was merely a construct of the human mind, a construct as devoid of objective reality as that which Presley projects onto the San Joaquin valley at the beginning of the novel. Moreover, and more important to Dewey, such "intellectual atavism" as he called it failed to solve any of the many problems confronting humanity as it headed into the twentieth century. And this is certainly evident within the context of *The Octopus*, for the "larger view" acquired by Vanamee, Annixter, and Presley changes nothing in the practical, material world in which they live. The Railroad maintains its strangle-hold on the people, and the people still suffer as a result. Neither does the "larger view" hold any hope for future change, as it implies the notion that "whatever is, is right," and therefore counsels acceptance rather than revolt. The belief in a transcendent principle, despite all the solace it may bring to the believer, resigns human beings to the uncertainties of faith in ameliorating their condition. As Dewey argued, regardless of the existence of an absolute, "truth and error, health and disease, good and evil, hope and fear in the concrete, would remain just what and where they now are."[20] And so they do in *The Octopus*.

The exigencies of the new century would thus force humanity to confront the Darwinian universe in all its austerity: godless, purposeless, and indifferent. In the work of Hemingway, which we shall look at next, human beings are denied the consolation of a philosophy predicated on the existence of an absolute—such as that which reconciles Vanamee, Annixter, and Presley to the natural world—and must therefore discover a new means of reconciliation. To this end, the self turns inward: to the human consciousness and its ordering, unifying power.

CHAPTER FIVE
THE RISE OF CONSCIOUSNESS AND
HEMINGWAY'S TRANSFORMATION
OF LITERARY NATURALISM

Unlike Frank Norris, Ernest Hemingway was not working off a new scientific paradigm—a new reading, as it were, of the book of nature. To Hemingway, the natural world was still largely Darwinian, a world of material force devoid of a moral and spiritual order and therefore of an ostensible purpose or meaning.[1] He was, however, working off a new conception of humanity. The rise at the turn of the century of the psychological and social sciences, of both pragmatic and Nietzschean philosophy, and of a new "modern" aesthetic, all pointed toward the efficacy of the human consciousness in confronting and ordering an otherwise meaningless universe. As a result, the self need no longer *necessarily* fall victim to natural force (as in *Vandover*), nor seek solace in an abstract order external to itself (as in *The Octopus*). Hemingway, in assimilating this modern view of humanity into his work, would transform the naturalistic novel by depicting a distinctly modern response—one in which the self creates its own order and meaning—to the naturalistic world of force.

The crisis in faith initiated by Darwinism reached its apogee with the cataclysm of World War I. This war, centered in predominantly Christian Europe, seemed to indicate undeniably the inefficacy of the Church and its ideals, their obsolescence in the modern world of the twentieth century. As in the wake of Darwinism, the aftermath of the war presented humanity with a material universe stripped of the comforting moral and spiritual order with which Christianity had formerly imbued it. Once again, the individual found himself alienated from that world, struggling to reconcile himself to it. The psychologist Carl Jung, whose essay "The Spiritual Problem of Modern Man" (1928) focused on the rift between the self and the natural world brought about by the war, summed up modern humanity's disillusionment with a Christian order that no longer seemed manifest when he proclaimed,

> we are the culmination of the whole history of mankind, . . . we are also the disappointment of the hopes and expectations of the ages. Think of nearly two thousand years of Christian Idealism followed, not by the return of the Messiah and the heavenly millennium, but by the World War among Christian nations with its barbed wire and poison gas. What a catastrophe in heaven and on earth![2]

Jung was one of several scientists at the turn of the century who turned their analytical techniques and skills inward—to the mind of the individual as something more than a biological organ. Jung directly ascribed the increased interest in psychology—and other marginal psychological "sciences" such as astrology, theosophy, and parapsychology—to the crisis in faith produced by the war. "Modern man," he claimed, "has suffered an almost fatal shock, psychologically speaking, and as a result has fallen into profound uncertainty."[3] Unlike medieval human beings, Jung argued, whose minds were integrated into a metaphysical order that had also embraced the material world, modern humans were cut off from any such integrative metaphysical system. The mind now existed as a separate entity, apart from and in opposition to the spiritless material world. Clearly alluding to the spiritual repercussions of the war, particularly to the war's effect on modern humanity's relationship to Christianity, Jung claimed that "as soon as he [man] has outgrown whatever local form of religion he was born to—as soon as this religion can no longer embrace his life in all its fulness [sic]—then the psyche becomes a factor in its own right which cannot be dealt with by the customary measures."[4] Jung thus saw modern human beings turning away from such "obsolete religious forms" and the external material world that they had once imbued with spiritual significance, and toward their own "inner processes."[5] "Modern man," he claimed, "expects something from the psyche that the outer world has not given him: doubtless something which our religion ought to contain, but no longer does contain."[6] In other words, Jung saw modern humanity's interest in the mind as an interest in the mind's ordering power, its ability to create an order that could fill the spiritual void left by the demise of "obsolete" Christianity. Such an order would necessarily integrate the self back into its world, would imbue that world with a human meaning.

Jung and other psychologists were thus moving away from the Darwinian conception of the mind as a biologically determined organ. Although Jung attributed a large portion of human behavior to instinct and therefore to "natural" causes — "human behavior," he argued, "is influenced by instinct to a far higher degree than is generally supposed"[7] — he did not go so far as Zola, who claimed that "a like determinism will govern the stones of the roadway and the brain of man."[8] In fact, Jung argued against reducing psychology to physiology, as Zola had advocated with his positivism and his heralding of "physiological man."[9] Jung asserted rather acerbically that psychology's "intrinsic value and specific quality would be destroyed if it were regarded as a mere activity of the brain, and were relegated along with the endocrine functions to a subdivision of physiology."[10] On the contrary, to Jung the domain of psychology was the "reality of psychic life,"[11] a reality independent of biology and biological determinants. The mind was truly its own place, distinct from the natural world. And along with this newly conceived independence came a newly conceived power: the power not just to perceive, but to create, and to validate that creation through the conscious experience of it. The human mind or consciousness, then, became a viable force in opposition to natural force.

At about the same time that psychology was moving away from an emphasis on biological determinism, so too were the social sciences. Charles Darwin, who in *The Origin of Species* had carefully avoided a discussion of human evolution, nevertheless proceeded in his later book *The Descent of Man* to draw a connection between animal and human behavior.[12] As Carl N. Degler has shown, Darwin in doing so established a link between biological and social evolution, a link that would infuse biological determinism into the study of diverse cultures and societies well into the twentieth century. Darwin, while denying advantageous traits among the physical attributes of different races, nevertheless contended that there were advantages in the intellectual, moral, and social faculties of the civilized races.[13] Cultural achievement — that is, the degree to which a culture had become civilized—was directly linked to the biological or "innate" capacities of that culture's people. The Social Darwinists, of course, exploited this belief to justify the struggle among the races—a struggle that often culminated in the suppression of "inferior" races by the white race.

The belief in biological determinism reached its peak in the eugenics movement. Initiated in 1883 by Francis Galton, a cousin of Darwin, this movement advocated "improving" the human species by eliminating the genes of "inferior" individuals and races. Its fundamental assumption, therefore, was that people were biologically determined via heredity, including their mental and behavioral capacities. By 1912, the year of the first International Congress of Eugenics, the eugenics movement had become a powerful social reform movement with strong supporters within the emerging social sciences of anthropology and sociology.

There was at the same time, however, a growing resistance to the eugenics movement and the credence it placed in biological determinism. The Columbia anthropologist Franz Boas led the charge within the academy against eugenics, and eventually he and others would succeed in overthrowing it. Boas's main contention was that differences in culture among people—that is, in *levels* of culture—were not due to the innate capacities of the individuals that composed them, but to the social history of the cultures themselves.[14] He argued, in other words, against biology and for culture as the predominant determining factor in social evolution.

Boas's student, the University of California anthropologist Alfred L. Kroeber, took Boas's ideas further. Kroeber advocated the absolute separation of biology and culture, claiming in his essay "The Superorganic" (1917) that cultural achievements "are uninfluenced by heredity."[15] To Kroeber, the connection Darwin had established between biological and social evolution was erroneous. Human evolution was not organic but "superorganic"—that is, effected by cultural rather than biological factors. He declared:

> it does seem justifiable to stand unhesitatingly on the proposition that civilization and heredity are two things that operate in separate ways; that therefore any outright substitution of one for the other in the explanation of human group phenomena is crass; and that the refusal to recognize at least the logical possibility of an explanation of human

achievement totally different from the prevailing tendency toward [a] biological one, is an act of illiberality.[16]

The ideas of Boas, Kroeber, and others soon pushed biology completely out of the social sciences. Even the concept of "instinct" fell out of favor as an explanation for human behavior. This substitution of cultural determinants for biological ones in the study of human societies was yet another of the contemporary movements away from the belief in biological determinism, at least as it pertained to humanity. The idea that culture was a shaping force, independent of biological factors, was akin to the psychologists' conception of the human mind as its own reality, equally independent of biology. Again, the self could create its own order, its own refuge apart from natural force.

If the human sciences were distancing themselves from Darwinism, philosophy at the turn of the century had incorporated Darwin's fundamentally materialistic conception of the universe. Paradoxically, though, this too moved philosophy toward a new confidence in the power of the human mind and a belief in its essential autonomy from biological determinants. We remember from chapter 1 John Dewey's critique of Gray, LeConte, and the other evolutionary theists whom he accused of "intellectual atavism." Dewey believed that Darwinism had moved humanity beyond the "old questions" that sought absolutes and transcendent causes, and that now human beings should turn their attention toward pragmatic solutions to the problems inherent in a world of flux. He rejected, in other words, any attempt to find an evolutionary substitute for Christianity by infusing spiritualism into natural process. Humanity, according to Dewey, must now confront the universe without the crutch of absolutes. Implicit in this, of course, is the belief in the ability of human beings to do so—again, in the ability of the mind to confront effectively the materialistic universe.

This view was given more forceful, and more influential, expression in the philosophy of Friedrich Nietzsche. Nietzsche's declaration in *Thus Spoke Zarathustra* that "God is dead"[17] was not only an unequivocal assertion of a godless universe but also a suggestion that the belief in a God had become obsolete. Whether aware of it or not, human beings now existed in a godless, indifferent universe, one characterized by meaningless flux and eternal recurrence. As a result, humanity was "beyond good and evil"—or, for that matter, any other absolute standards. Nietzsche's response to such a universe was his concept of the "overman" (or "superman"). "Man is something that shall be overcome," he declared.[18] In other words, the individual, the "all-too-human," had to go beyond or "over" any set definition of the self, had to create himself by his own actions and experiences. In this way, he gave meaning and justification to an otherwise meaningless existence, and affirmed life in the face of suffering and death. As Nietzsche was sure to point out in *Ecce Homo*, this overman was not a Darwinian end product, not an individual going beyond the rest of humanity *biologically*. On the contrary, the overman surpassed humanity through the powers of his mind, through his heightened consciousness. His self-creation was a creation of consciousness. Nietzsche, however, owed a debt to Darwin in his emphasis on the instinctual, the Dionysian in humanity that had the power to destroy old forms. To Nietzsche, the instincts were genuine impulses suppressed by the false doctrines and creeds of religion and the state. The individual had to unleash the Dionysian, had to destroy the old forms, so that new, more authentic forms could be created. The overman, then, was both destroyer and creator, both lawbreaker and lawgiver. "The breaker, the lawbreaker," Nietzsche declared, "he is the creator."[19] It is he who, after breaking the old "tables of values," writes "new values on new tablets."[20] These new values, of course, are highly personal, derived from the overman's subjective experience, rather than from established doctrine.

Hemingway's oft-cited "code" has much in common with Nietzschean philosophy, and with the other contemporary movements that emphasized the mind as a creative and ordering force. It is in this, in his stance toward a naturalistic universe and in the aesthetic that he brings to it, that Hemingway's transformation of the naturalistic novel is manifest. Like Nietzsche, Hemingway too posits a godless universe of meaningless flux. His conception of it is epitomized in "A Clean, Well-Lighted Place" when the old waiter ruminates "it all was nada y pues nada y nada y pues nada"[21]: "nothing and then nothing and nothing and then nothing" in endless, meaningless repetition. And like Nietzsche's overman, the Hemingway hero must accept this condition of existence, must confront it courageously and not hide in the shelter of obsolete creeds. All such creeds must be tested against one's own experience in the world, and if they are belied by that experience, must be rejected. So it is in *A Farewell to Arms* that Frederic Henry, after experiencing the war, can reject those "patriotic" words and values that perpetuate it:

> I was always embarrassed by the words sacred, glorious, and sacrifice and the expression in vain. We had heard them, sometimes standing in the rain almost out of earshot, so that only the shouted words came through, and had read them, on proclamations that were slapped up by billposters over other proclamations, now for a long time, and I had seen nothing sacred, and the things that were glorious had no glory and the sacrifices were like the stockyards at Chicago if nothing was done with the meat except to bury it.[22]

The Hemingway hero must therefore create his own values that he derives from experience. Experience must always come first: "Immorality," Jake Barnes thinks to himself in *The Sun Also Rises*, was what "made you disgusted *afterward*" (my emphasis).[23] Moreover, the Hemingway hero must create himself in the broadest sense, must give existence meaning through the courage, grace, and dignity of his actions. As we shall see in Chapter 7, Jake Barnes, whose injury precludes him from living the romantic male ideal, redefines himself and manhood in terms of a self-created ideal, one from which his handicap does not exclude him. By means of such redefinition and self-creation, the Hemingway hero affirms life in the face of an indifferent naturalistic world.

Hemingway's aesthetic goes hand in hand with his code; while it is certainly a modernist aesthetic in its emphasis on consciousness as an ordering principle, it is nevertheless uniquely his own. Reflecting his distrust of established creeds, doctrines, and ideals—what his contemporary Ezra Pound would metaphorically describe as the "broken statues" and "battered books" of Western civilization[24]—Hemingway in *Death in the Afternoon* claimed that the greatest difficulty for the writer was "knowing truly what you really felt, rather than what you were supposed to feel, and had been taught to feel."[25] Again experience must precede any standard of value. Even his quest for what he called the "real thing"—"the sequence of motion and fact which made the emotion"[26]—suggests this: experience (in this case, "motion" and "fact") must precede response ("emotion"). The reader, then, is involved in creating meaning through his response to the action described in the work of literature. Meaning is never declared from an authorial voice (as it is in both *Vandover* and *The Octopus*) but is evoked through dramatic action. In fact, Hemingway would often say that the successful literary work, the "real thing," would act as experience itself: "I have tried to eliminate everything unnecessary to conveying experience to the reader so that after he or she has read something it will become a part of his or her experience and seem actually to have happened."[27]

Hemingway's "iceberg principle"—his theory that the power of a work of literature resides in the seven-eighths of it that lies unexpressed—also works toward subverting any authorial creed divorced from immediate experience. The unexpressed element is intended to elicit an instinctual response—that is, a visceral or emotional response that is, in Jackson J. Benson's words, "prelogical."[28] It is evoked, in other words, before it can be intellectualized, and consequently before it can be distorted or repressed by the abstract beliefs the mind may harbor. The "iceberg principle," then, is necessarily iconoclastic—Dionysian, Nietzsche would say—because it is unaccountable to and ultimately undermines social, moral, and religious standards.

While Hemingway's aesthetic works on one level toward subverting such *a priori* standards, it also works on another level toward establishing new, *a posteriori* ones. The lyricism for which Hemingway's prose has often been justly praised involves a conscious reordering of experience. In Hemingway's work we see the self moving through experience and, in the process, creating its own aesthetic order from it; again, experience precedes order, a self-created order that in turn gives meaning to experience. As we shall see in Chapter 7, Jake Barnes learns that one means of living "in it"—that is, living in the meaningless material world—is to give it a meaning by transforming it aesthetically. The work of art then becomes an affirmation, a timeless stave against flux.

Robert Penn Warren once noted that Hemingway did not invent his world; it had already been invented by, among others Warren mentioned, the nineteenth-century literary naturalists.[29] Hemingway did, however, bring a distinctly modern twentieth-century consciousness to that world. Confronted with a universe devoid of absolutes, yet unable to take refuge in a new abstract philosophy as did Norris in *The Octopus*, Hemingway turned to the human consciousness as a means of ordering and justifying existence. It was a response consonant with other contemporary movements in the fields of psychology, sociology, anthropology, philosophy, and, of course, literature. No longer considered to be biologically determined, the mind became a viable force in its own right. In the work of Hemingway, it would become the means of transcending the meaninglessness of a naturalistic world.

CHAPTER SIX
A FAREWELL TO ARMS:
MODERN RESPONSE,
NATURALISTIC FATE

In *A Farewell to Arms*, Hemingway depicts a naturalistic world of natural force and a "modern" response to that world—yet a modern response that fails. Frederic and Catherine create their own order to fill the void left by Christianity's collapse, yet model that order on the traditional Christian concept of a fixed eternity—an order "above" and "beyond" natural, temporal cycles—rather than grounding it in their own experience in the natural world of flux. Without the accompanying Christian concepts of an eternal deity and a spiritual afterlife, such an order becomes an empty abstraction; it is doomed to die a physical death, perishing along with its human creator, for it provides no means of spiritual transcendence or regeneration. Death becomes the final end of spirit. As in nineteenth-century literary naturalism, the individual's spiritual self once again lies in opposition to his physical being, inevitably falling victim to that being, to natural force that operates through it. Thus, while Frederic and Catherine assert a characteristically modern response to their predicament, they nevertheless succumb to a distinctly naturalistic fate.

As in *Vandover* and *The Octopus*, in *A Farewell to Arms* a symbolic representation of the old, traditional Christian order provides a background against which the modern spiritual void can be contrasted. This is the Abruzzi, the mountainous region in central Italy that is the home of the priest.[1] The Abruzzi is an anachronism, a throwback to an earlier era; Christianity still "works" there, still provides human beings with a moral and spiritual order in which they can feel, like the priest, "at home." As the priest tells Frederic Henry, "in my country it is understood that a man may love God. It is not a dirty joke." [2] Yet the priest truly lives in another country; in contrast to the chaos and carnage of the war zone, the Abruzzi is a pastoral, idyllic land—much like the San Joaquin valley of De La Cuesta's day in *The Octopus*—a land of Christian brotherhood where "the peasants took off their hats and called you Lord" (13) and where, if you hunted, "you never took a lunch because the peasants were always honored if you would eat with them at their houses" (73). The rituals of hunting and fishing, rituals that create and reinforce a harmonious relationship between the self and nature, are the only forms of sacrifice. Unlike in the war where men are slaughtered and "nothing [is] done with the meat except to bury it" (184), in the Abruzzi the slaughtered animals are used for food, further indicating a regenerative harmony between humanity and the natural world.

It is significant that the Abruzzi is almost always described as a winter landscape, a "clear cold and dry" land covered with snow. Just as the snow-covered peak of Kilimanjaro represents an eternal, spiritual realm in "The Snows of Kilimanjaro," a realm above the rot and decay of the plain, so too do the snowy mountains of the Abruzzi.[3] And like the leopard that lies frozen near the summit of Kilimanjaro, forever removed from the decay of time and natural process, the peasants of the Abruzzi are themselves "frozen" in time. Throughout the novel, snow symbolizes the cessation of natural process and temporality. As we have seen, life in the Abruzzi is a throwback to an earlier era of Christian order, to a time when faith in Christ led to the belief in the spiritual transcendence of natural process and death. The snow-covered Abruzzi is somehow "above" and "beyond" physical decay, just as it is "above" and "beyond" the war. (Significantly enough, the priest—like Henry the artist in "The Snows," who *should* dwell on the immortal summit of Kilimanjaro yet instead rots on the African plain—lives "a *rotten* life in the *mess*" [73, my emphasis]). And it is the snow, when it begins to fall on the lowland battle zone, that finally brings a cease-fire and a respite from death. For the war, as we shall see in a moment, is intricately linked in *A Farewell to Arms* to natural force and can only continue, like life itself, with the coming of the spring rains.

The Abruzzi, however, is an anomaly in the modern world, and the Christian order it represents no longer exists beyond its boundaries. Frederic Henry, the epitome of the modern displaced hero, yearns nostalgically for that "other country" yet finds himself "banished" from it by his own modern sensibilities. In this way he is much like Vandover, who wished he had the faith of the Salvationist, yet whose modern insistence on natural facts kept him from such faith in the supernatural. Frederic, the priest's only friend in the war, "had wanted to go to Abruzzi" (13) while on leave but had not. Moreover, he is at a loss to explain to the priest why he had not gone: "I . . . could not understand why I had not gone. It was what I had wanted to do and I tried to explain how one thing had led to another and finally he saw it and understood that I had really wanted to go" (13). Instead, Frederic had gone to the bars and brothels of the city—the modern "churches" where only the senses are worshiped, where a man is caught in the temporal process of one thing leading to another. His carnal indulgence effectively undermines his spiritual yearnings, unconsciously denies to him the existence of a reality other than the material and biological. Like modern humanity in general, Frederic is a spiritual exile who cannot enter but can only imagine the Abruzzi, can only think abstractly about how life would be "in his [the priest's] own country" (73).

The priest, however, can and does enter Frederic's "country," yet he is clearly out of place there—an object of ridicule rather than reverence. Priest-baiting is the favorite pastime of the men in the mess. (Again, the words "rotten" and "mess" used in reference to the priest's existence in the war suggest that he has entered a foreign realm of decay and disorder, a world devoid of a transcendent vision and an ordering principle.) He is at best ineffectual, unable to prevent the death and destruction. "He can't do anything about it anyway" (14), says one captain. In addition, religion itself is inefficacious in this modern world. The Saint Anthony medallion that Catherine gives Frederic, telling him that "they say" it is "very useful" (43), does nothing to prevent his wounding; in fact, it is ironic that the first reference to his wounding occurs when he clasps the medallion around his neck, emphasizing the futility of religious faith:

I undid the clasp of the gold chain and put it around my neck and clasped it. The saint hung down on the outside of my uniform and I undid the throat of my tunic, unbuttoned the shirt collar and dropped him in under the shirt. I felt him in his metal box against my chest while we drove. Then I forgot about him. After I was wounded I never found him. Some one probably got it at one of the dressing stations. (44)[4]

Later, when Catherine's life is in danger, Frederic desperately pleads to God to save her:

Oh, God, please don't let her die. I'll do anything for you if you won't let her die. Please, please, please, dear God, don't let her die. Dear God, don't let her die. Please, please, please don't let her die. God please make her not die. I'll do anything you say if you don't let her die. You took the baby but don't let her die. That was all right but don't let her die. Please, please, dear God, don't let her die. (330)

Once again we are reminded of Vandover and his "instinctual" appeal to a deity—despite his own professed lack of faith—during his great spiritual crisis, as well as of Vanamee and his demand that God "do the miracle" and bring Angéle back to life. All are manifestations of a human being's powerful need for a deity whom he can supplicate, a spiritual presence who can intercede on his behalf in the face of apparently indifferent natural force. Yet, as with Vandover and Vanamee, Frederic's pleas are unanswered. Catherine dies.

Outside the symbolically timeless, spiritual realm of the Abruzzi, then, the universe is godless and indifferent, a spiritual wasteland with which humanity has no moral or spiritual affinity. It is essentially a Darwinian universe, one of natural force that "kills the very good and the very gentle and the very brave impartially" (249). And while it is similar to the Darwinian universe of *Vandover* in its implacability, it differs in form. Norris had conceived of nature as a "vast terrible engine" hurtling forward, indifferently crushing those that lagged behind the human herd. Hemingway, on the other hand, conceives of natural process not as a linear, forward progression but as a repetitive cycle. His central metaphor regarding the natural world is not of an unstoppable engine but of a car stuck in the mud, its wheels spinning but going nowhere, as we see during the retreat from Caporetto in chapter 29. Human beings are not crushed in such a world but trapped—in Frederic Henry's own words, "trapped biologically" (139).

We can most clearly see the contrast between the spiritual realm of the Abruzzi and the cyclical world "below" in an early description in which Frederic juxtaposes the two:

I had wanted to go to Abruzzi. I had gone to no place where the roads were frozen and hard as iron, where it was clear cold and dry and the snow was dry and powdery and hare-tracks in the snow and the peasants took off their hats and called you Lord and there was good hunting. I had gone to no such place but to the smoke of cafés and nights when the room whirled and you needed to look at the wall to make it stop, nights in bed, drunk, when you knew that that was all there was, and the strange excitement of waking and not knowing who it was with you, and the world all unreal in the dark and so exciting that you must resume again unknowing and not caring in the night, sure that this was all and all and all and not caring. Suddenly to care very much and to sleep to wake with it sometimes morning and all that had been there gone and everything sharp and hard and clear and sometimes a dispute about the cost. Sometimes still pleasant and fond and warm and breakfast and lunch. Sometimes all niceness gone and glad to get out on the street but always another day starting and then another night. (13).

This is Frederic Henry's vision of earthly heaven and hell: the one "frozen" in time, the other an endless temporal cycle of "always another day starting and then another night." The frozen "still point" of the Abruzzi (to borrow a phrase from T. S. Eliot) is contrasted with the rooms that "whirled" in the brothels of the city, the sexual act itself trapping Frederic within nature's whirling biological cycle. Frederic is forced to improvise his own still point to stop the whirling—as he will later attempt with Catherine above Montreux—but in the brothels there is nothing spiritual with which to do so, only a blank wall. In fact, the entire "civilized" world as Frederic describes it is spiritually blank. In contrast to the clarity of the Abruzzi (again, we note the immemorial association between light and spirit), the "smoke of cafés" is suggestive of an inferno in which, like Dante's, the damned are denied the light. And as in Dante's hell, the greatest punishment for a human being in Hemingway's world is his consciousness of his own damnation; of course, for Hemingway's heroes, such a consciousness must be endured *in* life, not after death, and it is a condition of being, rather than the result of a transgression. (Moreover, it will paradoxically be the only means he has of salvation, as we shall see later.) Alone in a room with a prostitute, indulging in the carnal excesses of sex and alcohol, Frederic "knew that that was all there was," was "sure that this was all and all and all." Such a consciousness is the only thing "hard and clear" in this world, and the ultimate irony is that it involves an awareness of a condition antithetical to the hardness and clarity of the Abruzzi, an awareness of one's existence in a world of cyclical movement devoid of a spiritual light. There is no spiritual force to transcend the material; the material is "all." And since one's materiality is biological, he is ensnared in the natural, biological cycle in which that "all" is endlessly repeated: "all and all and all." It is a world reminiscent of that described by Sweeney in Eliot's "Sweeney Agonistes: Fragment of an Agon," a biological world in which there is "Nothing at all but three things . . . Birth, and copulation and death. / That's all, that's all, that's all, that's all, / Birth, and copulation, and death." [5]

In fact, we see throughout *A Farewell to Arms* a rift between the world of spirit and that of biological force, a rift that is characteristic of literary naturalism. Without the traditional Christian conception of an ordered universe in which humanity is at home, the individual's spiritual self finds itself alienated from the natural world, even from its own biological being. Frederic had "wanted" to go to the Abruzzi; in the material, biological world in which he finds himself, his spiritual self still seeks a home. But the Abruzzi is an obsolete construct, a state of mind that only the priest and the *Abruzzesi* themselves can enjoy. Frederic will be forced to construct his own spiritual home, a new order to replace the old. However, as the libidinal drives of his biological being had kept Frederic from going to the Abruzzi, so too will the natural, biological world undermine the "religious" love of Frederic and Catherine—their new, self-created order. Nature, in and of itself indifferent and amoral, proves inimical to the spiritual self that yet remains unreconciled to it. In the natural cycle of birth, copulation, and death, there is no spiritual rebirth or resurrection. While sexual reproduction ensures that death is never final biologically, death is without a doubt the end of the cycle for the spirit.

The natural world in *A Farewell to Arms* is thus in all its facets associated with death and destruction. And the central symbol of that world—and one that I feel has been frequently misinterpreted—is the rain. Most critics have been content to accept the rain as merely a symbol of doom and disaster.[6] Philip Young has even gone so far as to defend it as an instance of the pathetic fallacy, something Hemingway himself would probably consider one of the most egregious of literary devices.[7] In fact, as most critics have described the rain, it is not so much a symbol—and here we must accept Richard Chase's definition of a symbol as "an autonomous linguistic fusion of meanings"[8]—as just that: an egregious literary device. But while the rain certainly symbolizes doom and disaster, it also symbolizes much more—indeed, a whole "fusion of meanings"—all of which are facets of natural force. It is the rain that provides the nexus between these various facets, that through its pervasiveness links them together.

Rain, of course, is fundamental to natural process, providing as it does the life-giving element of water. It is responsible for the seasonal growth of vegetation, and in this way can be said to begin the natural cycle or, more accurately, to re-begin it each spring. It has thus been immemorially associated with life in the human imagination. However, from the outset of *A Farewell to Arms*, we find the rain associated with death—specifically, with death as the inevitable end of one revolution of the biological cycle: "in the fall when the rains came the leaves all fell from the chestnut trees and the branches were bare and the trunks black with rain. The vineyards were thin and bare-branched too and all the country wet and brown and dead with the autumn" (4). As a symbol of natural process, then, the rain encompasses the full cycle of that process: from spring to fall, from birth to death. Yet the rain and the life and death that come with it are not confined to the earth and vegetation; the soldiers are also covered with rain, and in a curious image are also associated with sexuality and childbearing:

> the troops were muddy and wet in their capes; their rifles were wet and under their capes the two leather cartridge-boxes on the front of the belts, gray leather boxes heavy with the packs of clips of thin, long 6.5 mm. cartridges, bulged forward under the capes so that the men, passing on the road, marched as though they were six months gone with child. (4)

As several critics have noted, this image foreshadows Catherine's death in childbirth; yet it does more. The soldiers, as Frederic will later claim regarding himself, are "trapped biologically"; they are caught within natural process, symbolized by the rain that covers them. As such, they are all marching toward death, either death in battle or death by a "natural" cause—namely, the cholera that is a direct result of the "permanent" rain. The observation that they appear pregnant suggests that it is primarily an individual's sexuality that connects him to this process. Again, we see life and death intricately entwined in the biological cycle, for the "child" each bears is death itself: 6.5 mm. cartridges. More specifically, each "child" is an instrument of war, and the image seems to suggest that war is a product of natural process, that it is "born," like a child, from natural forces.

Whether Hemingway intended such a connection literally or metaphorically we can only speculate. Ray B. West has argued for the latter, claiming that the war in *A Farewell to Arms* is "really a symbol for the chaos of nature."[9] I would argue, however, that, shocking as it may be, the connection is literal. Certainly much anthropological evidence could be adduced to support such a view. Rene Girard and Walter Burkert have argued that war, like hunting, is a ritualized outgrowth of male sexual aggression.[10] (Again, we note the connection between war and sexuality—the "pregnant" soldiers.) Yet there is ample evidence within the text itself to corroborate this interpretation. In the same chapter, chapter 1, as the image of the rain-soaked, "pregnant" soldiers, we see another image in which the instruments of war appear to be an outgrowth of nature: "There were big guns too that passed in the day drawn by tractors, the long barrels of the guns covered with green branches and green leafy branches and vines laid over the tractors" (4). The vegetation that the springtime rain had produced now appears to be bearing strange fruit. Indeed, the war can only begin again with the coming of the spring rains, and, yet again in chapter 1, we see the war linked to the seasonal cycle:

> Troops went by the house and down the road and the dust they raised powdered the leaves of the trees. The trunks of the trees too were dusty and the leaves fell early that year and we saw the troops marching along the road and the dust rising and leaves, stirred by the breeze, falling and the soldiers marching and afterward the road bare and white except for the leaves. (3)

The use of the present participle—"marching," "rising," "falling," "marching"—suggests implacable process; in fact, a world *in the process*, and the autumnal "falling" leaves and the death-connoting "rising" dust imply that that process is a natural, biological one. The presence of the "marching" troops—the repetition of the word "marching" reinforcing the perennial repetition of the act itself—intimates that they too are a part of the natural process.

Frederic's entrapment within the war is also closely linked to his feeling of biological entrapment. In fact, his literal entrapment within the war—when the ambulances get stuck in the rain-soaked mud during the retreat from Caporetto—provides the central image in the novel for the biological cycle: a car endlessly spinning its wheels, going nowhere, leaving humanity helpless. Yet just before this scene, again during the retreat from Caporetto, Frederic himself associates this feeling of entrapment with both the war and sexuality. Significantly enough, he expresses himself through the image of rain. As the ambulance he and Piani are driving remains "trapped" in the column of vehicles fleeing the front in the rain, Frederic begins to dream about Catherine. It is clearly an erotic dream: "In bed I lay me down my head. Bed and board. Stiff as a board in bed. Catherine was in bed now between two sheets, over her and under her" (197). His mind, in the penumbra between sleep and wakefulness, then jumbles Catherine and the war together in an image of entrapment within wind and rain:

> Blow, blow, ye western wind. Well, it blew and it wasn't the small rain but the big rain down that rained. It rained all night. You knew it rained down that rained. Look at it. Christ, that my love were in my arms and I in my bed again. That my love Catherine. That my sweet love Catherine down might rain. Blow her again to me. Well, we were in it. Every one was caught in it and the small rain would not quiet it. (197)

The allusion to Shelley's "Ode to the West Wind" is unmistakable; that poem depicts a natural cycle, albeit one informed by a transcendent spirit, and the irony of Frederic's quotation of it in the spirit-less war-torn world is patent. Shelley's "destroyer and preserver" becomes primarily a destroyer, a snare in which "every one was caught." And it is the "big rain" that comes with the west wind that Frederic associates with the war. The "small rain" that he associates with Catherine and sexuality "would not quiet it"; it too is rain, and it is, of course, Frederic's natural sexuality that entraps him within the cycle.

Frederic's sexual drives had kept him caught within the "whirling" rooms of the brothels, preventing him from going to the spiritual realm of the Abruzzi. In essence, his biological being had undermined the spiritual aspirations of his self. In fact, Frederic's declaration that "you always feel trapped biologically" (159) implies that the self (the "you") is trapped by the body, that in the end it is always accountable to the natural, biological force of which the body is a part. As with Vandover, Frederic, while indulging his body, nevertheless feels alienated from it; it does not "belong" to him but to a natural world with which he has no spiritual affinity. For while there is much spiritual about Frederic and Catherine's love, there is nothing spiritual about the actual conception, gestation, and birth of their child. "It's a natural thing" (138), Catherine says, a creation of biological process, not of their conscious selves. Thus it is that, after the birth of their son, Frederic feels "no feeling of fatherhood" (325). It is not "his," but merely a biological "by-product of good nights in Milan" (320).

Another important aspect of the biological world, and one that is also united to the others through the symbol of the rain, is that of temporality. The natural world is a temporal world, the revolutions of the biological cycle measurable by such things as clocks and calendars. And for the individual who is biologically attached to this cycle, time is a force pushing him toward death. Thus when Catherine says, "I'm afraid of the rain because sometimes I see me dead in it" (126), the symbolic reference is not just to the biological world from which she cannot escape and by which she will eventually be killed, but also to the temporality of that world. She dies by a natural process—childbirth—but also *in* process. As foreshadowed in chapter 1, the rain generates life, but in so doing, it also begets death, death that will come *in time* and that will be the end of the cycle for the individual.

Time, then, as a feature of natural force, is something Frederic and Catherine must struggle against. Before returning to the front, in a tawdry hotel room (whose hall carpet, Frederic is careful to note twice, is worn—suggestive of the well-worn, repetitive path of sexual liaisons), Frederic quotes to Catherine a couplet from Marvell's "To his Coy Mistress": "But at my back I always hear / Time's winged chariot hurrying near" (154). The allusion is to his impending departure—to a war that is a product of natural force and from which, later, he will be retreating "against time" (208)—but it also refers to the biological force symbolized by the rain and manifest by their unborn child. Just before he quotes the line about "hearing" time, Frederic "hears" a klaxon and the falling rain. He then tells us that his head "felt very clear and cold"—similar to the clarity of his consciousness in the brothels of the city when he perceived that "this was all and all and all"—and that he now wants to talk "facts," facts that amount to details of the baby and its impending birth. Later, when Frederic and Catherine are living above Montreux, we will hear an echo of time "hurrying near" when Frederic tells us that the baby "gave us both a feeling as though something were *hurrying* us and we could not lose any *time* together" (311, my emphasis).[11] Significantly enough, another thing "hurrying" them then is the spring thaw and rain that breaks up the "cold, hard" snow above Montreux—and with it their self-created idyll—another instance in which the temporality of the biological cycle proves destructive.

We can also see Frederic and Catherine's struggle against temporal, biological cycles by their frequent use of the word "always"—sometimes in reference to those cycles, and sometimes in reference to the spiritual notion of a fixed eternity. Certainly the "always" in Marvell's poem alludes to the former, for it suggests humanity's inability to escape time or to flee from the temporal world; there is "always" Time with which to contend. And when Frederic tells Catherine that "you always feel trapped biologically," Catherine responds, " 'Always' isn't a pretty word" (139). Indeed, to be always bound to the "biological trap" is to be always subordinate to its cyclical revolutions, revolutions that lead to death. On the other hand, they often use "always" to refer to their love for one another, and in this case the word denotes a spiritual eternity that can transcend the temporal world (something we will look at more closely in a moment); however, such a transcendent eternity proves illusory, for the biological world always impinges.[12] At one point, Catherine asks Frederic, "And you'll always love me, won't you?" When Frederic responds, "Yes," Catherine asks, "And the rain won't make any difference?" (125). Her rationale for such a question is that she is afraid of the rain and, more specific, that the rain is "very hard on loving" (126). None of this makes sense on a literal level, but symbolically it does. The rain, as a symbol of natural force and process, is indeed hard on their "eternal" love; it destroys it in time. And while Frederic insists that he will "always" love Catherine, he also notes, ironically: "But outside it kept on raining" (126).

Frederic and Catherine, then, find themselves trapped in a temporal, biological world with which they have no moral or spiritual affinity, a predicament characteristic of literary naturalism. Without the consolation of an order external to the self or of a transcendent principle, Frederic and Catherine are forced to create their own order, an improvised moral and spiritual realm in which they can feel "at home." And the only means they have of creating such an order is their human consciousness. They must first recognize their predicament—that is, become "conscious" of it—and then use that consciousness to "build" a spiritual world that will transcend the biological. It is certainly appropriate that when Frederic and Catherine are arrested by the Swiss border police, and Frederic is asked what he has been doing in Italy, he responds, "studying architecture" (280).

Indeed, in comparison to Catherine, Frederic has much studying to do, for despite the occasional "sharp and hard and clear" consciousness he experiences in the brothels, Frederic's nostalgic yearning for the old Christian order often hinders him from clearly perceiving its absence in this biological universe. We have already noted Frederic's affection for the priest, his desire to go to the Abruzzi (even his belief in the *possibility* of his going to the Abruzzi), and his desperate plea for divine intervention during Catherine's difficult labor. But at a couple of points in the novel we also see Catherine acting as a type of mentor to Frederic, bringing him either through words or by example into consciousness of their predicament.[13] When they first meet, for example, Catherine tells Frederic that her fiancé "was killed and that was the end of it" (19). Frederic responds, "I don't know," intimating his belief in the possible existence of some regenerative spiritual force in the universe, or of a spiritual afterlife. Catherine, however, is thoroughly disabused in this regard, and reiterates, "Oh, yes, . . . That's the end of it" (19). Not until the end of the novel, when Catherine dies, will Frederic himself be disabused and truly see that death is, in fact, the end.

At another point, just before Frederic's return to the front, he and Catherine are walking through Milan in the rain when they come upon the cathedral. The image is stunning: this monument to Christian order wet with rain, covered with the symbol of natural force whose cyclical operation undermines any notion of a fixed order. In addition, Frederic and Catherine see an Italian soldier and his girl leaning against one of the cathedral's stone buttresses, his cape wrapped around them, hiding from the downpour. Again, the image speaks for itself: the ancient stone edifice sheltering them from the rain as the ancient petrified belief it represents shelters them from consciousness—consciousness of the biological reality ominously suggested by the pouring rain. Frederic tells Catherine, "They're like us," to which Catherine replies, "Nobody is like us" (147). Again, Catherine shows her awareness of their situation, her consciousness of their banishment from such a "shelter." While the Italian couple, in their innocence, "have the cathedral"—to use Catherine's own words—she and Frederic have no place. They must create their own.

In fact, in a parallel image a few pages later, we see them do just that:

> We turned down a side street where there were no lights and walked in the street. I stopped and kissed Catherine. While I kissed her I felt her hand on my shoulder. She had pulled my cape around her so it covered both of us. We were standing in the street against a high wall. (150)

A blank wall in a street with no light takes the place of the church buttress for Frederic and Catherine, the spirituality of their love the only spiritual force extant. And it is Catherine, the one who is fully aware of their situation, who wraps the cape around them. Yet the parallel imagery also suggests that Frederic and Catherine model their improvised spiritual realm on the traditional Christian concept of a fixed order that transcends biological process—in other words, on an abstraction. They mimic the Italian couple, attempting to "hide" themselves from the rain rather than integrating themselves into the natural process the rain represents. However, without the "support" of the Church and its doctrine of a spiritual afterlife, such hiding will prove futile.

Nevertheless, once conscious of their predicament, both Frederic and Catherine become obsessed with creating a home, the home a metaphor for a spiritual home—in this case, a self-created spiritual home to replace that which they have lost. They even manage to turn their tawdry hotel room where they stay before Frederic returns to the front, a room in which Catherine at first feels like a whore, into their home. With its red plush and mirrors, its worn carpet, and its obvious use as a place for illicit sexual liaisons, the room is certainly reminiscent of those in the brothels where Frederic had first become conscious of his existence in a spiritual wasteland. Yet as Frederic tells us, "in a little time the room felt like our own home. My room at the hospital had been our home and this room was our home in the same way" (153). Just as they create a home out of a cheap hotel room, they create, through their love for one another, a spiritual home amid the spiritless, biological world in which they find themselves. Moreover, this new home has its own moral order, one that they also create. Without a spiritual force in the universe, there is no moral force, no morality decreed from "above" and passed down through a church. Therefore, despite the fact that they are not married, Catherine can say that they are married "privately" (116) and that "I can't believe that we do anything wrong" (153).

Toward the end of the novel, Count Greffi tells Frederic that love "is a religious feeling" (263). Indeed, despite its rather cynical beginnings — "This was a game," Frederic tells us at the outset, "in which you said things instead of playing cards" (30) — Frederic and Catherine's courtship develops into its own moral and spiritual force. At one point, Catherine even tells Frederic, "You're my religion" (116), and throughout the serious stages of their affair they continually try to transcend their individual egos, even their physical beings, in order to merge with the other — clearly a religious experience. Catherine tells Frederic, "There isn't any me anymore" (106), and Frederic, later, tells her, "We're the same one. . . . I haven't any life at all anymore" (299-300). Each merges his or her self into a greater "self" that is the union of both, experiencing in the process not only a feeling of spiritual elation but also of physical death. By "dying" into a spiritual "oneness," they transcend, however illusory it may be, the biological trap: they no longer *feel* accountable to the physical world. Again, it is a religious experience modeled on the Christian paradigm of a spiritual afterlife, a life that begins with physical death, involves a spiritual merging with the indivisible "One," and ultimately transcends biological and temporal cycles.

It is fitting, then, that Frederic and Catherine's self-created "home" finds its most idyllic setting above Montreux in Switzerland — a mirror image of the priest's Abruzzi.[14] It too is a frozen realm "above" the chaos and rottenness of the war. Even the language used to describe it is similar: the roads are "iron hard with the frost" (289) and the air "cold and clear" (291). As in the Abruzzi, people treat one another with deference and respect. Time, too, seems to slow down — certainly in comparison to the rush of the war and the "whirling" rooms in the brothels. Yet there is a key difference. As we have already noted, the Abruzzi is a symbolic realm representing the old

Christian order. The priest is its native son; his family still lives there, and he plans to return after the war. The mountains above Montreux, on the other hand, serve as a symbolic expression of Frederic and Catherine's new, self-created spiritual order. While it is modeled on the former, it lacks the concept of a transcendent deity, and therefore lacks an everlasting spiritual presence outside temporal, biological cycles. As a result, despite its appearance, it is still accountable to those cycles. We thus see the rain impinge on this idyllic realm, forcing Frederic and Catherine—not natives, but only temporary visitors—to return to the city.

Of course, the rain is only a symbol of natural force in general, and while it puts an end to the setting for their spiritual home, it is another aspect of natural force—namely, their child—that ultimately destroys it. After all, it is the child that Frederic feels is "hurrying" them, pushing them back into the temporal, physical world they had hoped to escape. The child is a constant reminder that one can never escape the biological trap; as Frederic says, the child is "the end of the trap" (320). He is, in Frederic's words, "the price you paid for sleeping together" (32), a price not exacted by any external deity punishing a moral transgression, but one exacted by nature itself: "just nature giving her hell" (320). Moreover, the child forces Frederic and Catherine to realize that, despite the transcendent, religious feeling they had experienced in their love for one another, in reality they had never managed to transcend the physical and biological. As Catherine says, "It's just a dirty trick" (331): the means of expressing their "spiritual" love, the sexual act, is also a biological act. And the very natural child it produces biologically is the cause of Catherine's death. It is death by "natural" causes, by a "natural thing" (138)—death, as Catherine herself had presaged, "in the rain." [15]

At the end of the novel, after Catherine's death, Frederic is a man both alienated and disillusioned. He is completely alienated from the natural, biological world that has destroyed his and Catherine's self-created, spiritual home. He cannot even say good-bye to Catherine, for without her spirit, she is like a "statue"—a mere physical entity. He no longer harbors any sentimental notions of a spiritual afterlife or a spiritual regeneration. He does not "carry her with him" in spirit but leaves alone, finally realizing what Catherine had known from the beginning: that physical death is the end for the spirit. [16]

Frederic is also disillusioned at the end by love, a quality that he had apotheosized to an absolute, for it has ultimately failed to transcend the biological world. The Christian paradigm of a transcendent, fixed eternity does not work without the Christian God, becoming an empty abstraction. Without an eternal spiritual force "behind" nature, death is the end for any self-created spiritual home, as it is the end for the spiritual self that created that home. Frederic walks away from Catherine's body empty—empty of religion, empty of love—with nothing to fill the void and nothing to reconcile him to the rain that continues to beat down on him. As a character emblematic of modern humanity, Frederic must now find a new means of filling the void left by the demise of the traditional Christian order, a means modeled not on a religious abstraction but on his own experience in the natural world. And in *The Sun Also Rises*, a novel that begins where *A Farewell to Arms* ends, we see a protagonist who learns to do just that.

CHAPTER SEVEN
THE SUN ALSO RISES: LEARNING TO LIVE IN A NATURALISTIC WORLD

Even though *The Sun Also Rises* is an earlier novel than *A Farewell to Arms*, its protagonist finds himself in the same predicament at the beginning of that novel as Frederic Henry does at the end of the later work. Like Frederic Henry after the death of Catherine, Jake Barnes must find a way to live in a world in which there are no absolutes, must create a personal order that is neither based on an abstraction nor belied by experience. To this end, he learns to create a personal order within natural, temporal cycles—a means by which he can "live in it," as he says—rather than an order "above" and "beyond" those cycles as we saw in the case of Frederic and Catherine. Jake's personal order is thus grounded in his experience with the natural world. By asserting his consciousness in the face of natural forces, Jake gives meaning and justification to his existence. It is a "modern" response that, unlike Frederic and Catherine's, proves efficacious in reconciling the self to a naturalistic world.

As in *A Farewell to Arms*, Christianity has become obsolete in the postwar world of *The Sun Also Rises*. It no longer "works," no longer provides a moral and spiritual order in which the self can feel "at home." And although Jake, like Frederic Henry, yearns nostalgically for that absolute Christian order, for the comfort and solace that it had formerly provided, he nevertheless finds himself banished from it by his own modern sensibility. Jake is a Catholic, but, he laments, a "rotten Catholic."[1] Again, the word "rot-

ten," just as it is used in reference to the priest's experience in the war in
A Farewell to Arms, here too suggests decay and dissolution; in the case of
Jake's Catholicism, it connotes the demise of faith through Jake's experiences in a naturalistic world that moves ineluctably toward the ultimate rot
and decay of death. Catholicism for Jake, whether he is willing to admit it
to himself or not, has become an empty abstraction that no longer accords
with his own experience in the world. He tries to pray in the cathedral in
Pamplona, yet his prayers remain distinctly earthbound: he prays for good
bullfights, for good fishing, even for that root of all evil, money. To para-
phrase Emerson, Jake's "praying" is more akin to begging, for there is no
spiritual vision informing his prayers. He begins to sense this, for after a
long passage in which he describes himself as praying, he switches to describing himself as "thinking of myself as praying" (97). Prayer itself has
become alien to Jake's experience; he is reduced to vague nostalgia: "I only
wished I felt religious" (97).

The fiesta of San Fermin also illustrates the demise of Christianity and
Christian order. Jake tells us that "San Fermin is also a religious festival"
(153), but this casual, offhand remark—made after describing the peasants
drinking in the wine-shops and "shifting" their values for the fiesta—is indicative of the place to which Christianity has been relegated in the festival:
to a nominal or, at best, ancillary role. It may "also" be a religious festival,
but it is primarily a pagan ritual devoid of any Christian spirituality. The
Dionysian continually overshadows the Christian in Pamplona: drunken
revelers obscure the religious procession as it makes its way through the
streets; *riau-riau* dancers and various grotesques—"great giants, cigar-
store Indians, thirty feet high, Moors, a King and Queen" (155)—enclose
the procession, dwarfing and parodying the religious icon of San Fermin;
and after the procession disappears into a church, the revelers discover a
new icon to worship—Brett Ashley, who, ironically, had just been denied
entrance to the church for not wearing a hat. Brett, who, as we shall see
in a moment, is a "natural" woman—that is, a woman whose unrestrained
sexuality is emblematic of natural, biological forces—is transformed into a
pagan ordering principle: she becomes "an image to dance around" (155).
Even Jake and Bill Gorton are swept into the dance, the entire scene
suggesting the moral inversion—the overturning of absolute values—that

characterizes the fiesta. Shortly thereafter, the Christian aspect of the fiesta fades entirely; when the religious procession passes outside the wine-shop where the revelers are drinking, one of them responds to Mike Campbell's question—"Isn't that the procession?"—with "Nada.... It's nothing" (158). Indeed, for all the significance with which it now imbues the fiesta, Christianity itself has dwindled to nothing.

Yet this scene also points toward an alternative to the Christian moral and spiritual order—namely, a secular order imposed by the human consciousness in which natural force is celebrated and camaraderie, particularly male camaraderie, is exalted. Values may be overturned during the fiesta, but new values are established. And these new values are shown to be "truer" to one's experience in the world, generated as they are by that experience rather than by an antiquated creed. The wine-shop takes on connotations of a "new" church; in a parallel image, Jake describes it as a dark place just as he had earlier described the cathedral, yet a celebratory rather than solemn dark place in which people sing rather than pray. Brett replaces the Virgin as the central icon, her sexuality neither a sin nor a source of discord and strife but a source of order and power. She represents the natural life force, a pagan goddess of nature in stark contrast to the "unnatural" image of immaculate motherhood embodied in the Virgin. Money, something Jake had earlier prayed for in the cathedral and that, since the start of the fiesta, has lost its "definite value in hours worked and bushels of grain sold" (152), needs no value here; it is not really necessary, for it is subsumed to the value of human companionship.[2] When Jake tries to pay for his wine, someone puts his money back in his pocket. Jake then passes around his wine-bag, and in a type of secular communion, everyone drinks from it. And finally, in contrast to the Catholics on the train to Bayonne who preempt the dining car and thereby deny food to the other passengers, the peasants in the wine-shop show a true spirit of brotherhood by sharing their food with the expatriates. Jake tells a peasant who hands him a fork, "I don't want to eat up your meal," to which the peasant replies, "Eat, ... What do you think it's here for?" (157).

We see a similar instance of male camaraderie in the fishing scene at Burguete, and once again such an elemental celebration of life is put forth as a replacement to the obsolete Christian order.[3] Jake and Bill parody organized religion while eating and drinking beside the Irati River:

"Let us rejoice in our blessings. Let us utilize the fowls of the air. Let us utilize the product of the vine. Will you utilize a little, brother?"

"After you, brother." (122)

Yet their parody is certainly truer to the original acts of the Apostles than, say, the acts of the Catholics on the train to Bayonne. Again, it is performed in a true spirit of brotherhood, and it envelopes nature in its celebration. "Let no man be ashamed to kneel here in the great out-of-doors," Bill says. "Remember the woods were God's first temples" (122). Later, Jake and Bill, with the Englishman Harris, go through the monastery of Ronces-valles. The contrast between the monastery and "God's first temples" is made patent when Bill asks Harris, "It [the monastery] isn't the same as fishing, though, is it?" and Harris responds, "I say not" (128). They then "utilize" a nearby pub, the pub like the wine-shop a place of secular cele-bration. Again, money has no value: Harris will not let the others pay for the wine, and the innkeeper will not even take Harris's money. (Before going fishing for the first time, Bill had asked Jake jokingly, but signifi-cantly, if when he was digging for worms he was really "burying" his money, indicating its valuelessness in the country.) In the face of an indifferent uni-verse, Jake, Bill, and Harris assert their common humanity that gives their existence in that universe genuine value. Harris even tells the other two that they "don't know how much it *means*" (129, my emphasis) to him to have had their companionship. His gift to them when they depart—trout flies he himself has tied—is a gift from one human to another two whose worth transcends monetary value.

Even Jake and Brett find a peace and a genuine companionship in a bar that they are denied in a church. Their experience in the cathedral in Pamplona, an experience in which their praying "had not been much of a success," ends with Brett saying, "Let's get out of here. Makes me damned nervous" (208). Yet, at the end of the novel, they come to a quiet under-standing in the bar of the Palace Hotel in Madrid. It is a "clean, well-lighted place," a humanly ordered oasis that confronts and withholds the sum-mer heat just outside the window. Like the café in "A Clean, Well-Lighted Place," this bar of "wonderful gentility" (244) enables Jake and Brett to uphold their dignity and, in doing so, acts as a stave against the impinging forces of the world outside.

This becomes a recurring theme in Hemingway's work: the need for the individual to maintain his dignity and integrity in the face of powerful forces. He must create his own order—his own meaning and justification for existence—that preserves his dignity and integrity *within* a world of material force. This order may be metaphorically described as a clean, well-lighted place, as an island in the stream, as a trout holding himself steady in the current with wavering fins, or as a work of art that endures through changing literary fashions, but it always suggests stability within change. And it is this stability within change that Jake must learn to provide for himself in the course of the novel.

As in *A Farewell to Arms*, the universe in *The Sun Also Rises* is depicted as one of constant flux. With the collapse of the Christian conception of an ordered universe, natural processes are no longer conceived as moving toward a teleological goal; rather, they become indifferent material forces operating in repetitive cycles. We remember that the central metaphor in *A Farewell to Arms* was of a car stuck in the mud, its wheels spinning but going nowhere, leaving humanity trapped. We see similar metaphors in *The Sun Also Rises*. The epigraph from Ecclesiastes introduces us to such a world: it describes a universe of cyclical process—ironically, a universe that in the context of the novel is devoid of a transcendent principle which could give that material process meaning. The earth, the "hero" of the novel as Hemingway explained in a letter to Maxwell Perkins, can do no more than "abideth forever." [4] To abideth, to endure with patience and fortitude, maintaining stability within change, is all that the individual can do if he too is to become a "hero." The heroic self, in other words, must imbue the inherently meaningless, cyclical universe with meaning through his stoic endurance of its often destructive processes.

Death, of course, is the ultimate destruction, and as we saw in *A Farewell to Arms*, the dust that powders the leaves of the trees connotes its natural occurrence. Similarly, the revolving wheels of the car that takes Jake and Bill from Pamplona to Burguete churn up dust—"dust rose under the wheels" (105)—the image again suggesting natural, cyclical process leading ineluctably toward death. Dust, in fact, is everywhere in Spain, an elemental land more closely tied to the earth in Hemingway's imagination than France. It is a "white dusty road into Spain" (93), "dust powdering the trees" (104). The porter in the hotel in Pamplona brushes the dust off Jake's shoulders and collar, making a point that he could tell Jake was traveling in a motor car—that vehicle of aimless, circuitous movement in the novel—"from the way the dust was" (96). And after driving from Spain to Bayonne after the fiesta, Jake significantly rubs his fishing rod-case through the dust that covers the car, telling us that "it seemed the last thing that connected me with Spain and the fiesta" (232). Indeed, as we shall see, sexuality (intimated here by Jake's phallic rod-case) and the fiesta are both closely linked to cyclical natural processes of which death, of course, is a part and in which Jake must learn to live.

The structure of the novel also suggests a universe of cyclical process devoid of any meaning other than that which the self may give it. As Richard Lehan has pointed out, the action of the novel begins and ends with Jake and Brett in a taxi, first in Paris and then in Madrid.[5] Their movement through these two cities is also circular and aimless: "tell him [the taxi driver] to drive *around*" (24, my emphasis), Brett tells Jake in Paris. And, of course, Jake and the expatriates move aimlessly from place to place and back in the course of the novel; Jake even sleeps alone in the same room in Bayonne at the end of the novel as he did with Cohn and Bill toward the beginning.

In an echo of the epigraph from Ecclesiastes, Jake tells us early in the novel that "I had the feeling of going through something that has all happened before. . . . I had the feeling as in a nightmare of it all being something repeated, something I had been through and that now I must go through again" (64). He is referring to his futile relationship with Brett, who has just told him "I'm so miserable" (a sentiment she will repeat throughout the novel). The futility of their relationship is of course due to Jake's inability to consummate it; as in *A Farewell to Arms*, sexuality is depicted as the motive force behind natural process. "It always gets to be" *that* (i.e., sex), Jake tells Brett (26); it always comes back *around* to it.

As suggested earlier, Brett is the "natural" woman in the novel, the woman who "can't help" (183) her sexual promiscuity.[6] "It's the way I'm made" (55), she tells Jake. She often refers to herself as a "bitch," a term that connects her to natural animal sexuality and that is in stark contrast to the unnatural "stuffed dogs" to which Bill refers at one point. Just as Frederic Henry's sexuality had trapped him within the "whirling" rooms of the brothels—that is, within the whirling cycle of natural process—so too does

Brett's sexuality trap her "biologically," pushing her from man to man in an aimless circuit. She is the woman who never finishes sentences, according to Count Mippipopolous, nor does she finish anything else. She is constantly *in the process;* even her oft-repeated expression "rot" suggests a connection with natural process and its ineluctable progression toward decay.

As a pagan ritual, the fiesta is also closely connected to nature and natural process.[7] It is an annual occurrence, a festival that recurs with the seasons. Like the "nightmare" of Jake and Brett's repetitious relationship, it too is, in Bill's words, a "wonderful nightmare" (222). And just as in natural process, there are no values inherent in the fiesta other than those human beings give it. We immediately see that the fiesta requires a "shifting in values" (152), and that any preconceived or established values—"definite value" (152)—are overturned. Monetary value is shown to lie outside of "hours worked" and "bushels of grain sold" (152)—that is, outside *things.* Again, value or "meaning" is not intrinsic. It is imposed from without by humans: the prices of food, drink, and lodging are doubled for the fiesta. For some, even human life is devalued; there seems to be no great concern for the man killed during the running of the bulls. When Jake tells Bill of the death, Bill says indifferently, "Was there?" (204). Only a waiter—a man who seems to have a rigid set of values, values most likely derived from the established Christian belief in the sanctity of human life—is shocked. He sees no sense in a death "all for sport. All for pleasure" (197). And the value Pedro Romero places in killing the bull who had killed the man, and in giving its ear as a gift to Brett, is lost on Brett. She leaves the ear in the back of a drawer, along with several cigarette butts, at the Hotel Montoya.

In *A Farewell to Arms* Hemingway connects sexuality, war, and the "whirling" life of the city through the symbol of the rain: all are facets of natural force. The fiesta too, in addition to being repetitive, intrinsically valueless, and "whirling," is connected to those forces beyond one's control by its association in Jake's mind with the war. At a dinner during the fiesta with the expatriates shortly after some verbal fisticuffs between Mike and Cohn, Jake makes an explicit comparison:

> It was like certain dinners I remember from the war. There was much wine, an ignored tension, and a feeling of things coming that you could not prevent happening. Under the wine I lost the disgusted feeling and was happy. It seemed they were all such nice people. (146)

As in the war, Jake realizes that there are violent forces operating which he cannot forestall, only endure. There are other connections, too. Jake tells us that when the fiesta began, it "exploded." "There is," he says, "no other way to describe it" (152). He then compares the explosion of the rocket that signals the start of the fiesta to a "shrapnel burst" (153). Later, in describing the disastrous fireworks performance of Don Manuel Orquito, the "fireworks king," we sense a subtle, subconscious recognition of his wartime experience. Don Manuel sends up "fire balloons" as a military band plays; yet the fireworks, like the war itself, spin out of control, falling into the crowd and exploding. In what must be an allusion to Jake's particular wound, the fireworks, we are told, "charged and chased, sputtering and cracking, *between the legs* of the people" (179, my emphasis).

This sense of forces out of control, of process in repetitious cycles, is reproduced in another image that is also found in *A Farewell to Arms*. We remember Frederic Henry's experience in the "whirling" rooms of the brothels, his libidinal drives connecting him to nature's wheel. In *The Sun Also Rises*, just before the start of the fiesta, Jake experiences the same drunken sensation of a room going "round and round" (147). Later, toward the end of the fiesta, Jake must look at "some fixed point" (223) to make the room stop whirling. As does Frederic in the brothels, Jake in this instance finds only a blank wall on which to improvise a "fixed point." Outside, the fiesta too continues "going on," but, Jake remarks significantly, "it did not mean anything" (224).

It is in the midst of this whirling world that Jake must find some form of stability. And his ability to do so, an ability he develops as he goes through experience in the course of the novel, is a marked departure from the fate of characters in most works of nineteenth-century literary naturalism. Vandover, we remember, is crushed beneath the "iron wheels" of nature, his attempts at avoiding such a fate little more than "instinctual" reactions to circumstance. He never gains an awareness of his predicament great enough to enable him to create an order to fill the void left by the collapse of former ordering principles. In *The Octopus*, a much different naturalistic novel than *Vandover*, the source of order is ultimately discovered within nature itself, although this discovery does little to prevent the death and destruction produced by the Railroad. In Hemingway's work, we see a naturalistic world much like that found in *Vandover* (yet cyclical, rather than linear), a world in which there is no meaning immanent in natural process. Yet experience is not lost on the Hemingway protagonist; he gains an awareness as he goes through it, and it is this experience, in the form of consciousness, that he asserts in response to meaningless natural force. He can, in other words, create his own order, his own meaning, yet one that must be grounded in his experience—a fact that separates Jake Barnes from Frederic Henry. After all, it is only at the end of *A Farewell to Arms* that Frederic realizes that an abstract order—that is, any order not grounded in one's experience with the natural world—is doomed to failure. Jake, on the other hand, develops this awareness throughout *The Sun Also Rises*. He gradually moves away from Robert Cohn's form of sentimentality and romanticism and toward the personal and aesthetic order embodied by Pedro Romero, ultimately using the latter as a model on which to base his own personal order.

Robert Cohn is a character whose conception of the world has been formed by books, particularly romances.[8] It is thus a conception divorced from his own experience, a conception that implies there is an order external to the self, and it has the effect of preventing him from ever learning directly from life. He insists that life conform to his unrealistic conception. One of the first things we learn about Cohn is that "he read too much" (3). And the one book we learn that he has read, and that Jake claims was a major influence on him, is W. H. Hudson's *The Purple Land*. As its title might suggest, *The Purple Land* is a romance, accurately described by Jake as a book that "recounts splendid imaginary amorous adventures of a perfect English gentleman in an intensely romantic land" (9). Cohn obviously conceives of himself as such a perfect gentleman and believes that life holds out the possibility of such amorous adventures. He even goes to the absurd length of asking Jake to travel with him to South America, the setting of *The Purple Land*. When Jake tells him, "You can see all the South Americans you want in Paris," Cohn replies, "They're not the real South Americans" (9). Cohn is clearly confused about the nature of reality.

His view of women and love is likewise derived from romances. Cohn has an idealized view of love, one that never conforms to his own relationships. He had thought that it would be too cruel to leave his first wife, and then she subsequently leaves him. He is "sure" that he loves Frances, his current girlfriend, yet she treats him like something less than a lover. He is then sure that he loves Brett—or as he pompously tells Jake, "I shouldn't wonder if I were in love with her" (38)—even though he has only just met

her and really knows nothing about her. Jake, undercutting Cohn's romanticism, tells us that "I am sure he had never been in love in his life" (8).

It is Cohn's idealistic view of Brett that is the most absurd. He conceives
of her as one of the "ladies" in a romance, and of their brief and meaningless affair as an "amorous adventure" of the ages. His first address to Brett
at the Bal Musette could be a line of dialog right out of *The Purple Land:*
"Will you dance with me, Lady Brett?" (23). He later comments to Jake
about Brett's qualities of "fineness" and "breeding"—qualities we see Brett
distinctly lacks—and refuses to believe the "facts" Jake tells him about
Brett and her life, preferring his own idealized conception of her. He even
becomes ludicrously offended by Jake's knowledge: "I didn't ask you to in-
sult her" (39), he says.

Cohn never does see that Brett is nothing like a lady in a romance. And
Jake's descriptions of Cohn's behavior after his affair with Brett ridicule
Cohn's romantic delusions. Jake mocks Cohn's "affair with a lady of title"
(178), laughs at Cohn's readiness "to do battle for his lady love" (178) with
Mike. Cohn remains with Brett in Pamplona, Jake tells us, because Cohn
believes "love would conquer all" (199). Bill, too, laughs at Cohn's mis-
guided chivalry in beating up Romero and in wanting to take Brett away
with him "to make an honest woman out of her" (201). As if it were right
out of a romance, Bill comments, "Damned touching scene" (201).

The direct experience of life, apart from books, escapes Cohn. He misses
those moments of genuine value such as the fishing in Burguete and the
revelry in the wine-shop. His delusions regarding Brett and their relationship keep him from the former, and he passes out during the latter. He even
fails to appreciate the beauty of the Spanish land—a beauty both Jake and
Bill acknowledge—falling asleep in the car on the road to Pamplona.

Yet Jake has much in common with Cohn, especially at the beginning of
the novel. Both are outsiders: Cohn is a Jew among Gentiles, and Jake is a
de-phallused man in a world that exalts virile manhood. Even Jake's name—
a contraction of Jacob—connects him with the Jewish Cohn. There are
other subtle connections deliberately placed throughout the novel. Cohn
saves Jake a place on the bus to Burguete; Jake too falls asleep during the
fiesta when everyone else continues to carouse; Jake falls asleep on Cohn's
bed and wears his jacket. But, of course, the central connection between the
two, the connection that all the others reinforce, is their shared romantic

idealism.[9] Jake, too, reads too much, and his reading colors his apprehension of experience. He dislikes riding down the Boulevard Raspail in Paris because, he supposes, "I had read something about it once" (42). He goes on to say that "that was the way Cohn was about all of Paris" (42). Jake, like Cohn, also reads romances, as we see him do alongside the Irati River. Jake takes a break from fishing by reading a book by A. E. W. Mason containing a love story as ludicrous as those in *The Purple Land*. And Jake's relationship with Brett, at least until the end of the novel, is marked by sentimentality. He too idealizes her, crying over her even though he comes to realize that she is not worth the emotion. He also futilely follows her around as does Cohn.

Such romantic idealization threatens to destroy Jake emotionally, as it certainly does destroy Cohn. The imposition of a preconceived order on experience is doomed to failure in an implacable world of force, just as Frederic Henry's idealization of love is doomed in *A Farewell to Arms*. Jake must learn to move away from such romantic notions if he is to become "hard-boiled" (34). (Note how the term "hard-boiled" connotes arrested natural process, the creating of stability within flux.) Jake gradually abandons the belief in and the search for absolutes and settles for an approach to life that can give it a personal meaning—a genuine meaning because it is one derived from experience in the world. He succinctly sums up his slowly acquired philosophy when he says, "I did not care what it was all about. All I wanted to know was how to live in it" (148).

As do other protagonists in Hemingway's work, Jake learns to acquire a philosophy of life by observing and emulating another character who lives by it. Such a mentor for Frederic Henry in *A Farewell to Arms* is Count Greffi. In *The Sun Also Rises*, Jake learns from two mentors: Count Mippipopolous and Pedro Romero. The Count is a man who has "been around very much" (59); he has lived in the whirling world and, like Jake, has been wounded by his experience in it. His wound, or more precisely, the confrontation with death that it evinces, has made him appreciate life. As he says, "it is because I have lived very much that now I can enjoy everything so well" (60). He knows how to "get his money's worth out of life," a metaphor that Jake will reiterate when he meditates on learning "to live in it." The Count has already learned to live in it. He has gotten to "know the values" (60), values that are not decreed and absolute but that are self-discovered, grounded in his experience. He is not interested in titles—unlike Brett, who, in her own words, has had "hell's own amount of credit" (57) on hers—for he sees no intrinsic value in them. (Note the play on "credit.") They have no value unless the titled person's life and character give them value, something we see little of among the titled characters in the novel. Avoiding socially decreed values, the Count prefers the quiet of a restaurant in the Bois (another clean, well-lighted place) in order to drink and socialize with Jake and Brett to the smoke and noise of Zelli's in Montmartre, a place much like the city cafés Frederic Henry visits in *A Farewell to Arms*. The Count also embraces those values we have already examined: camaraderie and the celebration of life.

The Count, however, leads a retired life, a life Jake's financial situation, at least, prevents him from emulating. He finds a model for the active life, though, in Pedro Romero. Romero's bullfight becomes a visual metaphor for the way to "live in it": the self alone, confronting natural force with courage, grace, and dignity. The bull, of course, is the natural force, its blackness suggestive of the darkness of death it embodies. The bullfighter, like everyone, is up against that force, up against death, and the way in which he conducts himself in the face of it is all that gives the experience meaning. Natural force, then, becomes something more than the destructive process it had been, for example, in *Vandover*; it becomes a necessary component in one's self-definition, a necessary condition for imbuing life with meaning. It becomes, in other words, a means of transcending its own meaninglessness.

Yet, again, it is the individual himself who must effect that transcendence, who must create meaning through the integrity of his actions. In an era of decadent bullfighting, Romero has, in Jake's words, "the old thing" (168). His courage is evident to all but the Biarritz crowd. He does not needlessly wind the bull during his cape-work; he works closely to the bull and its horns; he does not counterfeit the danger and the emotion it produces; he doesn't quail when confronted with a difficult near-sighted bull. Romero's courage is contrasted with that of the aging Belmonte, a matador who once possessed courage but who has, with age and pain, lost it. Belmonte now handpicks his bulls, choosing small bulls with small horns in order to lessen the danger to himself. As a result, bullfighting—and, it is implied, life itself—no longer holds any meaning for him. "Things were not the same" for

Belmonte, Jake tells us, "and now life only came in flashes" (215). Even these flashes, these moments of his former greatness in the bullring, "were not of value because he had discounted them in advance" (215) by choosing bulls for safety. Again, we note the recurrent monetary metaphor, here again indicating that meaning, that "value," is not something intrinsic in things but something one bestows on them, something one creates for oneself.

In addition to courage, Romero demonstrates grace in the bullring. Everything he does is "straight and pure and natural in line" (167). There are no brusque movements, no contortions. He maintains "his purity of line through the maximum of exposure" (168), a quality that has become popularly known as "grace under pressure." In the face of brute force, Romero remains in control. Nor does he kill like the "butcher-boys" Hemingway describes in *Death in the Afternoon*, those practitioners of decadent bullfighting, but rather "like a priest at benediction"—that is, with a grace that confers dignity on the bull as well as on himself.[10]

Dignity, of course, is that other all-important element that the bullfighter must preserve. The decadent bullfighters have no dignity. By choosing the bulls for safety, by counterfeiting the danger, by using tricks rather than skill, by turning the aesthetic performance of the bullfight into a tawdry spectacle, they rob themselves, the bull, and the audience of the dignity that can give meaning to both life and death. Romero, however, does none of those things. His bullfight is an aesthetic performance that does not pander to the cheapest emotions of the audience. He ignores the Biarritz crowd, the English philistine tourists who know nothing about bullfighting but pretend to. Rather, Romero does it "all for himself inside" (216), and in that way he does it for Brett and for those in the audience who can appreciate the well-executed *corrida*. But, Jake emphasizes, he does not do it for others "at any loss to himself" (216). Bullfighting is Romero's craft, his *metier*, and it is an intensely personal *metier*. Regardless of its vicarious effect on the audience, bullfighting is above all else Romero's means of creating an order for himself, a means of defining himself and maintaining his human dignity in a naturalistic world that *by nature* undermines it. When bullfighting, Romero is always alone. Even in preparation for the bullfight at the Hotel Montoya, Romero is "altogether by himself" and "far away and dignified" (163). The electric light that illuminates him and sets him off from the surrounding darkness—an image recapitulated in "A Clean,

Well-Lighted Place"—suggests a personal illumination, a man-made order that holds off the impinging void.

It is important to note that outside the ordered medium of the bullfight, Romero is as flawed as any man and as susceptible to the whirling world.[11] This is Montoya's fear: that the young matador will fall among those who do not know what he is "worth" and who do not know what he "means" (172), particularly among women such as Brett. Indeed, Brett—the embodiment of sexuality and therefore of natural, biological force—pulls Romero into this whirling world, and it almost destroys him. Cohn's physical assault, brought about by sexual jealousy and romantic delusions, epitomizes the chaotic, orderless world outside the bullring. It is only through a return to the bullring, a return to his personal order, that Romero can "wipe out" Cohn. The bullfight, in other words, acts as a form of redemption: a personal redemption, man redeeming himself. With each well-executed *faena*, Romero purges the loss of dignity he suffered at the hands of Cohn. With each pass of the bull, he "wiped that out a little cleaner" (219).

As mentioned, Jake gradually moves away from Cohn's disastrous romanticism and toward the personal order embodied by Romero. The big break with Cohn comes when Jake panders Brett to Romero. Several critics have commented that by this act Jake gives the woman he loves but can never possess to the man whom he would like to be; but he also makes a break with the false chivalric code that, up to this point, he has shared with Cohn. It is a conscious break: "It was understood all right" (187), Jake says of the act. Shortly after this, Cohn knocks Jake out, and significantly enough, when Jake regains consciousness, "everything looked new and changed" (192). Cohn's punch brings about an epiphany. "It was all different," he says. "It was all new" (192).

Of course, just as Whitman's protégé cannot travel his own road by traveling that of his mentor, neither can Jake create his own personal order by imitating Romero. Rather obviously, Jake can never be a bullfighter, nor does he aspire to be one. He must create an order that is unique to his own personality, talent, and experience—one that nevertheless confronts the world with the same courage, grace, and dignity with which Romero confronts the bull. It is only in this way that he can bring meaning and stability to life. Yet, through parallel imagery—a device Hemingway employs quite often in his work, such as in the connections he draws between Jake and

Cohn—Hemingway links Jake and Romero quite closely. After the conclusion of the fiesta, Jake travels to San Sebastian. Significantly enough, he travels alone, the first time he does so in the novel. Moreover, unlike when he would be alone in his apartment in Paris, Jake never dwells on or even thinks about Brett, their relationship, or his wound. Instead, he carefully and deliberately goes through a private ritual that prevents him from thinking about those things and that recalls Romero's private ritual before the bullfight. He pays close attention to each detail, each seemingly insignificant act:

> After lunch I went up to my room, read a while, and went to sleep. When I woke it was half past four. I found my swimming-suit, wrapped it with a comb in a towel, and went down-stairs and walked up the street to the Concha. The tide was about half-way out. The beach was smooth and firm, and the sand yellow. I went into a bathing-cabin, undressed, put on my suit, and walked across the smooth sand to the sea. The sand was warm under bare feet. (234)

Jake awakes in the late afternoon, the time of the bullfights in Spain (cf., the title of Hemingway's book on the bullfight, *Death in the Afternoon*). The bay of San Sebastian—the Concha, or "scallop-shell"—is a nearly enclosed, circular bay here reminiscent of the bullring. And the beach with its smooth and yellow sand likewise recalls the sand of the bullring, which Jake had earlier described as "smooth-rolled and yellow" (211). Jake then ventures out into the sea; again, the self alone confronting nature. He is attentive to the aesthetics of his dives, diving "cleanly and deeply" (238), just as Romero plays and kills the bull.

The parallel imagery here is neither gratuitous nor overwrought; not only does it connect Jake to Romero, but it also shows Jake emulating the implicit philosophy of Romero's art—that is, ordering his life through the deliberateness, gracefulness, and dignity of his actions. Jake has learned to "live in it." He can now bear the solitude; in fact, he even enjoys it, for it keeps him safely ensconced within his own stoic order, holding off the whirling world outside. "I was through with fiestas for a while" (232), he says. He now finds company in a bottle of wine, the slow and deliberate enjoyment of it providing an island of repose amid the flux, in sharp contrast to the unbridled drinking during the fiesta. In addition, when he rejects the liqueur a waiter recommends to him—"the veritable flowers of the Pyrenees," the waiter had called it (233)—he is rejecting any preconceived or ordained "truth" in favor of his own experience of it. The waiter may call it what he will, but to Jake, who tastes it, it "looked like hair oil and smelled like Italian *strega*" (233). We even see that his attitude toward Brett and their relationship has fundamentally changed; even though he travels to Madrid after she wires him, he does so—as he had said of Pedro Romero's performance—without "any loss to himself" (216). He does not become maudlin, does not succumb to the sentimentality that would trap him once again in a repetitive cycle. Rather, he evinces a new awareness, stoically resisting Brett's own sentimentality. Regardless of the "damned good time together" they could have had if Jake had not been wounded, he was wounded. His famous closing retort to Brett—"Isn't it pretty to think so?"—shows that he has come to terms with his experience, that he realizes it is that reality which he must "live in," and not any romantic or idealized falsification of reality.

There is still, however, another dimension to *The Sun Also Rises:* the metafictional dimension. In addition to learning from Romero an approach to or a stance in life—a "code," as it has been called—Jake learns an aesthetic, one that also acts as a stave against implacable process. Several critics have pointed out the parallels between Jake's description of Romero's technique in the bullring and Hemingway's own literary style; Hemingway would draw those parallels between bullfighting and writing more explicitly in *Death in the Afternoon*, and in other works he would use hunting (cf., *Green Hills of Africa*) and fishing (cf., *The Old Man and the Sea*) as metaphors for, among other things, his own aesthetic. Certainly Hemingway's clean, stripped-down style possesses an affinity with Romero's smooth, controlled bullfight in which there are no brusque movements, no contortions. Hemingway argued in *Death in the Afternoon* that a writer should write clearly, that he should not mystify merely "to avoid a straight statement," [12] thereby hiding incompetence, just as a bullfighter should not contort himself "to give a faked look of danger" (168). Such tricks, both in writing and in bullfighting, inevitably "turned bad and gave an unpleasant feeling" (168) and, in writing, prevented the work from achieving immortality. In addition, to Hemingway, the writer, like Romero, was a man alone, working "all for himself inside," finding in his *metier* a means of ordering experience and using that order to hold off external forces. In the *Paris Review*, Hemingway told George Plimpton that the most difficult part of life to get through was the time between when he quit writing for the day and when he resumed writing the following morning.[13] Moreover, like Romero who works close to the bull's horns, the writer to Hemingway must work close to experience, must write about those things that he has experienced and therefore knows. The problem with Mencken, as Harvey Stone tells Jake, is that "he's written about all the things he knows, and now he's on all the things he doesn't know" (43).

The well-executed bullfight, like the well-wrought work of literature, also succeeds in achieving an aesthetic union between the self and the natural force that opposes it. Such a union involves a fundamental transformation, the creation of a new, distinctly human order and human meaning. During Romero's cape-work, Jake describes Romero and the bull as "*one sharply etched mass*" (217, my emphasis); when Romero kills the first bull, Jake says "for an instant he and the bull were one" (218), and when he kills the second bull, Jake reiterates, "he became one with the bull" (220). It is a transcendental moment; no longer opposites, the self and nature are one, the experience producing in the audience that sense of timelessness and immortality always associated with the transcendental—that is, a sense of arrested process (cf., "*for an instant* he and the bull were *one*"). Throughout *Death in the Afternoon*, Hemingway discusses the feeling of immortality produced by the well-executed bullfight; at one point he says:

> Now the essence of the greatest emotional appeal of bullfighting is the feeling of immortality that the bullfighter feels in the middle of a great *faena* and that he gives to the spectators. He is performing a work of art and he is playing with death, bringing it closer, closer, closer, to himself, a death that you know is in the horns because you have the canvas-covered bodies of the horses on the sand to prove it. He gives the feeling of his immortality, and, as you watch it, it becomes yours. Then when it belongs to both of you, he proves it with the sword.[14]

This "feeling of immortality" is also produced by the great writer. Like the bullfighter, the writer fundamentally transforms experience through the aesthetic act, imbuing it with order and meaning. If executed well enough, the work of art—the union of consciousness and experience—becomes the experience itself. In this way, it achieves immortality, the experience remaining valid for any reader at any time. It is this to which Hemingway refers when, in the *Paris Review*, he claimed, "I have tried to eliminate everything unnecessary to conveying experience to the reader so that after he or she has read something it will become a part of his or her experience and seem actually to have happened." [15]

In *The Sun Also Rises*, we see an example of this phenomenon when Jake reads Turgenev's *A Sportsman's Sketches* while drunk in his hotel room in Pamplona. He says,

> I turned on the light again and read. I read the Turgenieff. I knew that now, reading it in the oversensitized state of my mind after much too much brandy, I would remember it somewhere, and afterward it would seem as though it had really happened to me. I would always have it. (149)

Significantly enough, reading Turgenev stops the room from whirling; it is that metaphorical "fixed point" which arrests cyclical process. Turgenev, an influence Hemingway frequently acknowledged, has succeeded through art in transmuting his own experience into Jake's. He has created, in other words, a timeless experience. The work of art thus acts as a stave against process, serves as an island of stability within cyclical change. Art becomes a sanctuary, a man-made sanctuary, what Wayne C. Booth has called the "clean, well-lighted place of art." [16]

The Sun Also Rises, then, can be read as Jake's *Künstlerroman*. As the first-person narrator, Jake is of course the implied author of the novel; and by the end of the action of the novel, Jake has undergone those experiences and learned those things that make him able to write it. He moves away from the false aesthetics of Cohn—who is also a writer, though the writer of "a very poor novel" (6)—and toward the aesthetics evinced by Romero. He moves, in other words, away from romances and toward a literature that, rather than presuming an order in the world, creates that order and gives it meaning. In effect, Jake in *The Sun Also Rises* "re-writes" romances such as Hudson's *The Purple Land*, substituting a lyrical ordering of experience—that "clean, well-lighted place of art"—in place of a prefabricated and obsolete literary mode.[17]

Jake can never be the hero of a romance; he can never be like the narrator of *The Purple Land* because he is of course incapable of any "amorous adventures." He must, therefore, find a new definition of manhood—one that we have seen involves maintaining one's courage, grace, and dignity in the face of powerful forces. He must create an order that enables him to preserve those human qualities, an order that is true to his experience *in* the world. The self-created order of art, then, must also be true to his experience; it must not be an aesthetic Procrustean bed, a literary mode that experience is forced to fit. Rather, experience must shape the mode.

Jake's narrative, therefore, while it certainly maintains the external trappings of Hudson's romantic travelogue, is a very different travelogue, even in regard to its lyricism. Jake's descriptions of place—of the Spanish countryside, the fiesta, the streets of Paris—are lyrical compositions that go beyond description as mere recording, and become description as conscious aesthetic creation. Landscape becomes mindscape, revealing not just external features but the consciousness observing them. Jake's description, for example, of the café where he had left Brett with Romero, reveals not just the external "facts" but Jake's reaction to those facts:

> When I came back and looked in the café, twenty minutes later, Brett and Pedro Romero were gone. The coffee-glasses and our three empty cognac-glasses were on the table. A waiter came with a cloth and picked up the glasses and mopped off the table. (187)

Again, Jake reveals more than the external scene; he reveals his own disgust at the tawdriness of his actions and the profound emptiness he feels on account of them. Like the aesthetic union Romero achieves between himself and the bull, Jake here, as he does throughout the narrative, forges a union between his consciousness and the external world. We see the scene, but more important, we see a consciousness ordering that scene, a consciousness creating its own aesthetic "clean, well-lighted place."

Hemingway, in granting the human consciousness the power to order experience—in effect, to *create* order and meaning—moves away from nineteenth-century literary naturalism in which consciousness had little or no power to shape its world. While still existing in a largely naturalistic world—that is, a world of material force devoid of a moral and spiritual order—the Hemingway hero is nevertheless able to maintain his human dignity and integrity in the face of it by creating his own personal order.

Yet, as we have seen, any such order must be grounded in experience; it cannot be based on an abstraction, on an order decreed by authority, whether that authority be religious or aesthetic. Hemingway's "modernist" apotheosis of consciousness, however, would not make the transition into the postmodern world; for, as we shall see next with the work of Don DeLillo, in that world consciousness is no longer conceived of as an autonomous entity, but as itself absorbed into a greater system or "field" from which it cannot extricate itself.

CHAPTER EIGHT
FIELDS, SYSTEMS, AND DELILLO'S
POSTMODERN TRANSFORMATION
OF LITERARY NATURALISM

Just as Darwinism effected a revolution in thought during the late nineteenth century—a revolution that, as we saw in Chapter 1, went far beyond the field of biology—so too did the various discoveries and theories that comprise what we now call the new physics and systems theory during the early and middle twentieth century. Once again humanity was forced to reconceive of itself and its place in the universe. And as the naturalism of Zola and Norris was in part a literary response to the philosophical and theological repercussions of Darwinism, Don DeLillo's postmodern transformation of the naturalistic form is a literary response to these new sciences. Yet it is a literary response that undoes "classical" naturalism, for in many ways the new physics and systems theory that DeLillo incorporates in his fiction undermines the basic scientific assumptions on which literary naturalism was based: classical physics, positivism, and various interpretations of Darwinian evolution.

Classical, Newtonian physics posited a mechanistic universe, a universe that Boyle compared to a clock and Paley to a watch. As such analogies imply, the universe was considered a vast mechanism, a conglomeration of physical "parts" that functioned according to certain set laws. The parts in this scheme—physical phenomena—were discrete and isolatable; that is, they were capable of operating independently of one another, and therefore they could be separated and studied independently as well, much like a clock can be taken apart and its gears studied separately from its other components. The smallest discrete part was, of course, the atom. It was presumed that by studying these various parts in isolation, even at the atomic level, one could construct an accurate picture of the entire universe. The whole, in other words, was considered the sum of its parts.

Consonant with the clock analogy, the parts in this mechanistic universe were in constant motion. They too moved in a one-way direction — significantly enough, across measurable, chronological time. It was a linear movement, a chain of cause and effect that was irreversible. A cause remained distinct from an effect; and while an effect could in turn become a cause, it could never reverse the direction, could never influence reciprocally its own cause, but could only cause a future effect. After all, a clock cannot run backward. Such a process would continue until it ran out of energy — until the clock ran down and stopped. When all the discrete processes in the universe had reached this state — a state known as equilibrium in which all energy has been evenly distributed and therefore is incapable of doing work and continuing the process — the universe would be a lifeless, inert mass. Depending on one's religious convictions, it was believed to remain that way forever or to be "rewound" by divine intervention.

In the mechanistic scheme, the operations of these discrete, linear processes were governed by fixed natural laws such as gravitation, inertia, and those of thermodynamics. And because these processes were distinct and could be isolated, and because they moved in a linear chain of cause and effect, the laws governing them were ultimately knowable. By isolating the parts in a process, by studying the single effect of a single cause, one could unlock the secret of the process. Once the natural laws were known, humanity could then use this knowledge for its own ends: effects could be accurately predicted from causes.

These three main tenets of classical physics — the discreteness of physical matter, the linear cause-and-effect chain of natural processes, and the ultimate knowability of natural laws — all presupposed a tenet fundamental to the scientific method itself: the ability to separate the subject from the object, the observer from the observed, the scientist from the experiment. Since all physical matter was discrete, the scientist was discrete from his experiment; he could observe it unfold objectively without influencing its outcome in any way — at least in any way other than he may have originally intended. The cause-and-effect "line" of the unfolding experiment never bisected the cause-and-effect "line" of his own biological and mental processes. And because of his separateness, his knowledge—including his interpretive paradigms and his scientific biases—never influenced either the experiment itself or his interpretation of it. He remained an objective observer. Or so he believed.

Zola, in appropriating the scientific method for his own literary ends, also appropriated the basic tenets of classical physics. Zola, we remember, wanted to establish literature on the "solid ground" of science, for science dealt solely with physical phenomena, and to Zola, physical phenomena was all that was knowable. Moreover, like the positivists such as Auguste Comte who strongly influenced him, Zola believed that the deterministic linear causality manifest in the physical universe was recapitulated in the biological being and social milieu of humanity. "A like determinism," he claimed, "will govern the stones of the roadway and the brain of man." [1] He therefore argued that literature should not be concerned with the metaphysical "why" of events, but only with the "how"—that is, with their deterministic causes and effects. Like the classical scientist, Zola believed that once the "how" was known, once the "laws" governing human behavior in society were discovered, human beings would be able to use this knowledge to better society. They would be able to manipulate the environmental cause to produce a more desirable social effect. They would, in his own words, be able "to regulate life, to regulate society, to solve in time all the problems of socialism [i.e., sociology]." [2]

Zola's faith in the ultimate knowability of natural laws and in deterministic cause and effect went hand in hand with his methodological presumption that the subject could stand apart from the object—in his case, the novelist from his novel. He believed that the novelist, in writing the novel, in effect conducted an objective experiment. Just as a scientist might do with mice, the novelist placed a group of characters in a certain environment and "observed" them behave according to deterministic laws. He had no more influence on the outcome than that little granted to his individual artistic "temperament"—a quality that in Zola's mind only influenced the novel's stylistic features. He himself remained distinct from his characters, never interacting with them. They were an external, discrete object that he, the observing subject, studied. We discussed in Chapter 2 how such a methodology contradicted Zola's belief in materialistic monism, and how because of this the subject-object rift, the separation between the self and nature so characteristic of literary naturalism, remained unresolved. Yet the fact that Zola could earnestly believe that a novelist had no real influence on the behavior of characters he himself had created testifies to the enormous influence classical science had on him—and would have on his literary disciples.

Frank Norris, though not as programmatic in his approach to the novel as Zola, also appropriated aspects of classical science in his work. This was due in part, of course, to Zola's influence on him. Norris, we remember, moves toward a Zolaesque determinism at the conclusion of *Vandover.* Following the collapse of the ordering structures that had upheld him, Vandover degenerates into a physiologically determined brute. He becomes a victim of deterministic cause and effect, his actions beyond his control. As in Zola, the laws of physics are shown to be recapitulated in the laws of biology.

Joseph LeConte, Norris's other main influence, had also assimilated aspects of classical physics into his interpretation of Darwinism, and these too show up in Norris's work, particularly *The Octopus.* While LeConte denied materialistic determinism, he did advocate a type of divine determinism, one in which natural phenomena were determined by God's will. The rationale for such a view was his belief in God's immanence within nature and natural process. There was, he claimed, a "complete *identification* of first and second causes."[3] "All is natural—i.e., according to law, but all is supernatural—i.e., above Nature, as we usually regard Nature, for all is permeated with the immediate Divine presence."[4] LeConte's belief in distinct evolutionary stages through which biological forms progress also paralleled the one-way linear progression of classical physics. In LeConte's paradigm, species are continually moving toward higher forms; no species ever de-evolves. Thus, in *The Octopus,* despite the apparent catastrophe that befalls the ranchers, humanity as a whole continues to evolve toward a greater good. Moreover, and perhaps most important, LeConte's view of an order external to the self, an order that the self need only learn to perceive, implied classical physics' separation of subject and object. Once again, perception is viewed as a strictly objective act, the observer standing apart from the observed. Despite the spiritual connection with nature that Vanamee, Annixter, and Presley finally experience, the means of coming to that experience is presented in an image suggestive of the classical subject-object rift: each character, the subject, standing on a hill observing the wheat, the object, and perceiving an order manifest in it—that is, an ultimately knowable order.

The new physics of the early and middle twentieth century radically altered the classical, Newtonian conception of physical reality, and as a result would alter the form of the naturalistic novel. N. Katherine Hayles has referred to the new physics as the "field concept," a broad term intended to encompass the wide-ranging permutations of twentieth-century theoretical physics.[5] Taken as a whole, these theories—such as Gödel's Incompleteness Theorem, Einstein's Relativity theories, and the various interpretations of quantum mechanics—all share principles that undermine those of classical physics. The most fundamental transformation involves the shift from the Newtonian view of a physical universe composed of parts to one consisting of an all-encompassing field. Everything, in this conception, is connected; nothing operates independently of anything else. As Hayles puts it:

> a field view of reality pictures objects, events, and observer as belonging inextricably to the same field; the disposition of each, in this view, is influenced—sometimes dramatically, sometimes subtly, but in every instance—by the disposition of the others.[6]

Parts cannot be detached, as they could be in the Newtonian conception, without affecting the whole—including our understanding of the whole. To do so would be to distort "reality," to perceive an inaccurate picture of the physical universe. The whole, in other words, is not just the sum of its parts. "The whole is composed of parts," as Hayles phrases it, "but cannot be reduced to them."[7]

Another feature of the field concept that is closely related to the former is the notion of reciprocity. The linear cause-and-effect chain of classical physics does not hold in the new view; there is no one-way, linear movement in which the cause is distinct from the effect. Instead, there is a mutual, reciprocal interaction between events so that each is both a cause *and* an effect. Physical reactions, then, move in at least two directions simultaneously.

Implicit in the concept of a universal field is that the observer is no longer discrete from the observed, the subject no longer separable from the object. Both are part of the same field. Since there is nothing outside the field, there can be no frame of reference outside it either. The observer

must observe from within. As such, any observation he may make necessarily refers back to him—again, ignoring one-way, linear cause and effect.
He is simultaneously observing himself or, as we shall see in a moment, he
is simultaneously observing his own interpretive paradigms. "We are involved," says Hayles, "in what we would describe." [8]

This inseparability of subject and object in the field concept goes hand in
hand with perhaps the most significant epistemological shift brought about
by the new physics: the shift from Newtonian certainty and knowability
to uncertainty and indeterminacy. Gödel's Incompleteness Theorem is of
course seminal here—it is often referred to as the indeterminacy principle
—for he demonstrated mathematically that indeterminacy was inevitable,
that one could never prove a theory that was not false was completely true.
Einstein's Special and General Theories of Relativity are also of central
importance, for they were the first to conceptualize the notion of an interconnected field that contained the observing subject, and that therefore
rendered objective observation and analysis impossible. But it is the quantum theory developed and interpreted by such scientists as Planck, Bohr,
and Heisenberg that is the most pertinent in this regard and to this study,
and therefore a brief summation of its central features is necessary here.

Heisenberg begins *Physics and Philosophy*, his lucid history and interpretation of quantum theory, by declaring that "the change in the concept of
reality manifesting itself in quantum theory is not simply a continuation of
the past; it seems to be a real break in the structure of modern science." [9]
This break originated in Planck's discovery that light did not always behave
like the electromagnetic wave it had been thought to be, but often behaved
like energy particles or "quanta." Heisenberg, speaking retrospectively,
asks the question: "How could it be that the same radiation that produces
interference patterns, and therefore must consist of waves, also produces
the photoelectric effect, and therefore must consist of moving particles?"
(35). The attempt to resolve this dilemma, to reconcile the wave-particle
duality, led the scientists Bohr, Kramers, and Slater to introduce in 1924 the
concept of the "probability wave." They interpreted electromagnetic waves
not as real waves, but as indicators of the probability that a light quantum
was present at any given point on the wave. The more intense the frequency,
the higher the probability that a light quantum was being absorbed or emitted at that point. Such a concept was revolutionary. According to Heisen-

berg, it possessed an affinity with Aristotle's *potentia:* "it introduced something standing in the middle between the possibility and the reality" (41).

Thus uncertainty superseded certainty or knowability in physics.
Heisenberg's Uncertainty Relation—a mathematical formula proving the
impossibility of locating accurately both the position and velocity of a
particle—demonstrated the limitations of Newtonian physics. As Heisenberg noted, "One had learned that the old concepts fit nature only inaccu-
rately" (43). Bohr, too, added to this epistemological shift. His concept of
"complementarity"—that the wave and particle "pictures" were "comple-
mentary descriptions of the same reality" (43), each with its limitations in
accuracy—again demonstrated that our observations, our descriptions, and
therefore our knowledge can only be partial.

Heisenberg went even further. He introduced uncertainty not only into
our knowledge but also into our methodology for obtaining it. As a result,
he illustrated the impossibility of separating subject from object, of having
an experimentor who was not simultaneously a participant in his own experiment. Heisenberg describes a hypothetical experiment in which a scientist observes the movement of an electron using a microscope that emits
gamma rays. He reasons that the light quantum emitted by the microscope
must hit the electron—otherwise the electron could not be "seen"—and
that when it does so it must necessarily change the electron's position and
momentum. Thus the ability to observe objectively, and therefore to grasp
reality objectively, is impossible. The act of observation itself becomes part
of the experiment.

Heisenberg was certainly well aware of the implications of his argument.
"In classical physics," he says, "science started from the belief—or should
one say from the illusion?—that we could describe the world or at least part
of the world without any reference to ourselves" (55). Now, however, the
act of observing something happen in effect makes it happen; it effects the
transition from the possible to the actual that Heisenberg had adumbrated
in his discussion of Aristotle's *potentia:*

> What happens depends on our way of observing it or on the fact that
> we observe it . . . the term "happens" is restricted to the observa-
> tion. . . . The observation plays a decisive role in the event and . . . the
> reality varies, depending upon whether we observe it or not. (50–52)

Moreover, the inevitable "reference to ourselves" in any observation goes beyond the act itself, for the act of observation is never disinterested. It is, in Hayles's words, "always theory-laden." [10] Our theoretical constructs and paradigms limit what may be observed or, at least, what may be considered important or significant in the observation. In other words, we only find what we are looking for, and what we are looking for depends on our theoretical perspective. The answers depend on the questions. Thus it is that Heisenberg makes the revolutionary statement, "We have to remember that what we observe is not nature in itself but nature exposed to our method of questioning" (58).

At about the same time that quantum theory was revolutionizing physics —during the 1920s—a parallel movement was realigning the field of biology. I use the term "parallel" because the systems theory developed and promulgated by Ludwig von Bertalanffy, though not as well known nor as widely accepted as the new physics, nevertheless sought to undermine the fundamental assumptions and methodology of classical science—namely, the belief in the discreetness of parts, in the linear cause-and-effect chain of natural process, and in the division of subject and object. Like Heisenberg, who claimed that quantum theory represented "a real break in the structure of modern science," Bertalanffy called systems theory "a change in basic categories of thought," "a basic re-orientation in scientific thinking." [11] Tom LeClair, who has studied the influence of systems theory on novelists such as DeLillo, has similarly described the theory as "a new paradigm for thinking about reality." [12] Moreover, like the new physics—and, we might add, Darwinism—whose ramifications went far beyond its particular field of inquiry, systems theory continues to influence thought in disciplines other than biology. In fact, Bertalanffy himself advocated that it should; he felt strongly that systems theory, while originating as an "organismic" approach to biology, ought to be codified into a "general system theory": "a theory," he stressed, "not of systems of a more or less special kind, but of universal principles applying to systems in general" (32). It was to be a universal, cross-disciplinary science of systems. The organization he founded, the Society for General Systems Research, stated in its program that its mission was, among other things, to "investigate the isomorphy of concepts, laws, and models in various fields, and to help in useful transfers from one field to another" (15).

Bertalanffy's main point of contention with classical biology was its re-ductiveness. He argued that biology should not be focused solely on the molecular level—which he claimed reduced biology to physics—but also on the higher levels of "living organization" (6). He wrote that, in the early 1920s, "the then prevalent mechanistic approach [to biology] . . . ap-peared to neglect or actively deny just what is essential in the phenomena of life" (12). In place of this approach, one that viewed biological organisms as collections of often-unrelated chemical processes, Bertalanffy advocated viewing them as wholes or "systems." A biological system, to Bertalanffy, was not a loose collection, but a complex organization of many interrelated and interdependent systems.

Given such a view, Bertalanffy naturally disagreed with the assumption in classical science that phenomena could be broken down into discreet, iso-latable parts, and that from studying those parts one could grasp the whole:

> It is necessary to study not only parts and processes in isolation, but also to solve the decisive problems found in the organization and order unifying them, resulting from dynamic interaction of parts, and making the behavior of parts different when studied in isolation or within the whole. (31)

He even cited Heisenberg's Uncertainty Relation as proof that it was "im-possible to resolve phenomena into local events" (31).

The belief in a "dynamic interaction of parts" precludes of course a be-lief in the linear causality of classical science. Bertalanffy distinguished be-tween two types of systems: closed and open. Classical science dealt with closed systems, those presumed to be isolated from the environment and therefore incapable of interacting with other systems. These closed sys-tems, as adumbrated in the Second Law of Thermodynamics, move lin-early toward maximum disorder (entropy) and a state of equilibrium (the end of the cause-and-effect process). Open systems, on the other hand, which form the central paradigm of systems theory, are living systems that are continually interacting with their environment. They are continu-ally building up and breaking down components and, rather than moving toward disorder and equilibrium, tend toward complex organization and a steady state (homeostasis). Another characteristic of the open system is a phenomenon Bertalanffy called "equifinality." In contrast to closed systems in which the final state (equilibrium) is determined by initial conditions, the open system can reach the same final state via different initial conditions and processes. Bertalanffy illustrates this with the example that either a single fertilized egg or two separate fertilized eggs (different initial conditions) can lead to twins (the same final state). Thus the open system—by moving toward greater complexity and organization, by maintaining itself in a steady state, and by equifinality—defies linear causality.

Bertalanffy went further, however, in attacking the linear paradigm. As part of his program for a "general system theory," Bertalanffy extrapolated his conception of the open system into the fields of psychology and history. He inveighed against deterministic psychology or behaviorism (the psychological theory that Zola had enthusiastically embraced), calling it the "robot concept" (194). "Man is not a passive receiver of stimuli coming from an external world," he argued, but is instead an "active personality system" (192) interacting with his environment. He creates as well as is created by his world, determines as well as is determined.

History, too, was to Bertalanffy an open system. While not denying the role played by "great men," Bertalanffy did not subscribe to the notion that they "caused" history to happen. Rather, he viewed them as "acting like 'leading parts,' 'triggers' or 'catalyzers' in the historical process" (116). They too are as much caused by history as they are the cause of it. Once again, it is a mutually interactive, nonlinear process. Causality is never one-way.

As with the field concept in physics, the denial of discrete parts and linear causality in systems theory controverts any notion of a separation of subject and object. Just as the "personality system" of the "great man" of history must interact with broader historical "systems," so too must the "system" of the scientist interact with the "system" of his experiment. Again, the interpretive paradigm he brings to bear on his experiment colors his observations and his subsequent analysis of them. No objective observation or analysis is possible.

Bertalanffy, though, was not content simply to undermine the assumptions of classical science. He also attacked humanity's application of the classical scientific paradigm—the paradigm of the closed system—to its interactions with its environment and with itself. Writing in 1968, having lived through two world wars and currently in the midst of the Vietnam debacle, Bertalanffy blamed classical science for "the catastrophes of our time" (49). He attacked the Enlightenment legacy, the belief in progress that, in his view, had led not to a better world but to an entropic wasteland, a world destroyed by its own technology. He put forth systems theory as an alternative to classical science and as a possible panacea for its inherent destructiveness:

> The mechanistic world view, taking the play of physical particles as ultimate reality, found its expression in a civilization which glorifies physical technology that has led eventually to the catastrophes of our time. Possibly the model of the world as a great organization can help to reinforce the sense of reverence for the living which we have almost lost in the last sanguinary decades of human history. (49)

LeClair agrees, citing the "mechanistic world view" as the cause for what he calls humanity's scientific "mastery" of nature: the human attempt to dominate and control the natural world that has led to the destructive exploitation of its resources. LeClair further blames scientific mastery for emptying the world of its "mystery," a term he appropriates from DeLillo and which he takes to mean "spiritual enchantment." Humanity's knowledge of the natural world has destroyed any spiritual or emotional affection human beings may once have had for it. Paraphrasing Morris Berman, LeClair claims that systems theory "creates a 'Reenchantment of the World,' restoring to living systems their complexity and mystery lost since medieval times and re-placing humanity within its natural environment." [13]

By undermining and even attacking the assumptions of classical science, both the new physics and systems theory inadvertently undermined the foundation of the naturalistic novel. Preeminent was the destruction of the subject-object dichotomy, the methodological foundation of literary naturalism. In fact, in the work of DeLillo we see the end of Zola's experimental novel. An author can no longer presume to stand apart from his created universe as a classical scientist from his experiment. As he is not discrete from, but is instead a part of the same field as his creation, the author must necessarily interact with it. As a result, DeLillo positions himself differently in relation to his material than did either Zola or Norris, or for that matter Hemingway. In the "historical" novel *Libra*, for example, we do not see an objective, if still fictional, account of the Kennedy assassination, an attempt at re-creating the causes and effects of that event. (On the contrary, we see what amounts to a parody of such an attempt in the character of Nicholas Branch.) Rather, the author becomes a part of the event itself, his fiction an addition to the historical fact of the assassination that is no longer present itself but only preserved in other forms of discourse—histories, biographies, television footage. DeLillo and *Libra*, in other words, become part of the historical event that continues to grow toward greater uncertainty and complexity.

Neither can the fictional self stand apart from the material world in which he finds himself—a man-made, built world that also has grown in complexity beyond human comprehension. He cannot grasp it objectively as could Norris's characters, who needed only to learn to perceive an order external to the self, a divine order immanent in "objective" nature. Nor can he presume to stand in conscious opposition to the natural world, as in Hemingway, and create his own order which imbues that world with a human meaning. Such a power implies an autonomous, efficacious consciousness capable of creating a union between an otherwise separate subject and object. On the contrary, the self in DeLillo's postmodern reworking of literary naturalism is ineluctably and inextricably a part of the universal field or systems universe—whichever way we may choose to describe it. He is part of an all-encompassing system of mutually interacting systems. However, such a situation does not resolve the rift between the subjective self and the objective world that we have seen is a fundamental feature of the naturalistic form. Rather, it presents the self with a new dilemma: how to locate the subjective self in and reconcile it to a world in which there is no distinction between subject and object.

We also see in DeLillo's work the undermining of linear causality. Zola's deterministic causes—heredity and environment—are now merely two factors in a warren of factors. Moreover, the self is no longer helplessly determined by its environment, but also displays features of Bertalanffy's "active personality system" in reciprocally influencing it. History, too, becomes not a linear narrative of causes and effects brought about by the actions of "great men," but a complex, whirling system of often arbitrary and accidental events that are simultaneously causes and effects of still other events—often actuated by seemingly insignificant figures. Nor does either the psychological self or human history move inevitably in a one-way line toward equilibrium and entropy—as in Vandover's psychological demise in

Norris's novel or Western civilization's demise in Hemingway's *A Farewell to Arms*—but builds toward greater disequilibrium and complexity. In all of the above, *Libra*, of course, comes immediately to mind.

The collapse, then, of humanity's conception of an order in the material world—a feature fundamental to literary naturalism—is not that of a divine order or unifying myth, as in the collapse of Christianity in Norris's and Hemingway's work. Rather, it is the collapse of the secular paradigm that went hand in hand with that divine order and myth: the scientific conception of a universe of discrete subject and object and of linear causality that paralleled Christian dualism and teleology and that therefore made humanity believe it could know and master nature. Human beings now find themselves in a material universe that defies their comprehension and control, knowledge and certainty giving way to indeterminacy and uncertainty. And humanity's attempt to apply this now obsolete paradigm to experience—an attempt that, despite its futility, humans persist in—leads to an inaccurate and often catastrophic picture of reality. In *Libra*, for example, Nicholas Branch is frustrated in his attempt to reconstruct the Kennedy assassination primarily because of this interpretive paradigm; the conspiracy defies both objective analysis and linear causality, and therefore any reconstruction Branch may make using such a paradigm is doomed to be false. In *End Zone*, we see the paradigm's destructive capabilities. Football, war, and science are all a part of the same mind-set, which glorifies mastery and strives for the "end zone"—the entropic closure to the closed system, nuclear devastation.

DeLillo has said that the fiction writer's role is "to restructure reality," that the novel is "a new map of the world." [14] Indeed, such is the case with DeLillo and his work. By working off a new scientific paradigm, a new way of conceiving of the universe and of humanity's place in it, DeLillo undoes the "reality" on which literary naturalism was based, and therefore—as we shall see more closely in the next two chapters—undoes the naturalistic novel itself.

CHAPTER NINE

END ZONE:

THE END OF THE OLD ORDER

DeLillo's early novel *End Zone*—like Norris's *Vandover*, which depicted the collapse of the traditional Christian order brought about by Darwinism, and Hemingway's *A Farewell to Arms*, which depicted the collapse of the same order due to the cataclysm of World War I—also depicts the end of an order. In this case, it is the classical scientific order that went hand in hand with Christian dualism. DeLillo exploits the hackneyed analogy between football and war as a means of attacking the paradigm that makes such an analogy possible: the scientific paradigm that conceives of the universe as a collection of discrete parts operating according to the laws of linear causality.[1] As we saw in the previous chapter, such a paradigm also presupposes the discreteness of subject and object, as well as the ultimate knowability of physical phenomena. Football and war are expressions of this paradigm; both are closed systems in which a comfortable but illusive order ineluctably moves toward disorder and exhaustion—in scientific terms, toward entropy and equilibrium. Yet continually impinging on these closed systems—and continually affecting the novel's characters, particularly the protagonist Gary Harkness—are greater, interconnecting systems that point to a new, possibly regenerative order modeled on that of the new physics and systems theory.

While Norris and Hemingway dramatized the demise of the Christian order in their respective modes of literary naturalism, they left intact, at least implicitly, the classical scientific order. Zola, of course, was explicit in this regard, adamantly championing science as the only foundation on which the novel should rest. DeLillo, however, demonstrates in *End Zone* that Christianity and classical science are two sides of the same construct, that the demise of the one necessitates the demise of the other. Both are dualistic, the Christian dualism of spirit/flesh and God/humanity paralleling the scientific separation of subject and object and the discreetness of parts. Moreover, Christian teleology recapitulates linear causality: Christian history is a one-way linear progression beginning with the Creation and ending with the Apocalypse. And at least since the Enlightenment, science has not been purely a disinterested inquiry into the secrets of natural phenomena, but has also carried with it the Faustian notion of unlocking the Christian mysteries; like natural phenomena, these mysteries at last appeared knowable.

From the outset, then, DeLillo establishes a connection between classical science and Christianity. The name of the West Texas college, Logos College, itself suggests such a connection—the "Word" as both religious authority and rational truth. The wife of the deceased founder, Mrs. Tom Wade, tells Harkness that her husband "built it [the college] out of nothing. He had an idea and he followed it through to the end. He believed in reason. He was a man of reason. He cherished the very word."[2] We see here the cosmogonic archetype—building something out of nothing, forming cosmos from chaos. Mr. Tom Wade reenacts the Creation at Logos College, or at least Western humanity's conception of the Creation, one that is rooted in the same rationality as classical science. It is creation from an "idea"; Mr. Tom, "a man of reason" ("He cherished the very *word*" [my emphasis]—again, Logos as both secular and religious rationality) is reminiscent of the rational God of the Enlightenment, the designer of the universal "clock." As does the God of the mechanistic universe, Mr. Tom imposes his idea on the external world, his subjective idea creating an objective order that is closed off from the nothingness that surrounds it. Moreover, his idea contains its own telos; he follows it "through to the end." Again, we see the connection between linear causality and Christian teleology, both of which have end points, or "end zones." Ironically, the end of each is destruction—on one hand, the Biblical Apocalypse, on the other, entropy or, it is intimated, nuclear devastation. The creation of order out of chaos, in both the Christian and classical scientific conceptions, inevitably leads back to chaos.

Emmett Creed also illustrates the connection between classical science and Christianity. His name, Creed, carries clear religious connotations, and as we learn of his football "creed," we see that it is an expression of the classical scientific paradigm. Like Mr. Tom, Creed "became famous for creating order out of chaos" (10). He is the savior of the football program at Logos College, an American Christ figure born "in either a log cabin or a manger" (9). And again like Mr. Tom—or the Enlightenment God or, for that matter, the classical scientist—Creed begins by imposing an order on the external world, an order that is characterized by separation. He puts up canvas blinds to fence in the football field, builds a tower from which he can observe the field, and establishes separate living quarters for the football team. The blinds are ostensibly designed to prevent spying by other teams, but as Harkness tells us, "There was nothing out there but insects" (10). In effect, Creed is fencing out chaos from his arbitrary order—ironically, a chaos filled with insects, which, we later learn, will inherit the earth after the nuclear holocaust, the "end zone" of Creed's paradigm of order. The Texas wasteland thus lies beyond like a grim portent, and as such is a real threat from which Creed "blinds" himself.

The tower that separates Creed from the closed rectangle of the football field gives him a vantage point from which he can view "overall patterns" (9). He is simultaneously the objective observer and the omnipresent God, a presence that is nevertheless separate from the closed system. Like the classical scientist, Creed believes that he can stand apart from the patterns unfolding "within the chalked borders of the playing field" (4), that he can observe them without affecting them. And like the Christian deity, Creed is enthroned on high, looking down on his men. The player Raymond Toon even refers to Creed as "the man upstairs" (97). Toon, or Toony as he is called, tells Harkness that he cannot crack the starting lineup because "the man upstairs wants it that way," that "He has his reasons. . . . But they're probably beyond our scope" (97–98). Again we see reason associated with God, and we cannot miss the parallel between God and the "objective" scientist. Such objectivity, however, is an illusion; the players are well aware of Creed's presence in the tower, and that awareness cannot help but affect their play. Creed, too, is a part of the "field"—a field greater than the limited perimeters of the gridiron. There is no frame of reference outside that greater, universal field.

Harkness tells us that the separate living quarters Creed establishes for the football team were designed "to instill a sense of unity" (9) among the players. "Oneness" is Creed's byword, a word with clear religious connotations, such as in the oneness of God in the Trinity or the oneness of the blessed with God. Yet, as Harkness tells Creed, his oneness is really "elevenness or twenty-twoness" (19). It is a finite oneness, a oneness of components within a closed system. By separating the players from the rest of the student body, Creed closes them off from a more universal oneness that would include other "systems" on campus or in the outside world. Harkness is aware of the contradiction, a contradiction that is endemic to both Christian dualism and classical science. As he says: "It was a good concept, oneness, but I suggested that, to me at least, it could not be truly attractive unless it meant oneness with God or the universe or some equally redoubtable super-phenomenon" (19).

Creed, as the embodiment of both the scientific and the divine mind, is clearly a Faustian character. He is even compared to another great Faustian character in American literature, Ahab. Harkness refers to Creed as "a landlocked Ahab who paced and raged, who was unfolding his life toward a single moment" (54). Again we see the connection between Christian teleology—"unfolding . . . toward a single moment" (i.e., toward the Apocalypse)—and linear causality (i.e., toward the entropic end). For Ahab, of course, the "single moment" was to be the destruction of the whale, and we realize that for Creed it is to be the defeat of Centrex. Both of these apocalyptic events are to bring about a revelation—the unlocking of the secrets of the universe. Ahab would find out what lay beyond the symbolic "white wall"; Creed, too, would learn the metaphysical truth. (Taft Robinson tells Harkness that Creed had recruited him with the promise that, by finding out "how much we could take," "we would learn the secrets" [237].) Neither event, though, comes to pass. Ahab and his crew are destroyed by the whale, and Logos College is trounced by Centrex. After the game, the football team begins to disintegrate; several players are badly injured, one is killed, and both Harkness and Taft Robinson quit. Creed, very much like a latter-day Ahab, is confined to a wheelchair. The apocalyptic revelation—either through Christian mysticism or scientific knowledge—is no revelation at all. It is only collapse, the "end zone" of the paradigm.

The game that Creed calls "the only game" (15) is thus an expression of the classical scientific and Christian paradigms. Football is an outgrowth of the mind-set of the closed system; it is itself a closed system. Toward the end of the novel, Creed explains his conception of football to Harkness:

> Football is a complex of systems. It's like no other sport. When the game is played properly, it's an interlocking of a number of systems. The individual. The small cluster he's part of. The larger unit, the eleven. People stress the violence. That's the smallest part of it. Football is brutal only from a distance. In the middle of it there's a calm, a tranquillity. The players accept pain. There's a sense of order even at the end of a running play with bodies strewn everywhere. When the systems interlock, there's a satisfaction to the game that can't be duplicated. There's a harmony. (199)

Again, the unity—the "oneness"—that Creed stresses is finite. While football may be "an interlocking of a number of systems," the maximum number, according to Creed, is eleven. His description, then, of football as a "complex of systems" is ironic; on the contrary, football is a reduction of systems, a simplification. ("Simplicity" is a term, as we shall see in a moment, that is frequently used in reference to the game.) Creed's "systems" are more accurately discrete parts: offense, defense, home team, opposing team. Then there are the coaches and spectators whose frames of reference are removed from the closed system of the playing field, watching "objectively" as the discrete parts collide in a human parody of the mechanistic universe. Harkness says of one practice: "I moved about not as myself but as some sequence from the idea of motion, a brief arrangement of schemes and physical laws abstracted from the whole" (62). Of course, like the closed system adumbrated in the Second Law of Thermodynamics, this motion unfolds linearly, the progress of the game measured by yardage and the time clock.

The "sense of order," the "harmony" in football that appeals to Creed is also characteristic of the closed system. DeLillo himself has said that "most games . . . satisfy a sense of order and they even have an element of dignity about them."[3] He goes on to say, however, that "in my fiction this search [for order] sometimes turns out to be a cruel delusion."[4] Alan Zapalac, the exobiology teacher at Logos College and the voice of skepticism in the novel, concurs, telling Harkness that "sport is a benign illusion, the illusion that order is possible" (112). As noted, the order in a closed system is indeed illusory, as it inevitably moves toward disorder, or entropy. We certainly see this in the game against Centrex, as the initial order of the game breaks down into a chaotic and destructive clash of opposites. As mentioned earlier, injuries are rife and the team of Logos College begins to disintegrate. Taft Robinson, the possessor of speed—in Harkness's words, "The one thing we haven't used up" (5)—is indeed "used up" by the end of the novel; he refuses to move, much less run. He becomes symbolic of spent energy. Taft, one of Coach Creed's intricate "systems," has reached the entropic state of equilibrium.

In addition, with the advent of the new physics and systems theory, the closed system itself seems to be illusory, an inaccurate conception of reality. We see in the course of the novel that the order of football is arbitrary; it is as much a construct—and as out of place—as Logos College is in the middle of the West Texas wasteland. Yet it provides a comforting order in which most of the players and coaches find refuge. Harkness enjoys football practice, for as he says, "Life was simplified by these afternoons of opposites and affinities" (56). (Again, we note the language of classical physics—"opposites and affinities"—as well as the reductiveness inherent in the Newtonian scheme.) He feels "reduced in complexity" (31). In fact, Harkness claims that football players have a "passion for simplicity," and admonishes himself to "keep things simple" (4):

> Football players are simple folk. Whatever complexities, whatever dark politics of the human mind, the heart—these are noted only within the chalked borders of the playing field. At times strange visions ripple across the turf; madness leaks out. But wherever else he goes, the football player travels the straightest of lines. His thoughts are wholesomely commonplace, his actions uncomplicated by history, enigma, holocaust or dream. (4)

The "chalked borders of the playing field" are, of course, the arbitrary, man-made borders that both create the order of the closed system and shut out the surrounding chaos. And the "straightest of lines" that the players follow (the assistant coach Tweego also "thinks in one direction, straight ahead" [49]) recall the linear causality of the closed system. Yet the ripples of madness come from without the chalked borders, from the chaos itself, and they impinge on this safe sanctuary. Certainly the chaos to which the closed system inevitably leads is foreshadowed in Harkness's reference to a "holocaust," for we soon see that war is as much a closed system as football, that it too is an expression of the same paradigm. But we also see the possibility of new paradigms—"strange visions"—that expose the arbitrariness and inaccuracy of the closed system. Harkness's experiment with marijuana changes his perception of the game, and the free-for-all in the snow—football with all rules abrogated—removes football's illusion of order.

Football, however, is not the only closed system in the novel, not the only expression of this destructive paradigm. Since the paradigm of the closed system is a means of conceptualizing reality, it manifests itself in all aspects of human experience. We learned from Heisenberg that there is no objective encounter with the physical world; the interpretive paradigm we project onto it colors our perceptions of and affects our interactions with it. We are therefore limited by any paradigm we may choose to employ, and we are especially limited by the inherently reductive paradigm of the closed system. Thus it is not surprising that Harkness's father, not a football player but certainly a product of the same American mind-set, chooses "to follow the simplest, most pioneer of rhythms" (17) in his life, namely the Protestant work ethic that the "simple folk" (4) of football players also follow. "Beyond these honest latitudes," according to him, "lay nothing but chaos" (17). Clearly, this world view springs from the same source as that which finds order "within the chalked borders of the playing field," an order that likewise acts as a stave, however illusory, against impinging chaos.

Anatole Bloomberg, the overweight Jewish football player who comes to Logos College to "unjew" himself, also follows this paradigm. The very process of "unjewing" is a movement from high order and uniqueness (the specificity of "Jew") to low order and uniformity (the generality of "American")—a type of racial and cultural entropy that America perhaps demands of its ethnically diverse people. The specific "parts" that are specific ethnic groups intermingle until, genetically or culturally, they become a uniform mass. Like the entropic end of a chemical reaction in which all energy is spent, such a culture, DeLillo seems to be saying, is equally spent; it is oversimplified, unable to produce anything of cultural value. Bloomberg illustrates this in his description to Harkness:

The desert was an ideal place in which to begin the process of unjewing. I spoke aloud to myself in the desert, straightening out my grammar, getting rid of the old slang and the old speech rhythms. I walked in straight lines. I tried to line myself up parallel to the horizon and then walk in a perfectly straight line. I tried to become single-minded and straightforward, to keep my mind set on one thought or problem until I was finished with it. It was hot and lonely. I wore a lot of clothing to keep the sun from burning me and causing my skin to peel. Sometimes I read aloud from a children's reader. I wanted to start all over with simple declarative sentences. Subject, predicate, object. Dick opened the door. Jane fed the dog. It helped me immensely. I began to think more clearly, to concentrate, to leave behind the old words and aromas and guilts. (187–88)

The desert, a landscape suggestive of an entropic wasteland, of the return to chaos after a nuclear holocaust, is the "ideal place" for Bloomberg to reduce himself culturally. He begins "straightening out" his grammar, walks in "straight lines," thinks "straightforward." The "unjewing" process, we see, recapitulates the linear unfolding of the closed system, an unfolding that is inherently reductive. Bloomberg is reduced to thinking only one thought or solving only one problem; he reads from a children's reader and speaks in "simple declarative sentences" in which "subject, predicate, object" follow in a predictable, linear pattern. His cultural reduction is even accompanied by a physical reduction: he begins to lose weight.

Zapalac, the exobiology teacher, attributes the depredation of the global environment to this paradigm of the closed system. To him, science, religion, and middle America all embrace this same paradigm that, while pushing for progress and mastery, leads to entropy. He says of his fiancé's people, the Midwesterners:

They're masters of the categories of things. They've been raised to believe everything they're told by their elders. They do things in alphabetical order. They know their place. They've known it since early childhood. Drummed into them by respectable parents. The same people who are ripping up the forests with their engines, their money-building machines. (164)

They seek to be "masters" of "categories," to control with their paradigm those things that it will enable them to control. Its categories, in other words, are constructs of its own devise—arbitrary, illusory, and discrete—

that permit them only a limited comprehension of the physical world. One result is that they perceive phenomena as a sequence of discrete processes, and they emulate such processes in their own lives: they follow their elders; they "do things in alphabetical order." And the application of this paradigm to the environment leads to the destruction of the forests and, ultimately, to the same entropic wasteland in which Zapalac and Harkness now find themselves.

During one of his lectures, Zapalac implicates science and religion in this destructive process:

> Science fiction is just beginning to catch up with the Old Testament. See artificial nitrates run off into the rivers and oceans. See carbon dioxide melt the polar ice caps. See the world's mineral reserves dwindle. See war, famine and plague. See barbaric hordes defile the temple of the virgins. See wild stallions mount the prairie dogs. I said science fiction but I guess I meant science. (160)

Again, science and religion (the "Old Testament") are presented as two facets of the same paradigm. (At an earlier lecture, Zapalac had said that "science is religion" [92].) And along with the destruction of the environment, this paradigm of the closed system, according to Zapalac, leads to global war. Beyond the facile analogy, then, between football and war lies a real and frightening connection. Football, as Zapalac says, is not warfare: "Warfare is warfare. We don't need substitutes because we've got the real thing" (164). But both are closed systems, each leading to its own "end zone" of destruction. We see the connection between the two perhaps most clearly in the war game Harkness plays with Major Staley in a motel room. Like football, it too is confined within measurable borders—in this case, within the grid of a world atlas. It also unfolds linearly: it is a twelve-step process, each step numbered in sequence. (During an earlier conversation, Major Staley had told Harkness that global nuclear war would, like football, have "all sorts of controls. You'd practically have a referee and a timekeeper" [82].) Harkness also describes the game in the same language that he uses to describe football, and he experiences similar emotions: "There were insights, moves, minor revelations that we savored together. Silences between moves were extremely grave. Talk was brief and pointed. Small personal victories (of tactics, of imagination) were genuinely satisfying.

Mythic images raged in my mind" (223). During the twelfth and final step—
the advent of the "spasm response"—the telephone rings, and the Major is
startled and, in Harkness's words, "terrified" (225). The telephone suggests
an intrusion—or perhaps it would be best described as a *connection*—from
outside the closed system of the war game. The Major, of course, is un-
aware of such a connection, and here we are reminded of Emmett Creed,
the commander of the closed system of football, of whom the player Tim
Flanders says, "You never see him in a phone booth" (57). The unaware-
ness or denial of outside connections—of other systems interacting with
the closed system or other fields incorporating a limited field—does not
preclude their existence. And DeLillo seems to suggest, the awareness of
such connections is perhaps the first step toward avoiding the occurrence
of "spasm response," the final "end zone" of the closed system.

  Harkness, as the novel's protagonist, best illustrates the struggle to escape the destructive closed system and to find a new regenerative and integrative paradigm. He is certainly fascinated with the closed system, enjoy-
ing the simplicity of football and becoming obsessed with global nuclear
conflict. He desires the comforting, simplified order that it brings, yet as
the novel progresses he begins to see its dark underbelly, its inherent destructiveness. Our first intimation of his growing awareness of this is his
consciousness of the pervasive silence, a silence that the "familiar things"
(31) of home dispersed, but that he finds inescapable in the strange wasteland of West Texas. "Of all the aspects of exile," he says, "silence pleased
me least" (30). It is "difficult," "menacing" (31). He feels "threatened by the
silence" (31). As in DeLillo's later novel *White Noise*, silence is a symbol for
entropic collapse, the end of communication, meaning, knowledge. The
certainty of the Logos degenerates to the jargon of football (e.g., "Zone set,
triple tex, off-hit recon dive" [136]) and war (e.g., "SIMcap dictates spasm
response" [225]), and finally to a silence containing the "broken codes" (192)
of human communication. As in *White Noise*, silence is thus not so much
the absence of sound as it is undifferentiated noise: a static hum. Harkness
calls the silence "the big noise," "the big metallic noise" (48). Bloomberg
calls it "the rumble" (48). For both of them it exists "out there," "out over
the desert" (48). Harkness says, "It hung over the land and drifted across
the long plains. It was out there with the soft black insects beyond the last
line of buildings, beyond the prefabs and the Quonset hut and the ROTC

barracks" (31). While the silence exists beyond the order of Logos College, it is the inevitable product of that closed order. It exists in the portentous landscape suggestive of the entropic end of all natural process, of the earth after humanity's depredation and exploitation of its resources, or after nuclear holocaust. Its metallic timbre points toward the latter. (Harkness will later compare the silence to "a clash of metals no louder than heat on flesh" [192]—in other words, to the sound of war that has progressed from the clash of swords to the explosion of radioactive heat.) The insects, the inheritors of the nuclear wasteland, also suggest a post-holocaust silence.

At one point, wandering in the West Texas wasteland, aware of the silence, Harkness searches for "something that could be defined in one sense only, something not probable or variable, a thing unalterably itself" (88). He is searching for certainty within the end product of the science of certainty, the wasteland. Once again, he desires the comfort that order and certainty bring; he even lists his surroundings, categorizing phenomena as unalterable discrete parts: "The sun. The desert. The sky. The silence. The flat stones. The insects. The wind and the clouds. The moon. The stars. The west and east. The song, the color, the smell of the earth" (87).

In his search, he thinks of a solitary painted-black stone he had come across on an earlier walk through the desert, but rejects the stone for he finds it "too rich in enigma" (88). When he does discover the "thing un-alterably itself," he is shocked: "It was three yards in front of me, excre-ment, a low mound of it, simple shit, nothing more, yet strange and vile in this wilderness, perhaps the one thing that did not betray its definition" (88). The discovery is epiphanic; to his horror, he sees the essential value of certainty, of something that does not "betray its definition," as well as the essential nature of the closed system. The excrement stands as a symbol of entropy; it is the end product of a process that moves toward decomposi-tion. He says of the sight:

> It was overwhelming, a terminal act, nullity in the very word, shit, as of dogs squatting near partly eaten bodies, rot repeating itself; defe-cation, as of old women in nursing homes fouling their beds; feces, as of specimen, sample, analysis, diagnosis, bleak assessments of disease in the bowels; dung, as of dry straw erupting with microscopic eggs; excrement, as of final matter voided, the chemical stink of self dis-

continued; offal, as of butchered animals' intestines slick with shit and
blood; shit everywhere, shit in life cycle, shit as earth as food as shit,
wise men sitting impassively in shit, armies retreating in that stench,
shit as history, holy men praying to shit, scientists tasting it, volumes
to be compiled on color and texture and scent, shit's infinite treachery,
everywhere this whisper of inexistence. (88–89)

The series of images are characterized by finality: "a terminal act," "nul-
lity in the very word," "final matter voided," "self discontinued," "the whisper of inexistence." Such finality is associated with the scientific method:
"specimen, sample, analysis, diagnosis," "scientists tasting it, volumes to
be compiled on color and texture and scent." It is also associated with war
and religion: "armies retreating in that stench," "holy men praying to shit."
For the first time, Harkness senses where the paradigm of science and religion leads, and he begins to think of a new way, a "fresh intelligence": "I
thought of men embedded in the ground, all killed, billions, flesh cauter-
ized into the earth, bits of bone and hair and nails, man-planet, a fresh
intelligence revolving through the system" (89). As with his reflection on
the black stone, Harkness dismisses this unfamiliar thought, rebuking himself for "misspent reflections" (89). But he does begin to rethink existence,
speculating that "perhaps there is no silence," that "in some form of void,
freed from consciousness, the mind remakes itself" (89). In other words,
he begins to sense that there is an alternative to entropy—to silence and
the void. And although he never fully grasps what that alternative is, we
begin to see it. Juxtaposed throughout the novel are the metaphor of the
straight line and that of the circle. We have already noted that the former
suggests the linear causality of the closed system, the one-way cause-and-
effect line leading inevitably to entropy. The metaphor of the circle, on the
other hand, suggests a different type of causality: a nonlinear, systems causality that moves back on itself and that therefore contains within it the
possibility of regeneration. Bertalanffy calls this "negative entropy," the
movement not toward breakdown and simplification but toward rebuilding
and greater complexity.

Harkness's difficulty in grasping this systems pattern manifest in the
physical world is due to his perceptual limitations—limitations endemic to
human beings. He is forced to view the external world in pieces; the seg-

ment of the circle he can see at any given time thus appears to be a discrete line, unrelated to other causal lines. As Hayles says, "the static 'patterns' [one may have seen] never in fact existed as discrete entities."[5] So it is that when Harkness first comes on the painted-black stone he attributes it to someone who had "preceded" him—presumably in chronological time. He refers rather casually to a "vandal," "stone-painter," and "metaphorist of the desert" (43), all suggesting an ancient predecessor. Yet he discovers that the "metaphorist" is not some ancient poet or language-builder but Bloomberg—the one who tried to walk "in a perfectly straight line," but who gives it up on his mother's death. Bloomberg had painted the stone, the only round stone in a desert of flat stones, as a burial marker for his mother. Bloomberg's "Jewishness," his separateness from middle American culture and from the other players on the football team, is only an illusion. He is intricately involved with them; his "system"—cultural, familial, and personal—interacts with theirs. His mother's death, someone Harkness never knew, affects Harkness in ways unknown to him, the pattern more complex than he had imagined. The "metaphorist," then, does not build the language but rebuilds it; he points toward that "new way of thinking about reality."[6] The metaphor of the circle—"the fresh intelligence *revolving* through the system" (89, my emphasis)—replaces that of the line.

Zapalac, Myna Corbett, and Bing Jackamin, characters who impel Harkness to look at the world from a different perspective, are also associated with the circle. Zapalac, during his lecture on the entropic decline of the earth, circles his desk, his movement a stark contrast to the linear paradigm he inveighs against. And in Myna, Harkness seeks "a perfect circle whose reality overpowered the examiner's talent for reducing in size and meaning whatever variety of experience he was currently engaged in sampling" (65). In other words, she counters his desire for simplicity and reductiveness, the desire of the "objective" examiner. She tells him of the science fiction writer Tudev Nemkhu, whose book she calls "a whole total experience" (167). The fantastic creature at the center of the book—called monodanom, "the thing that's everything" (170)—"sees itself seeing what is outside it being seen by itself" (169). It is a creature that transcends human perceptual limitations, those same limitations that prevent Harkness from perceiving the complete systems pattern. It is both observing subject and observed object, both cause and effect—indeed, "the thing that's everything." Like this new reality depicted by Tudev Nemkhu, Bing Jackamin posits a football game of "double consciousness," one with "old form superimposed on new" (129). He tells Harkness that the game involves "a breaking-down of reality. . . . This is not just one thing we're watching. This is many things" (129). Part of these "many things" is the act of observation itself, akin to both mono-danom's circular perception and Heisenberg's Uncertainty Relation. Bing and Harkness are observing the effects of their own observation; in effect, they are observing themselves, their "objective" observation circling back on them, giving them what Bing calls "primitive mirror awareness" (129).

Bing also perceives the arbitrariness of the "old form," its tenuous reality. Referring to the green and white colors of both the playing field and the Logos College uniform, Bing tells Harkness that "we melt into our environment" (138). Indeed, without the "old form" in which these colors determine the "field" and distinguish the opponents—in other words, in which they create order—these colors gain new meaning and assume new relations to one another. Viewed in a new context, a "new form," they highlight the arbitrariness of the old and point toward new possibilities—toward a new conception of the game and, by extension, of the universe. Rather than closing off and dividing, these colors now open and bind. They join subject and object, player and field. Bing perceives this and tries to make Harkness aware of it: "There's a lot more out there," he tells him, "than games and players" (129).

Yet it is not until the free-for-all in the snow that Harkness realizes these new possibilities. As noted earlier, the free-for-all is football with all rules abrogated. It begins spontaneously, a way to "get it going again" (193) after the end of football season. In many ways, it illustrates the movement of the closed system of football from beginning to end: from high order (a game with rules) to entropy (a chaotic free-for-all). As the game progresses it becomes more and more chaotic. John Jessup steadily "outlaws" certain plays and features of the game until it becomes a straight-ahead clash of forces, devoid of strategy or even objectives. It becomes even more closed and limited; after the passing game is outlawed, Harkness says that the game's "range was now limited to a very small area and its degree of specialization diminished" (195). Yet it is in the midst of this entropic end that Harkness's mind "remakes itself." This is the void that enables him to do so. Rather than yearning for a return to the old order, to its solace—

like the others, he is no longer concerned with rules or objectives—Harkness instead conceives of a different order. He experiences "melting" into his environment, what he calls "environmental bliss": "We were part of the weather, right inside it, . . . We were adrift within this time and place and what I experienced then, speaking just for myself, was some variety of environmental bliss" (194). The players begin "seeking harmony with the weather and the earth" (195), a harmony that is not Creed's harmony between limited systems within limited fields, but a more universal harmony between humanity and the planet: "man-planet." It is a harmony between interdependent and interconnecting systems, regenerative rather than reductive. As the game of football is a metaphor for the old paradigm, this new game becomes a metaphor for the new systems paradigm.

Of course, by the end of the novel Harkness loses sight of this new vision, succumbing to the destructiveness of the old order. He disintegrates as a human being, no longer eating or drinking, being fed through plastic tubes. Significantly enough, he tells us that "high fevers burned a *thin straight channel* through my brain" (242, my emphasis), again using the metaphor of the line to suggest the closed system's linear progression toward entropy. The final sentence of the novel, in fact, begins with, "In the end." Harkness has reached the "end zone."

By depicting both the destructiveness and the inaccuracy of the classical scientific paradigm, DeLillo in *End Zone* depicts its collapse. He also dramatizes the effect of that collapse on his protagonist—much like Norris and Hemingway did with the collapse of the Christian order in *Vandover* and *A Farewell to Arms* respectively. Of course, the end of the classical scientific conception of the physical universe and of humanity's place in it, a conception Norris and Hemingway implicitly upheld, sends the naturalistic novel in a new direction. There is still the alienation of the self from a world of force, as well as the struggle to reconcile the self to that world. But the perception of order in the physical world is a perception that the self cannot fully make, for the self is indistinguishable from it. Nor can the self create an order, as in Hemingway, for such an order would presume the essential separateness of subject and object. Rather, the self must rethink its constructs, its interpretive paradigms, and begin to conceive of the world not as a mechanism but as a system of systems. In this Harkness ultimately fails. Yet *End Zone* is not a fully developed novel, and in it DeLillo does not present a convincing systems universe nor fully explore the naturalistic possibilities of placing a protagonist in it. In his later novel *Libra*, however, DeLillo succeeds in presenting such a universe and, in doing so, in rethinking "reality." The result, as we shall see in the next chapter, is both a reworking of the naturalistic leitmotiv and the end of the Zolaesque experimental novel.

CHAPTER TEN
LIBRA:
UNDOING THE
NATURALISTIC NOVEL

While *End Zone* depicted the collapse of the classical scientific paradigm and its effect on the self, DeLillo's later novel *Libra* focuses on the predicament of that self trapped within the "new" order adumbrated by the new physics and systems theory. The individual must now try to locate himself in and reconcile himself to this new world of nonlinear causality and uncertainty, the comforts of the old order—knowability and the subsequent possibility of control or "mastery" over the external world—no longer available to him. "Mystery" replaces "mastery"—or even the illusion of mastery. *Libra* is thus a novel more firmly in the naturalistic vein, for it is a reworking of the naturalistic leitmotiv of the self caught in a universe of force, a universe that defies the reason and with which the self has no moral or spiritual affinity. Yet it is a reworking that effectually "undoes" the naturalism of Zola and Norris, for it plays out this naturalistic leitmotiv within a universe whose conception by definition undermines the basic tenets of classical science—the foundation, as we have seen, of nineteenth-century literary naturalism.

We remember that Zola had compared the novelist to a scientist and argued that, like the scientist, the novelist in writing a novel essentially conducted an experiment. Such a comparison implicitly granted the novelist the same working assumptions of the classical scientist—namely, that the universe was a conglomeration of discrete parts, that these parts interacted according to the laws of linear causality, that by studying these parts and the laws governing their behavior one could comprehend the universe, and most important, that the scientist could stand apart from his experiment and watch it unfold objectively. In *Libra*, we see what amounts to a parody of Zola's "experimental novelist" in the character of Nicholas Branch. While Branch in writing his "history" of the Kennedy assassination is certainly not conducting an experiment, nor—he hopes—is he writing fiction, he nevertheless approaches his material and the task of assembling it into a cohesive narrative with the same assumptions that Zola's novelist had in mind. His interpretive paradigm, in other words, is the same; however, the world in which he finds himself is far different, the material resisting such a paradigm. We first encounter Branch in a "small room," a metaphor that recurs throughout the novel. On its most fundamental level of meaning, the small room suggests isolation, and in the context of Branch, it initially seems to suggest an objective distance from the assassination that he is trying to piece together. In this way, Branch is akin to the rational man of science, alone in his "book-filled room, the room of documents, the room of theories and dreams."[1] Yet such objectivity is immediately undercut when we learn that he is also in "the room of growing old" (14), his isolation granting him not perspective on the assassination but trapping him within the interpretive paradigm he brings to it. He cannot escape his paradigm, can never see the assassination in itself, and as a result can never construct a cohesive narrative that will render a "true" picture of the event. Branch and his facts, theories, and dreams grow old together. We learn that he has written very little since the CIA hired him to write the secret history of the assassination, that he cannot even reach the "end" of his accumulated data.

It is, of course, his paradigm that is primarily at fault, for it is based on a false conception of reality. Despite his growing frustration and despair, Branch continues to view his intractable data as an assembly of parts that can be linked, given enough rational analysis, into a cohesive pattern. "Everything is here" (181), we are told, in his room of theories and facts:

> Baptismal records, report cards, postcards, divorce petitions, canceled checks, daily timesheets, tax returns, property lists, postoperative x-rays, photos of knotted string, thousands of pages of testimony, of voices droning in hearing rooms in old courthouse buildings, an incredible haul of human utterance. (181)

This is but one list of several that are given in reference to Branch's data, the list itself indicative of the disjunctiveness of the parts as he perceives them. The implication is that while "everything" may be here, nothing is here, for reality is not composed of discrete parts but of those parts *in relation* to one another. As Hayles has commented, in the field concept of reality, "The whole is composed of parts but cannot be reduced to them."[2] Branch wants such reductiveness, such simplicity—the same desire we saw in Harkness and in other characters in *End Zone*. Yet only after years of study and frustration does Branch begin to see that such simplicity is impossible. He begins to doubt that "the true nature of the event" (299) is contained in the various exhibits that the Curator sends him: "There is nothing to understand," he muses, "no insight to be had from these pictures and statistics" (299). Yet he remains at a loss as to an alternative paradigm.

In the course of the novel we begin to see that the various parts that comprise the Kennedy assassination are all connected in a nonlinear, looping pattern of interconnecting systems. This systems pattern is the "true" relation of parts to one another, and therefore is the more accurate picture of the event itself. Branch, however, like Harkness in *End Zone*, can only see fragments of this pattern due to his inherent limitations as a human being and to his interpretive paradigm that discounts those limitations. The looping pattern thus appears to him to be linear, and his *ex post facto* attempts to connect the parts into a cohesive whole are constrained by his imposition of the laws of linear causality. He wants to analyze the "six point nine seconds of heat and light" (15), as if the linear, chronological unfolding of events must contain the truth of the assassination. He searches in vain for a beginning, for an original cause of the assassination. Likewise, he searches in vain for an end—the linear paradigm, of course, positing a clearly defined beginning and end. In fact, Branch wonders "if he ought to despair of ever getting to the end" (59). "It is impossible," we are told, "to stop assembling data. The stuff keeps coming" (59). The assassination, just as it defied reduction to discrete parts, defies linear causality. Branch cannot bracket the event within a spatial or temporal frame. He cannot discern a linear pattern with a clear beginning and end. The pattern stretches beyond both space (i.e., Dallas) and time (i.e., six point nine seconds). The past is even "changing as he writes" (301).

Thus, rather than the accumulated data leading to greater knowledge, to greater certitude regarding the assassination, it leads to greater uncertainty. The more isolated "facts" Branch knows, the less he knows about the entire picture. "It is essential," he tells himself, "to master the data" (442), but it does him no good. The facts themselves are too ambiguous, their meaning too uncertain; moreover, they point in too many different directions, each direction resisting closure. As a result, Branch has no hope of coming to a definitive end to his investigation. In his frustration, he yearns for certitude, wanting "a thing to be what it is" (379). We are reminded here of Harkness, who wanted to find the "thing unalterably itself," and, like Harkness's, Branch's wish goes unfulfilled. Toward the end of the novel he begins to accept uncertainty, abandoning his search for a linear pattern of cause and effect, and resigning himself to the indeterminate conclusion that "the conspiracy against the President was a rambling affair that succeeded in the short term due mainly to chance" (441).

Of course, of all the assumptions of classical science that Zola granted his experimental novelist, the most fundamental to his methodology was the separation of observing subject from observed object. As Branch's "objective" investigation progresses, we become increasingly aware that such a separation is an illusion. Branch is indeed a "branch" of the event: a part of it, not separate from it. He is part of the same field. In fact, in the same way that Heisenberg's scientist made something happen merely by watching it happen, Branch creates the "reality" of the assassination by writing about it. The event cannot remain isolated and discrete; it becomes something different when it is interpreted, assuming aspects of the interpretive paradigm applied to it. Laurence Parmenter's comment to his secretary—"Every bit and piece and whisper in the world . . . doesn't have a life until someone comes along to collect it" (143)—can be applied to the data that Branch himself imbues with meaning. So too can the narrator's comment regarding Oswald's Historic Diary: "the writing of any history brings a persuasion and form to events" (211). Again, that form is determined by the writer and his paradigm. Heisenberg's statement that "what we observe is not nature in itself but nature exposed to our method of questioning" comes to mind here, and we can see why, on another level, "the past is changing as he [Branch] writes": the act of writing changes it.

Thus Branch's "history" of the Kennedy assassination does not give us an objective picture of the event, but rather a picture of someone taking a picture of the event. Branch is like the second woman at the scene of the assassination: "There was a woman taking a picture and another woman about twenty feet behind her taking the same picture, only with the first woman in it" (398-99). And like the experience of the first woman who, when she turns to see the other woman taking her picture, feels that that other woman is she and, simultaneously, that she herself is the person whom she had just seen shot in her own viewfinder (in other words, that she is both observing subject and observed object), Branch too is both observer and observed. He is observing himself observing the event. As a result, Branch's "history" inevitably becomes a self-referential fiction. Branch at one point senses this:

> it has taken him all these years to learn that his subject is not politics or violent crime but men in small rooms. Is he one of them now? Frustrated, stuck, self-watching, looking for a means of connection, a way to break out. (181)

Branch *is* "one of them," a man in a small room, watching other men in small rooms such as Oswald, Ruby, the CIA, FBI, Alpha 66—indeed, "self-watching." He has become the subject of his own history.

Nicholas Branch thus comes to represent the impossibility of the objective observer and, by extension, the experimental novelist. He cannot presume to stand apart from events, to watch them unfold objectively. Neither do those events conform to the classical scientific paradigm he would subject them to: they are not discrete and isolatable, nor do they follow the laws of linear causality. Knowledge and certainty, then, the ends of classical science and Zola's experimental novel, are necessarily replaced by uncertainty. All this, of course, raises the question of the novelist's "position" in a postmodern text that reworks the conventions and concerns of literary naturalism. DeLillo, in an interview with Anthony DeCurtis, claimed that the fiction writer tries to "redeem" the despair felt by Branch in the face of his overwhelming data.[3] We find a clue as to the means of this redemption in DeLillo's "Author's Note" at the conclusion of *Libra:*

> In a case in which rumors, facts, suspicions, official subterfuge, conflicting sets of evidence and a dozen labyrinthine theories all mingle, sometimes indistinguishably, it may seem to some that a work of fiction is one more gloom in a chronicle of unknowing.
>
> But because this book makes no claim to literal truth, because it is

only itself, apart and complete, readers may find refuge here—a way of thinking about the assassination without being constrained by half-facts or overwhelmed by possibilities, by the tide of speculation that widens with the years.

DeLillo in effect privileges fiction over history, for fiction provides a new "way of thinking" about reality without being accountable to "facts" or the necessity of historical accuracy. It provides, in other words, a new paradigm, one that we shall see is based on that of the new science. As such, the novelist does not presume to stand apart from his material, for he knows he cannot. He and his fiction become a part of the event itself, a part of the cultural consciousness that is the Kennedy assassination. (Note the reaction to the publication of *Libra*. Many seemed to think, despite DeLillo's disclaimer, that he was promulgating yet another "conspiracy theory." George Will was incensed enough to call DeLillo a "bad citizen."[4] After the publication of *Libra*, the past, indeed, has changed. The assassination, or at least our way of thinking about it, will never be quite the same.) Nor does the novelist make any claim to certainty. After all, even "history" is fiction, and therefore the open acknowledgment of the text as such precludes any pretension to the contrary. Like Oswald's mother, who at the end of the novel claims that "it takes stories to fill out a life" (453), the novelist, too, must tell a story. Significantly enough, the story is not the linear narrative of Zola's experimental novel, complete with clearly discernible causes and effects. Rather, to use Marguerite Oswald's words, "there are stories inside stories" (450). It is a narrative of looping, interconnecting stories.

DeLillo, though, does more than "undo" the naturalistic, experimental novelist in the character of Nicholas Branch; he undoes the naturalistic novel throughout *Libra* by undermining its scientific foundation. The most salient victim is linear causality. Just as our first image of Branch is that of the objective analyst in his "book-filled room," an image that is soon undercut by the patent futility of such objectivity, so too is our first impression of the cause of the Kennedy assassination a set-up. We are led to believe that Lee Harvey Oswald, who at the beginning of the novel we assume will be the sole assassin—the immediate cause of the assassination—is himself caused by the classic Zolaesque determining factors: heredity and environment.[5] His mother is slightly crazy, narrating her story in a rambling, disjointed monologue. At one point, she alludes unconsciously to an oedipal relationship with her son: "This boy slept in my bed out of lack of space until he was nearly eleven" (11). Her contradictions—at one point dismissing Oswald's troubles in school as "the accepted fact of a fatherless boy" (4) and then later denying such "environmental factors" (451) as the cause of his attempted assassination of Kennedy—seem to have been passed on to her son, the United States Marine and defector to the Soviet Union. And these "environmental factors" are for the most part the same ones that Zola, in his preface to *L'Assommoir*, attributed to "the polluted atmosphere of our urban areas":[6] poverty, violence, and psychological torment. Oswald's life with his mother is "a dwindling history of moving to cheaper places" (5), a life lived in "the meanest of small rooms" (11). (Again, the small room is used as a metaphor for isolation, and in this context adduced as an environmental cause.) While growing up in the Bronx, Oswald is exposed to the violence typical of urban slums: a man murdered in a nearby candy store, a cat tortured and killed by neighborhood kids. Moreover, whether in the poor sections of New York or New Orleans, Oswald is an outcast; he is teased in New York for his southern accent and beaten up in New Orleans for talking "like a Yankee" (33).

Oswald even begins to blame his position in society on environmental factors—namely, on the capitalistic system. His reading of Marxist doctrine pushes him toward this explanation, since Marxism posits a type of economic determinism in which the weak—that is, those without capital—are oppressed and crushed by the monied classes. In a passage that would not be out of place in a Zola novel such as *Germinal*, we see Oswald working out a Marxist interpretation of his place in social history:

> He saw himself as part of something vast and sweeping. He was the product of a sweeping history, he and his mother, locked into a process, a system of money and property that diminished their human worth every day, as if by scientific law. (41)

This is a purely deterministic vision of economics, society, and history, complete with "scientific law" as the ultimate authority. Marxism aside, this passage is typical of the authorial interjections we find in naturalistic texts: the "scientific" explanations, for example, that Dreiser gives us for Carrie's behavior in *Sister Carrie*, or that Norris gives us for Vandover's fall in

Vandover. (We remember the passages concerning the "enormous engine" of Nature crushing under its wheels those that lagged behind the human herd.) And when Oswald is thrown in the Marine brig, he once again gives a deterministic explanation: "He could see how he'd been headed here since the day he was born. The brig was invented just for him. It was just another name for the stunted rooms where he'd spent his life" (100). Indeed, the brig is another "small room," a variation of his and his mother's basement room in the Bronx with its "barred window" (5). To Oswald, the brig is the inevitable "effect" of the former "cause."

We soon see, however, that such deterministic explanations based on the laws of linear cause and effect are too reductive. As Oswald's mother says in trying to explain her son's behavior, we "cannot pin it down to a simple statement" (450). After presenting us with the naturalistic determining factors of heredity and environment, and in doing so satisfying our own reductive expectations, DeLillo undercuts those expectations by putting forth a plethora of causes that all interact to produce the culminating effect: the assassination of President Kennedy. Almost immediately we see the beginnings of the anti-Castro conspiracy, the most apparent cause other than Oswald's upbringing. This involves a plot to counterfeit an attempt on Kennedy's life in order to dupe the American public and government into thinking that it was the work of pro-Castro agents. The anti-Castro forces, mostly intelligence planners or veterans of the Bay of Pigs invasion, believe that this false event would then shock the United States into over-throwing Castro. Yet it is more complex than this. Win Everett, one of the CIA planners of the Bay of Pigs who is, significantly enough, referred to as a man with "a sense of cause" (18), implies that this new scheme, like that of the Bay of Pigs, is only the result of "a diehard and fool" (25). He puts forth, in other words, a personal cause for the assassination, one that will dove-tail with Oswald's personal cause and with still other causes. Part of this personal factor is each conspirator's sense of a personal destiny. "Stalking a victim," Everett ruminates, "can be a way of organizing one's loneliness, making a network out of it, a fabric of connections. Desperate men give their solitude a purpose and a destiny" (147). Everett, who is inventing such a desperate man, is, of course, one himself. He too organizes his disrupted life—he had been "retired" by the CIA after the Bay of Pigs debacle—by plotting the counterfeit assassination attempt. He begins to feel that this is his "purpose," his "destiny." He tells Laurence Parmenter and T. J. Mackey, two other conspirators, that "some things we wait for all our lives without knowing it" (27). Oswald, of course, also organizes his loneliness in this way; he identifies with Trotsky, who, like Oswald, had once lived in the Bronx and, Oswald believes, "waited" for history to sweep him to his destiny. Oswald, too, feels that in time he will be swept along. We are told that "he believed religiously that his life would turn in such a way that people would one day study [his] Historic Diary for clues to the heart and mind of the man who wrote it" (212). Later, of course, he feels that he can fulfill his destiny by killing Kennedy, thereby becoming a Cuban national hero.

There are still other causes. There is the innate human passion for secrets—a theme that runs throughout the novel—that appears to be the main attraction for the conspirators. Everett tells Parmenter and Mackey: "Secrets are an exalted state, almost a dream state. They're a way of arresting motion, stopping the world so we can see ourselves in it. This is why you're here" (26). Parmenter seems to agree. He calls the CIA "a natural extension of schoolboy societies, secret oaths and initiations, the body of assumptions common to young men of a certain discernible dash" (30). Oswald too is attracted to secrets and secret organizations, though from the opposite end of the political spectrum, finding in them a similar extension of boyhood fantasy: "They [the communist cell] would give him tasks to perform, night missions that required intelligence and stealth. He would wear dark clothes, cross rooftops in the rain" (37).

Then there are the financial causes, the oil, sugar, and gambling interests in Cuba that were lost after the revolution and that stayed lost after Kennedy's failure to support fully the Bay of Pigs invasion. Parmenter lost his investment in a leasing company that would have facilitated oil drilling on the island; he also lost his investment in a sugar company that he had made immediately before the Bay of Pigs; the Mafia lost their gambling casinos. Carmine Latta, a mobster, funnels money to the anti-Castro arms supplier Guy Banister—money that will go toward the Kennedy conspiracy—as a "bid for gambling concessions after Castro fell" (175).

Still other causes arise, more involving the Mafia. We learn that Robert Kennedy, the attorney general and brother of the president, had in recent months been clamping down on organized crime. To get rid of the pressure, Latta suggests getting rid of the head man, the president: "You cut off the head, the tail doesn't wag" (174). In addition, according to Jack Ruby, Kennedy had been carrying on a two-year affair with the mistress of another mobster, Sam Giancana. Such an offense, according to the Mafia code, is of course punishable by death.

Then there are the seemingly less significant, more nebulous causes. There is Banister's irrational hatred of Kennedy and his charisma, a hatred that "had a size to it, a physical force" (62). (Note the play on "physical force" as a deterministic cause.) There is the boredom of the former CIA, former Bay of Pigs conspirators: Banister asks Mackey, "how do we retire to a chair on the lawn? Everyday lawful pursuits don't meet our special requirements" (63). There is Parmenter's need for revenge for the personal humiliation of his forced retirement by the CIA for something that he feels was Kennedy's fault. There is even Banister's suggestion of a mystical cause: "there are forces in the air that compel men to act" (68). (Again, we note the play on "forces.")

We soon see, then, that it is impossible to isolate a single cause or a single chain of cause and effect that leads to the Kennedy assassination. There are too many causes, none of which can be called the original or "first cause"— as Zola was able to call the "lesion" that resulted in the effects he depicted in his *Rougon-Macquart* series of novels. And while all these causes point in different directions, their causal chains intersect at various points along the way, until they all meet in Dallas, Texas, on November 22, 1963. In other words, rather than these causal chains unfolding linearly, they unfold in a circular, looping pattern. As DeLillo himself has said,

> It is . . . my sense that we live in a kind of circular or near-circular system and that there are an increasing number of rings which keep intersecting at some point, whether you're using a plastic card to draw money out of your account at an automatic teller machine or thinking about the movement of planetary bodies. I mean, these systems all seem to interact to me.[7]

Where these interacting systems do intersect, they mutually influence one another so that each point of intersection becomes simultaneously both cause *and* effect. This marks a fundamental difference between the paradigm of the old science and that of the new, between the linear causality of Newtonian physics and the nonlinear causality of the field and systems concepts.

DeLillo has also said that with the Kennedy assassination we lost "a sense of a manageable reality," that "we seem much more aware of elements like randomness and ambiguity and chaos since then."[8] Perhaps this explains why the predominant metaphor in *Libra*, one that illustrates this new systems causality, is that of "no-control." It suggests humanity's inability to control or master nonlinear phenomena, and by implication the human inability to know or comprehend them. The novel begins with Oswald riding the New York City subway, going "so fast sometimes he thought they were on the edge of no-control" (3). This feeling occurs when the train goes around a curve in the track, suggesting the difference between the control of linear movement and the lack of control experienced in curved, looping systems. Later, the Soviet KGB man Kirilenko, when thinking about the "lesson" of Lee Harvey Oswald, reflects that "we are living in curved space" in which the "classical axioms" of geometry and arithmetic—those that give one a sense of control—fail when applied to experience (164). The climax of the novel is an explosion of "no-control," first with the surging crowd around Kennedy's motorcade, and finally with the assassination itself, which is the convergence of so many diverse causal systems. And the novel concludes as well with "no-control": Marguerite Oswald's rambling monologue, trying to make sense out of a life and an event characterized by "no-control," and, like Branch, unable to do so.

But throughout the course of the novel the unfolding conspiracy is the primary expression of "no-control," for despite the conspirators' efforts, it develops its own "powerful logic" (28) and "logical end" (221). "Secrets build their own networks" (22), Everett believes. At the Bay of Pigs, he had felt that "the system [i.e., the plan] would perpetuate itself in all its curious and obsessive webbings" (22), and indeed it did, to the point of the planners losing control over that system. The same thing happens with the Kennedy conspiracy: not the effect of a single cause, as we have seen, it seems to be born of itself, existing apart from its primary "conceiver," Everett. He tells Parmenter and Mackey that it is "like a dream whose meaning slowly becomes apparent" (28). As it develops, moving toward greater complexity as is characteristic of an open system, it moves further and further from their control. The conspiracy whose end was originally to counterfeit an attempt on the president's life, killing nobody, becomes a conspiracy to assassinate him without fail, and then to murder the suspected assassin. "Too many people," Mackey muses, "too many levels of plotting" (304). Too many systems interacting.

Toward the end of the novel, Branch puts forth the commonly held, albeit mistaken view of a conspiracy as a closed system:

> If we are on the outside, we assume a conspiracy is the perfect working of a scheme. Silent nameless men with unadorned hearts. A conspiracy is everything that ordinary life is not. It's the inside game, cold, sure, undistracted, forever closed off to us. We are the flawed ones, the innocents, trying to make some rough sense of the daily jostle. Conspirators have a logic and a daring beyond our reach. All conspiracies are the same taut story of men who find coherence in some criminal act. (440)

By this time, however, Branch begins to doubt this view, concluding that the conspiracy against the president succeeded mainly because of chance. "Chance" is what he calls the apparently random intersection of systems loops. David Ferrie calls it "coincidence." But Ferrie, unlike Branch, senses a pattern of chance or coincidence; that is, he senses an order behind it, a "hidden principle" (172). He tells a young Oswald, "Coincidence is a science waiting to be discovered. How patterns emerge outside the bounds of cause and effect" (44).[9] Apparently random occurrences, in other words, are random in appearance only. They form a pattern — not a linear pattern, but a looping, circular pattern of interconnecting systems. As we have seen, however, this pattern is ultimately impossible to perceive, for the observing subject is a part of it, and his actions — even the action of observing — affect it. Moreover, since his frame of reference is inside rather than outside the pattern, he cannot perceive the whole, only a part. Part of the pattern often appears to be either a straight line or a random intersection of lines. Of course, if one cannot perceive something, one cannot know it or master it. Again, we return to "no-control."

We can, however, chart certain patterns of connection within *Libra;* as a novel, *Libra*, in DeLillo's words, "attempts to provide a hint of order in the midst of all the randomness."[10] We see, for example, that Oswald's sudden appearance at 544 Camp Street in New Orleans—the location of Banister's office and the center of the conspiracy against Kennedy—is not the result of blind chance or coincidence. It *appears* to be that at first, and Banister and the other conspirators—with the exception of Ferrie—continue to believe that to the end. But in the course of the novel we find out that the FBI, wanting to crack down on anti-Castro activities that have been embarrassing the Kennedy administration, enlist Oswald as a spy to gather information on Banister's activities. An agent Bateman tells Oswald that he can distribute his Fair Play for Cuba leaflets, free of hassle from the FBI, if he will consent to go to Banister at 544 Camp Street and ask to work for him as a spy. Banister had been looking for Oswald, and now he appears, allegedly to set up a Fair Play for Cuba office in his building as a means of spying on pro-Castro people. Banister, whose Alpha 66 is affiliated with the CIA, knows nothing of the FBI's activities. Oswald's appearance, in other words, is the intersection of three systems: Oswald, the FBI, Alpha 66/CIA. There is a fourth system too: David Ferrie, who had known Oswald as an adolescent in New Orleans, and who now works for Banister. Ferrie, again, senses a pattern: not blind coincidence, but coincidence as a manifestation of a hidden order.

We have already noted the preponderance of the metaphor of the "small room" and have indicated that it suggests isolation and alienation. Oswald's oft-repeated expression—"There is a world inside the world"—is analogous to the small-room metaphor, for it too suggests an isolated, or "closed," system within the greater world. Yet there are only open systems in DeLillo's conception of the universe, some of which may appear closed. The various "men in small rooms," apparently closed off from the greater world, not only interact with that world but also with one another. So it is that the closed systems of Oswald, the FBI, and the CIA intersect at 544 Camp Street. So it is that Everett's "invention" of the assassin—a desperate man seeking to organize his loneliness by giving it a destiny, "making a network out of it, a fabric of connections" (147)—intersects with Oswald. Everett's desperate, lonely man is himself: he invents a fiction of himself, a "second existence" that intersects with Oswald's "second existence." Oswald, too, feels "a sense of destiny . . . [as he sits] locked in the miniature room, creating a design, a network of connections" (277). These two men in small rooms, then, two men who do not know one another nor would appear to interact, do interact. Their two systems intersect at the point of their one fiction, their self-invented destiny.

"Something in us has an effect on independent events," Ferrie tells Oswald. "We make things happen" (330). These "independent events," of course, are only *seemingly* independent; everything is interdependent. Thus Oswald is not just a product of his environment, nor is he a dupe of history as he would be, for example, in a Zola novel. As we have seen, causality is never one-way or linear, but is a looping system interacting with other systems. But while the end of linear causality may be the end of materialistic determinism, and therefore of the determined self, it is not the end of the self's alienation. The self still feels cut off from the material world, for it remains a world he can neither know nor master—a world of "no-control." Thus, while DeLillo "undoes" the naturalistic novel by undermining linear causality, he maintains and reworks a central feature of literary naturalism: the rift between the self and a material world of force.

The same is true of DeLillo's undermining of the subject-object duality of classical science, for as this certainly undoes the methodological foundation of Zola's experimental novel—as we saw in regard to Nicholas Branch—it does not reconcile the self to the material world. Rather, it presents the self with a new dilemma: how to locate the subjective self in and reconcile it to a world in which there is no distinction between subject and object. The pervasiveness of the mass media, primarily television, has produced in the postmodern world what amounts to a "cultural consciousness": a uniformity of thought and desire that effaces the individual. There is no autonomous individual consciousness that can stand apart from the cultural matrix in the same way, for example, that the Hemingway protagonist could stand apart from the natural world. As such, there is no way that the individual can reconcile himself to the "objective" world, as the Hemingway protagonist could by confronting it with his ordering consciousness. As Hayles has argued, the culture is a "field" from which the individual consciousness cannot extricate itself; consciousness is a part of it, its frame of reference contained within it.[11] One result—as we saw in the case of Branch, and as we shall see in a moment in the case of Oswald— is that the self is continually self-referring: the subjective self becomes the performing self, watching its own performance. It is simultaneously both subject and object. DeLillo attributes this new self-referentiality largely to the power of television and traces its origin in the cultural consciousness to the "media event" of the Kennedy assassination:

This has become a part of our consciousness. We've developed almost a sense of performance as it applies to televised events. And I think some of the people who are essential to such events [such as Oswald] . . . are simply carrying their performing selves out of the wings and into the theater. Such young men have a sense of the way in which their acts will be perceived by the rest of us, even as they commit the acts. So there is a deeply self-referential element in our lives that wasn't there before.[12]

We can see the absorption of the individual consciousness into the cultural matrix throughout *Libra*. Kennedy—the first great political manipulator of television—is present in the novel primarily through the various forms of mass media: "he floats through television screens . . . floats from the radio" (324). Oswald's wife is infatuated with Kennedy's media presence, fantasizing that he enters her bed through the radio, dreaming of the president "in pictures taken near the sea" (324) while Oswald makes love to her. She also imagines that she is not alone in her fantasies: "It's as though he floats over the landscape at night, entering dreams and fantasies, entering the act of love between husbands and wives" (324). Kennedy, not the man but the media presence, insinuates himself through that media into the very consciousness of the culture, into its "dreams and fantasies." He is part of a shared consciousness.

When Kennedy does appear "in person" in Dallas at the end of the novel, the crowd's reaction is immediately to privilege the authenticity of his media presence over his actual presence: "He looked like himself, like photographs" (392). "*They're real* [i.e., Kennedy and his wife]" (394), the crowd responds, as if surprised. The event of Kennedy's presence in Dallas, the dynamics of his interaction with the crowd, is treated as a cultural performance, a "media event":

Street by street the crowd began to understand why it was here. The message jumped the open space from one press of bodies to the next. A contagion had brought them here, some mystery of common impulse, hundreds of thousands come from so many histories and systems of

being, come from some experience of the night before, a convergence
of dreams, to stand together shouting as the Lincoln passed. They
were here to be an event, a consciousness. (393–94)

While the event involves the interaction of numerous "systems of being,"
these systems, we find, possess a single consciousness. They were there, in
fact, to be "a consciousness," the "convergence of dreams" the convergence
of facets of the same dream—namely, the American culture's desire to par-
take in the aura of the rich, the famous, and the star of the screen, to perform alongside that star. The "mystery"—or the "contagion" as it is more
pejoratively referred to—is the pervasiveness of this dream. Everyone is a
performer; everyone is filmed with the president in Dallas, performing the
role of adulating audience. Everyone is absorbed by the media, watching
himself watching.

Oswald, too, is an individual who, despite his ideological struggle against
the American system, has nevertheless been co-opted by that system
through the media. He shares a belief in what DeLillo calls "the promise of consumer fulfillment in America."[13] Shortly before the assassination, Oswald fantasizes about the "new" life he and Marina will live, a life
surprisingly middle-class, suburban, and materialistic: "They'd get their
own furniture, modern pieces, and a washing machine for Marina" (382).
And Oswald is also a performer, "an actor in real life" (56), as George de
Mohrenschildt calls him, as does DeLillo in his interview with DeCurtis. DeLillo goes on to say that "there is a sense in which he [Oswald] was
watching himself perform. I tried to insert this element into *Libra* on a
number of occasions."[14] Indeed he did. From the beginning, we see Oswald
the performer, a Walter Mitty who imagines himself, even in the squalor of
his mother's Bronx apartment, as "Oswald-hero" (46). His sense of himself as "hero" is a product of the movies; he sees himself as one of the "men
in dark coats, like men on movie posters" (46). And he continues to play to
his own audience throughout his life. His attempted suicide in Moscow is a
consummate performance. His actions are dictated by the movies and television. (He even thinks of a Gillette commercial while he prepares to slash
his wrists with a razor blade.) He rolls up one sleeve, fills the sink with cold
water, fills the tub with hot, loosens his tie, follows "step one" (numbing
the pain with the cold water), and "step two" (letting the blood flow into

the hot). He even wonders, while filling the tub, "why it had to be filled?" (152). The answer, of course, will later be supplied by Wayne Elko as he waits for the "proper" moment to murder Oswald, significantly enough, in a theater: "Because that's the way they do it in the movies" (412). Oswald, in fact, is described as "watching himself do it" (152); he could "picture himself" (153), and he simultaneously wonders how those who will find him and those who know him will react, as if they, too, were present watching. His entry in the Historic Diary, which obviously had to be written *before* the performance, reads like stage directions in a play, right down to the musical direction of violins: "7:00 P.M. I decide to end it. Soak rist in cold water to numb the pain. / My fondes dreams are shattered / Then slash my left wrist. / somewhere, a violin plays, as I watch my life whirl away. / I think to myself, 'How easy to die' / and 'A sweet death, (to violins)' " (151–53). Oswald's Historic Diary, of course, is itself a performance—with posterity or "history" as the presumed audience—one that ultimately refers back to him. We remember that Oswald believes one day people will study his diary for clues to himself. Of course, with the Historic Diary, as with his attempted suicide, the only real audience, the only present audience, *is* himself. Again, he is both observing subject and observed object.

But it is Oswald's final performance that is perhaps his most interesting. Oswald seems to watch his own murder at the hands of Jack Ruby, to watch it on television in "someone's TV den" (440):

> He could see himself shot as the camera caught it. Through the pain he watched TV. . . . Through the pain, through the losing of sensation except where it hurt, Lee watched himself react to the augering heat of the bullet. . . . The only thing left was the mocking pain, the picture of the twisted face on TV. (439–40)

"Someone's TV den" turns out to be Beryl Parmenter's, the wife of Laurence Parmenter the conspirator. Of course, the implication is that a similar experience, conscious or otherwise, occurs in the TV dens across America. But Mrs. Parmenter becomes conscious of it—that is, conscious of television's power to efface the distinction between subject and object. Mrs. Parmenter had liked to hide from the world in her "small and darkish" (123) house in Georgetown, outside the "heat and light," sending newspaper clippings of current events to friends. The newspaper clippings made it seem possible to objectify the world—to cut it into discrete, isolatable parts—much as Branch would like to do. "These pictures from the other world" are different, however, "not at all like the news items she clipped and mailed to friends" (446). She finds that there is no separation possible between observer and observed, that the television—heat and light itself— erases the comfortable illusion. "These men were in her house with their hats and guns," the violence "spilling in" to her room. And she notices the effect of the camera on Oswald:

> There was something in Oswald's face, a glance at the camera before he was shot, that put him here in the audience, among the rest of us, sleepless in our homes—a glance, a way of telling us that he knows who we are and how we feel, that he has brought our perceptions and interpretations into his sense of the crime. Something in the look, some sly intelligence, exceedingly brief but far-reaching, a connection all but bleached away by glare, tells us that he is outside the moment, watching with the rest of us. . . . He is commenting on the documentary footage even as it is being shot. Then he himself is shot, and shot, and shot, and the look becomes another kind of knowledge. But he has made us part of his dying. (447)

Again, Oswald seems to be watching himself perform. But he is also watching them, the American public, watching him. The subject-object duality, the distinction between observer and observed, collapses. Everyone is watching; everyone is being watched. And what everyone is watching is themselves being watched. Oswald's tacit commentary on the documentary—a film genre that, like Branch's "history," purports to provide an objective narrative of an event—is that such objectivity is impossible. The camera, like Branch's observing historian and Heisenberg's observing scientist, by filming this event "happen" in effect makes it happen. It, and its implied "subjective" audience, become part of the "objective" event.

We see, then, that Oswald is inseparable from those observing him and inseparable from the American consciousness. As Mrs. Parmenter says, Oswald "has brought our perceptions and interpretations into his sense of the crime"; he "has made us a part of his dying." He becomes an expression of that cultural consciousness: the culture, in observing Oswald, observes itself. Again we return to the individual consciousness effaced by the cultural matrix, and the dilemma confronting that consciousness: how to locate itself in and reconcile itself to a world devoid of subject-object distinctions. Oswald's response—a response we have seen reproduced by Everett, among others—is to create an identity, a destiny, and then to merge that destiny with history. As Everett says, creating a destiny is a way of "organizing one's loneliness" and giving it "a purpose" (147). To organize, of course, is to provide an order. And to give one's loneliness a purpose is to give it a teleology, a unique and distinct goal that can be fulfilled individually. Teleology, too, presumes linear causality, and linear causality implies discreetness and certainty—the separation of subject from object and the knowledge of that separation. Yet in *Libra*, the creation of an identity and a destiny, like linear causality, is an illusion. Oswald's identity and destiny are not autonomous creations but are encoded in the cultural matrix. He draws on two sources for his identity: books and movies. His early reading of Marx, Engels, Lenin, and Trotsky connects him to these historical figures: "The books made him part of something" (41). Trotsky in particular appeals to Oswald. Trotsky had lived in the Bronx like Oswald, had suffered in isolation like Oswald, had waited for history to sweep him along like Oswald. Once again, the distinction between subject and object is blurred: Oswald's reading of Trotsky becomes a reading of himself; subject becomes object.

We have already seen how "Oswald-hero" is an identity co-opted from popular films. He identifies with the heroes of suspense thrillers in the same way that he identifies with Trotsky. When he sees *Suddenly*, a film starring Frank Sinatra as a veteran who attempts to assassinate the president, Oswald again reads himself into the lead role. "He felt connected," we are told, "to the events on the screen. . . . They were running a message through the night into his skin" (370). The message, of course, is that he is to attempt the same thing: the assassination of the president. "They" who are conveying the message are the culture and Oswald himself—the culture that is fascinated by such figures, and Oswald who is a part of that culture and who can read himself into the role. He thus gives himself an identity and a destiny that are already encoded within the culture.

The same thing occurs when he watches *We Were Strangers* starring John Garfield as an American who plans to assassinate a Cuban dictator. Oswald "felt he was in the middle of his own movie. They were running this thing just for him" (370). In fact, Oswald begins to see everything that happens as a reference to himself. He reads in the newspaper of a Yale professor who was arrested as a spy outside a hotel where Oswald had once stayed in the Soviet Union. Oswald believes the story is about him: "Everything he heard and saw and read these days was really about him" (383). Later, he is not surprised to see a textbook salesman showing a rifle to his boss at the Texas School Book Depository and then carrying the gun up to the sixth floor where Oswald works and from where he will shoot the president: "Everything that happened was him." (385). In other words, despite his attempts to create a distinct identity and destiny, Oswald loses even the illusion of a distinction between the I and the not-I, between subject and object. He sees himself in everything; the observing subject and the observed object are the same.

Oswald's desire to merge himself or his destiny with history thus becomes an impossibility. What he desires in effect is a type of Romantic transcendence, a means of escaping the self by uniting with something greater. This of course implies an initial separation between subject and object, and, as we have seen, there is no such separation. Oswald believes his destiny is a teleology, and he believes history, too, is teleological. He refers to history alternatively as a "tide" (85) or a "stream" flowing in a "single direction" (101). This is the paradigm of one-way linear causality, a paradigm that proves inaccurate. Applied to history, it becomes the "great men" theory, the belief that certain key figures can cause historical events to happen. Oswald believes that by merging the line of his destiny with the line of history—the point of intersection, "the *point* where he was no longer separated from the true struggles that went on around him" (248, my emphasis)—he too can effect historical events. "How strangely easy," Oswald muses, after defecting to the Soviet Union and thinking about all the changes the U.S. military will have to make because of his defection, "to have a say over men and events" (163). Later, while contemplating murdering General Walker, Oswald thinks to himself "how simple, how strangely easy it is to make your existence felt" (373). Bertalanffy, in attacking the "great men" theory of history, had argued that these great men acted only as " 'leading parts,' 'triggers,' or 'catalyzers' in the historical process," that they did not in fact "cause" history to happen.[15] Significantly enough, neither does Oswald: his defection has little impact on the United

States; he fails to kill Walker; and most revealingly, he even fails to assassinate Kennedy. Oswald cannot merge with history because history is not something separate to begin with; it, too, is a field, or a system of interconnecting systems, encompassing Oswald.

Libra is a remarkable achievement. In it, DeLillo not only manages to undo the naturalistic novel by undermining its classical scientific foundation, but he also manages to rework a central leitmotiv of the naturalistic form: the self's struggle within a material world of force. Unlike Norris and Hemingway, DeLillo is not so much concerned with the loss of a moral and spiritual order, but with a scientific order that had made the universe knowable and therefore controllable. The self must now exist in a universe of "no-control," a universe of looping systems that defies human mastery. Moreover, with the natural world giving way to the built environment, a man-made world dominated by forms of mass media, the self enters a self-referring loop, the individual consciousness absorbed within the encompassing field of the cultural consciousness. The naturalistic struggle thus becomes not a struggle to perceive an order or to create one's own order, as in Norris and Hemingway respectively, but to accept a world where order lies beyond rational comprehension. It becomes, in other words, a struggle to accept uncertainty and indeterminacy, to accept "no-control."

NOTES

Introduction

1. Charles Child Walcutt, *American Literary Naturalism: A Divided Stream* (Minneapolis: University of Minnesota Press, 1956), 3.

2. Both Walcutt and Pizer focus on the tension of opposites within naturalistic works. Walcutt argues that American literary naturalism derives from and dramatizes the tension of the "divided stream" of American transcendentalism—that is, the split between intuitive and scientific modes of thought. Naturalism, to Walcutt, alternates between or combines these two modes, at times positing a spiritually monistic universe (consonant with intuition), at other times a materially monistic one (consonant with science), and, at other times, a philosophically muddled mixture of the two. Pizer, in *Realism and Naturalism in Nineteenth-Century American Literature* (Carbondale: Southern Illinois University Press, 1966), conceives of naturalism as embodying the tension between a debased subject matter and "the concept of man which emerges from that subject matter," and that between materialistic determinism and a "humanistic value . . . which affirms the significance of the individual and of his life" (10–11). Richard Lehan, in his study of Theodore Dreiser, *Theodore Dreiser: His World and His Novels* (Carbondale: Southern Illinois University Press, 1969), posits a similar tension in naturalism, which he refers to as the "romantic dilemma": the conflict between the individual's aspirations and his or her physical, environmental limitations

3. Pizer, in *The Novels of Frank Norris* (Bloomington: Indiana University Press, 1966), discusses the ideas of the late nineteenth-century "evolutionary theists" and traces the influence of one of them, Joseph LeConte, on Norris. Ronald E. Martin, in *American Literature and the Universe of Force* (Durham: Duke University Press, 1981), also focuses on late nineteenth-century science and philosophy, examining in depth that era's concept of the "universe of force" and its various cultural ramifications, including its expression in the works of literary naturalism. In *The American 1890s: Life and Times of a Lost Generation* (New York: Viking, 1966), Larzer Ziff

explores the broader cultural and literary climate of the period in his analysis of American naturalism.

4. Lars Ahnebrink, in his early influence study *The Influence of Emile Zola on Frank Norris* (1947; Cambridge: Harvard University Press, 1976), concentrates on formal parallels between Zola's novels and those of Norris. He examines similarities in such literary features as theme, image, scene, and style, arguing in the process that Norris was heavily indebted, as a novelist, to Zola. In Ahnebrink's later work, *The Beginnings of Naturalism in American Fiction* (Cambridge: Harvard University Press, 1950), he broadens his study of literary influence to include Turgenev and Ibsen as European mentors, and Garland and Crane as American protégés. More important, he examines the social, philosophical, and literary climate in late nineteenth-century America that made young writers amenable to the naturalism and naturalistic theories of Zola and the other Europeans. Richard Lehan, like Ahnebrink, discusses the parallels between Zola and the American naturalists in "American Literary Naturalism: The French Connection," *Nineteenth Century Fiction* 38.4 (1984): 529–57, but does so by focusing on the "social/historical/cultural dimension of naturalism" (530). He argues that naturalism cannot be divorced from historical processes and cogently examines the social and historical similarities between the Second Empire of Zola's *Rougon-Macquart* novels and post–Civil War America, the domain of the American naturalists. In particular, Lehan notes the effect of the parallel, though not exactly coeval, movement from a landed to an urban economy in both France and America, and its many social ramifications, on these writers and their work.

5. Charles L. Crow, in "Gnawing the File: Recent Trends in *McTeague* Scholarship," *Frank Norris Studies* 13 (Spring 1992): 1–5, usefully labels these two schools of recent theorists "neo-Naturalists" and "anti-Naturalists." The main thrust of the anti-Naturalists—such as Don Graham, Joseph R. McElrath, Jr., and Barbara Hochman among Norris scholars—is to argue for the aesthetic merits of naturalistic works that they feel have taken, unnecessarily, a back seat to theoretical and philosophical considerations. They have cogently demonstrated the artistic complexities of Norris's work, complexities that they believe cannot be discerned by judging it against theoretical standards or credos of "naturalism." See Don Graham, *The Fiction of Frank Norris: The Aesthetic Context* (Columbia: University of Missouri Press, 1978); Joseph R. McElrath, Jr., "Frank Norris's *Vandover and the Brute:* Narrative Technique and the Socio-Critical Viewpoint," *Studies in American Fiction* 4.1 (Spring 1976): 27–43; also McElrath, *Frank Norris Revisited* (New York: Twayne Publishers, 1992); and Barbara Hochman, *The Art of Frank Norris, Storyteller* (Columbia: University of Missouri Press, 1988).

The neo-Naturalists have either built on the work of the early theorists and history-of-ideas critics of naturalism, or have radically departed from it. John J. Conder and Harold Kaplan fall into the first group. Conder, in *Naturalism in American Fiction: The Classic Phase* (Lexington: University of Kentucky Press, 1984), approaches naturalism from the philosophical background of materialistic determinism, claiming that naturalism is philosophically coherent and that apparent inconsistencies in its deterministic vision are due to the broad spectrum of views contained within the traditions of philosophical determinism itself—a spectrum ranging from what he terms "hard" determinism to "soft." Kaplan, in *Power and Order: Henry Adams and the Naturalistic Tradition in American Fiction* (Chicago: University of Chicago Press, 1981), concedes that naturalism "remains a useful term for describing a literary practice and a set of programmatic ideas reflecting the laws of thermodynamics, Darwinian theory, and the sociological thought derived from Adam Smith, Malthus, Marx, and Spencer" (5), yet propounds that naturalism's most significant contribution consists of "a myth of power and conflict charged with apocalyptic themes of order and chaos, creation and destruction, purgative crisis and redemptive violence" (xi).

Among those who have departed from the early theorists and the history of ideas critics, the most prominent are June Howard, Lee Clark Mitchell, Mark Seltzer, and Walter Benn Michaels. Howard, in *Form and History in American Literary Naturalism* (Chapel Hill: University of North Carolina Press, 1985), argues that naturalism as a literary genre is "a distinctive response to its historical moment" (ix); yet, for Howard, "historical moment" refers to social, rather than intellectual, history. Her reading is heavily Marxist, one that views class conflict and class anxieties as the central concerns of literary naturalism. Mitchell, in *Determined Fictions: American Literary Naturalism* (New York: Columbia University Press, 1989), focuses on the language and style of naturalistic works—that is, on the "bad writing" often dismissed by critics—to show that they, rather than contemporary science and philosophy, are responsible for narrative determinism. He attempts, in his own words, to "[shift] attention away from scientific to linguistic forms of determinism" (xv). Seltzer and Michaels both approach naturalism from a New Historicist perspective, focusing on how naturalistic works "participate"—to use Seltzer's term—in various nineteenth-century discourses, particularly those that represent contemporary economic and aesthetic conflicts. They attempt, in other words, to locate or relocate naturalistic discourse within the discourses of a broad historical episteme, "shifting the focus of literary history," as Michaels phrases it, "from the individual text or author to structures whose coherence, interest, and effect may be greater than that of either author or text" (174-75). See Michaels, *The Gold Standard and the*

Logic of Naturalism (Berkeley and Los Angeles: University of California Press, 1987); see also Seltzer, "The Naturalist Machine," in *Sex, Politics, and Science in the Nineteenth-Century Novel*, ed. Ruth Bernard Yeazell (Baltimore: Johns Hopkins University Press, 1986): 116–47.

6. Ronald E. Martin, for example, contends that American literary naturalism was the culminating expression of the nineteenth-century "universe of force" concept, and that after Dreiser both naturalism and the belief in a universe of force disappeared (*Universe of Force*, 256). It is beyond the scope of his study to explore where they may have disappeared to, or how they may have been transformed.

Although Donald Pizer, Charles Child Walcutt, and June Howard address naturalism in the twentieth century, they do so in ways quite different from my own. All keep naturalism distinct and separate from modernism and postmodernism, thereby implying, in effect, that naturalism in the twentieth century is a literary atavism, rather than a dynamic narrative mode that has undergone several transformations. Pizer, in *Twentieth-Century American Literary Naturalism: An Interpretation* (Carbondale: Southern Illinois University Press, 1982), argues that naturalism in the twentieth century recurs in two "waves," which he specifically locates in the 1930s and in the late 1940s and early 1950s (xii). These new waves of literary naturalism, according to Pizer, are the result of social and historical pressures as well as literary influences, and while they each exhibit "a degree of innovation," they nevertheless remain firmly in the naturalistic tradition first established in the 1890s (14). Walcutt, while he discusses Ernest Hemingway's work—and that of Sherwood Anderson, James T. Farrell, John Steinbeck, and John Dos Passos—in terms of literary naturalism, he does so, as we might expect, within the context of his own particular definition of it. He thus views *For Whom the Bell Tolls* as Hemingway's culminating work of literary naturalism: "the most explicit, sustained, and triumphant reunion of its divided stream that American naturalism has seen" (*Divided Stream*, 276). Such a statement implies that Hemingway's work is the fulfillment of a nineteenth-century literary ideal—something Hemingway certainly was not out to accomplish, nor which, in my opinion, accurately assesses his achievement. Howard, too, identifies several twentieth-century works as "naturalistic"—such as Upton Sinclair's *Jungle* and *King Coal*, Farrell's *Studs Lonigan* trilogy, Dos Passos's *U.S.A.*, and Hubert Selby, Jr.'s *Last Exit to Brooklyn*—yet her brief discussions of these novels concentrate mainly on their appropriation of naturalistic "narrative strategies." These include the documentary strategy, the plot of decline, and the anatomy of a particular milieu—as well as the implicit class separation between the narrator and reader, on one hand, and the characters of the novel, on the other, that provides the voyeuristic thrill Howard finds characteristic of literary naturalism.

While claiming that these writers and their works are "inheritors of naturalism," and while acknowledging that a relatively recent novel as *Last Exit to Brooklyn* must involve a *"reinvention"* of the form, she never broaches what might constitute such a reinvention, and thus never provides a framework for conceiving of twentieth-century naturalism as anything other than a throwback to an antiquated and conventionalized form (*Form and History*, 156–67).

Finally, the methodology of the New Historicists such as Walter Benn Michaels and Mark Seltzer precludes them from treating history, including literary history, temporally—that is, as process; rather, they view history spatially, as episteme, and therefore confine their studies of American literary naturalism to the late nineteenth century. For an interesting critique of the New Historicist spatialization of history, see Richard Lehan, "The Theoretical Limits of the New Historicism," *New Literary History* 21.3 (Spring 1990): 533–53.

7. Harold Kaplan is the one exception, for he does conceptualize naturalism in the twentieth century in terms of modernism's transformation of it. He argues, as I do, that modernism was both a reaction against and a continuation of literary naturalism, and that the work of modernists such as Hemingway, Fitzgerald, and Faulkner "cannot be deeply understood without reference to the philosophic context of naturalism." Yet, unlike my own, Kaplan's focus is on what he calls naturalism's "metaphysics of power" or "myth of power" (*Power and Order,* 5).

8. Quoted in Tom LeClair, *Anything Can Happen* (Urbana: University of Illinois Press, 1983), 80.

Chapter One. Man, God, and Natural Law: Darwinism and the Darwinian Debate

1. In *Principles of Geology* (1830–33), Charles Lyell promulgated his theory of "uniformitarian" geological evolution—that is, the view that the earth has gradually evolved through geological processes that have operated over immense periods of time, and that are still in operation. See Charles Lyell, *Principles of Geology; or, The Modern Changes of the Earth and Its Inhabitants*, 9th ed. (New York: D. Appleton and Co., 1853). Lyell's theory countermanded that of "catastrophism," which postulated that past geological changes were caused by a series of abrupt, unrelated catastrophes, between which the earth remained in stasis.

2. Lamarck, in *Philosophie zoologique* (1809), proposed that organisms evolved by acquiring traits, or "characters," through the use or disuse of particular organs, and that these "acquired characters" were then inherited by their offspring. See Jean-Baptiste Lamarck, *Zoological Philosophy*, trans. Hugh Elliot (Chicago: University

of Chicago Press, 1984). However, as Richard W. Burkhardt, Jr. has noted in his introduction to the above translation, "Lamarck's problem was that he was unable to relate his broad hypotheses to factual evidence in such a way as to cause his contemporaries to treat his hypotheses as profound insights rather than unfounded speculations" (xvi). For a thorough examination of Lamarck's life and work, see also Burkhardt, *The Spirit of System: Lamarck and Evolutionary Biology* (Cambridge: Harvard University Press, 1977).

3. See Thomas Robert Malthus, *An Essay on the Principle of Population*, ed. Philip Appleman (1798; New York: Norton, 1976). Malthus's first essay was published in 1798, and an expanded version published in 1803.

4. In 1865, Gregor Mendel delivered two lectures to the National History Society of Brunn—published as a single paper the following year—in which he explained his eight-year experiment that inaugurated the science of genetics. See Mendel, *Experiments in Plant Hybridisation*, trans. the Royal Horticultural Society of London (Cambridge: Harvard University Press, 1965). However, his lectures and paper were largely ignored until they were rediscovered in 1900 by the botanists Hugo de Vries, Carl Correns, and Erich von Tschermak-Seysenegg. For a history of the science, see L. C. Dunn, *A Short History of Genetics: The Development of Some of the Main Lines of Thought, 1864–1939* (New York: McGraw-Hill, 1965).

5. The Dutch botanist Hugo de Vries is credited with first promulgating a theory of genetic mutation in *Die Mutationstheorie* (1901–3). See de Vries, *The Mutation Theory: Experiments and Observations on the Origin of Species in the Vegetable Kingdom*, trans. A. D. Darbishire and J. B. Farmer (Chicago: Open Court Publishing Company, 1909). See also Dunn, *Short History of Genetics*, 55ff.

6. Cynthia Eagle Russett, *Darwin in America: The Intellectual Response, 1865–1912* (San Francisco: Freeman, 1976), 35.

7. Quoted in Russett, *Darwin in America*, 26.

8. Charles Darwin, *The Origin of Species* (1859; New York: Penguin, 1968), 133.

9. Ibid., 65.

10. Ibid., 133.

11. Ibid., 129.

12. Morse Peckham, "Darwinism and Darwinisticism," *Victorian Studies* 3.1 (September 1959): 19–40. Edwin H. Cady makes a similar distinction between "science" ("the functional application of ideas to specific natural phenomena") and "scientism" ("the application of ideas derived from science to phenomena not specifically natural or properly scientific: like history, social behavior, theology, or the arts") in *The Light of Common Day: Realism in American Fiction* (Bloomington: Indiana University Press, 1971), 46.

13. See Herbert Spencer, *First Principles* (1862; New York: D. Appleton and Co., 1864). For a clear exposition of Spencer's life and work, see Hugh Samuel Roger Elliot, *Herbert Spencer* (1917; Freeport: Books for Libraries Press, 1970).

14. Pizer, *Novels of Frank Norris*, 4–5.

15. Asa Gray, *Darwiniana: Essays and Reviews Pertaining to Darwinism*, ed. A. Hunter Dupree (Cambridge: Harvard University Press, 1963).

16. Gray, "The Origin of Species by Means of Natural Selection," *American Journal of Science and Arts* (March 1860). Quoted in Gray, *Darwiniana*, 45.

17. Gray, "Darwin and His Reviewers," *Atlantic Monthly* 6 (October 1860): 406–25. Reprinted as part 3 of "Natural Selection Not Inconsistent with Natural Theology," in *Darwiniana*. Quoted in Gray, *Darwiniana*, 119.

18. Gray, "Design Versus Necessity: Discussion Between Two Readers of Darwin's Treatise on the Origin of Species, Upon Its Natural Theology," *American Journal of Science and Arts* 30 (September 1860): 226–39. Quoted in Gray, *Darwiniana*, 55.

19. Gray, "The Origin," in *Darwiniana*, 47.

20. Gray, "What Is Darwinism?," *Nation* (May 28, 1874). Quoted in Gray, *Darwiniana*, 226.

21. Gray, "Evolutionary Teleology." Originally published in *Darwiniana* (1876). Quoted in Gray, *Darwiniana*, 294.

22. Gray, "The Origin," in *Darwiniana*, 47.

23. Gray, "Darwin and His Reviewers," in *Darwiniana*, 144.

24. Gray, "The Origin," in *Darwiniana*, 11.

25. Ibid.

26. Ibid., 18.

27. Ibid., 47.

28. Ibid., 43.

29. Ibid.

30. Joseph LeConte, *Evolution: Its Nature, Its Evidences, and Its Relation to Religious Thought* (1888; New York: D. Appleton and Co., 1908), 300. Subsequent references to this edition are provided within the text.

31. Pizer, *Novels of Frank Norris*, 22.

32. John Dewey, "The Influence of Darwin on Philosophy," in *The Influence of Darwin on Philosophy, and Other Essays in Contemporary Thought* (New York: Holt, 1910). Reprinted in *Darwin*, ed. Philip Appleman (New York: Norton, 1970), 402. Subsequent references to this edition are provided within the text.

33. Ernest Hemingway, *The Sun Also Rises* (New York: Scribners, 1926), 148.

Chapter Two. *Zola and Determinism*

1. Walcutt, *Divided Stream*, 30.
2. See Emile Zola, *The Experimental Novel and Other Essays*, trans. Belle M. Sherman (1880; New York: Haskell, 1964). Subsequent references to this edition are provided within the text.
3. Walcutt, *Divided Stream*, 155.
4. Ibid., 29.
5. Ibid., 39.
6. Emile Zola, *L'Assommoir*, trans. Leonard Tancock (1876; New York: Penguin, 1970), 21.

Chapter Three. Vandover and the Brute *and the Post-Darwinian Condition*

1. Frank Norris, *Vandover and the Brute* (1914; Garden City: Doubleday, 1928), 7. Subsequent references to this edition are provided within the text.
2. Perhaps this is a good time to acknowledge two important and influential, although different, interpretations of Vandover's "divided self." McElrath, in "Frank Norris's *Vandover*, 27–43, sees a tension in Vandover between his natural, sexual impulses and the genteel morality—inculcated in him by society—which would repress them. To McElrath, then, Vandover becomes a victim, not of his biological drives, but of that morality, for he places his faith in it and perceives experience through it—even though experience belies it. Don Graham concurs, arguing that Vandover's fall is precipitated by the division between experience and the abstract morality he imposes on it. Graham concludes: "Far from being a social-Darwinist or deterministic tragedy, *Vandover and the Brute* is a tragedy of the reification of experience into unrealistic and deadening rigidities of behavior. It is a tragedy of imperception, not of forces greater than the self." See Graham, *Aesthetic Context*, 42.

While both these interpretations differ from my own, they do not do so in as marked a way as they may initially seem; after all, the genteel morality McElrath and Graham correctly attribute to Vandover and his society had its roots, we may presume, in the Christian conception of an ordered universe, and is itself a manifestation of the human need to live within such a universe. That Vandover's experience now seems to belie universal moral and spiritual order is the crux of my argument, as it is theirs. The key difference, as I see it, is that McElrath and Graham read this conflict between moral vision and experience as social critique, whereas I read it as a representation of a post-Darwinian metaphysical crisis. They are also not as sympathetic as I am to such characters as Vandover's father and Turner Ravis, as will become evident.

3. Don Graham reads these "ordering principles" differently, seeing them as "categories of abstracted good" that Vandover's experience belies. See Graham, *Aesthetic Context*, 20, 29–30.

4. Barbara Hochman, who reads *Vandover* as "the story of a self crippled by a loss it can neither integrate nor transcend," interprets this loss quite differently; to Hochman, it has strictly personal, rather than metaphysical, implications. Vandover's inability to come to terms with his childhood feelings of loss after his mother's death, according to Hochman, condemns him to relive those feelings throughout his life. In this sense, Hochman contends, "the novel seems to point more directly to Freud than to Darwin." See Barbara Hochman, *Art of Frank Norris*, 43, 56.

5. Don Graham finds the "Old Gentleman" to be more mercenary than moral, one for whom money is the "central criterion of value." See Graham, *Aesthetic Context*, 27.

6. Several critics would disagree with such an assessment. Joseph R. McElrath, Jr., Don Graham, and Barbara Hochman all find Turner to be a moral hypocrite. Hochman calls her "priggish and self-interested"; Graham sees her falling far short of the "idealized picture" that Vandover and Dolly Haight hold of her; McElrath claims that Flossie, not Turner, is more akin to Norris's "man's woman" type. He calls Turner "self-centered," "intellectually and emotionally shallow," and, finally, "simply not much of a human being." See Hochman, *Art of Frank Norris*, 57; Graham, *Aesthetic Context*, 23–24; McElrath, "Frank Norris's *Vandover*," 32–38.

7. It also echoes a comment by the religious social reformer Charles Loring Brace, who, in *The Dangerous Classes of New York* (1872), described the difference between sexual vice in men and women as follows: "For there is no reality in the sentimental assertion that the sexual sins of the lad are as degrading as those of the girl. The instinct of the female is more toward the preservation of purity, and therefore her fall is deeper—an instinct grounded in the desire of preserving a stock, or even the necessity of perpetuating our race." See Brace, *The Dangerous Classes of New York, and Twenty Years' Work Among Them* (1872; Montclair: Patterson Smith, 1967), 115–16.

8. Donald Pizer has argued that, to Norris, nature "is above all moral," that it contains a "moral order . . . which abhors evil and punishes the wrongdoer." See Pizer, *Novels of Frank Norris*, 22, 10. While Pizer is certainly correct in such a view regarding *The Octopus*, I believe he errs in attributing that same LeContean moral order to the natural world and natural force in *Vandover*. Pizer, it seems to me, reads

a moral vision into Norris's early work that Norris did not fully embrace, or at least dramatize, until the later novel.

9. Donald Pizer would disagree, having previously argued that "Norris' immense attraction for Zola . . . did not mean that he fully accepted Zola's view of human nature," that Zola's influence was primarily literary rather than philosophical. See Pizer, *Novels of Frank Norris*, 26. Pizer adduces as evidence Norris's critical emphasis on Zola's "Romantic" literary style rather than on his philosophy of determinism, a philosophy that Norris only refers to once (*Wave*, XV; June 6, 1896) in his many critical studies and reviews of Zola's work. To Pizer, Zola only provided Norris with a sensational and contemporary style with which to portray LeConte's philosophy of humanity's dualism—what Pizer calls humanity's "ethical duality" of rationality/animality or spirit/flesh. According to Pizer, then, Vandover's fall is self-induced, a moral failure in a LeContean, not Zolaesque, universe. As we saw in Chapter 1, LeConte believed that nature was God Himself, that natural law was His will. For humans, natural law involved the willful subordination of their animality to their rationality, of flesh to spirit. In addition, human beings were not to eradicate their animality, but use its energy to "nourish" and "strengthen" their higher rational and spiritual beings. Vandover, then, sins and consequently falls, according to Pizer, by failing on two levels to align himself with and his conduct to this LeContean natural law. His sensuality, including his sexual indulgence through which he contracts his debilitating disease, indicates his failure to subsume the animal to the rational. And his easy adaptability to any environment involves a failure to employ rationally his animal vigor to compete successfully in the struggle for existence. Nature, then, essentially destroys Vandover for being morally weak.

10. The first phrase is Pizer's, *Novels of Frank Norris*, 15; the second is Walcutt's, *Divided Stream*, 155.

11. See Frank Norris, "The Novel with a 'Purpose,'" in *The Literary Criticism of Frank Norris*, ed. Donald Pizer (Austin: University of Texas Press, 1964), 90–93; see also Frank Norris, "The Responsibilities of the Novelist," in *Literary Criticism*, 94–98.

12. Walcutt, *Divided Stream*, 121.

13. Pizer, *Novels of Frank Norris*, 42.

14. Barbara Hochman comes to a different conclusion regarding the effect of Vandover's fall on Norris. She surmises that, rather than proving ultimately unbearable for Norris, the deterministic explanations for Vandover's fall in fact make it tolerable by rendering it a physical, not psychological or spiritual, collapse. See Hochman, *Art of Frank Norris*, 58–59.

15. Joseph R. McElrath, Jr. speculates that Norris's artistic transformation from

Vandover to his later work may have been caused by changes in his personal life, particularly his marriage to Jeannette Black and the stability and domesticity it brought to him. In "Frank Norris's *The Octopus:* The Christian Ethic as Pragmatic Response," in *Critical Essays on Frank Norris,* ed. Don Graham (Boston: G. K. Hall, 1980), McElrath asserts: "Norris was, by 1901, no longer the 'boy Zola' whose hard Darwinism was voiced in *Moran* and whose other early works were set in a Godless universe of insentient forces. As his personal life became more stable (largely because of his 1900 marriage) and his future as a successful writer began to seem assured, he turned from the sensational negativism, flamboyant hard Darwinism, and lurid ultra-Realism of his apprentice days to a more sober and thoughtful analysis of contemporary issues. The first fruit of this new phase is seen in his turning away from the fashionable, attention-winning clichés of Naturalism to a more common-sensical, tradition-tested investigation of broadly applicable verities" (147). See also McElrath, "Frank Norris: A Biographical Essay," *American Literary Realism, 1870–1910* 11.2 (Autumn 1978): 219–34.

Chapter Four. The Octopus: *Norris's Response to the Post-Darwinian Condition*

1. Pizer, *Novels of Frank Norris,* 113–62.

2. Frank Norris, *The Octopus* (1901; New York: Penguin, 1986), 22. Subsequent references to this edition are provided within the text.

3. Stuart L. Burns, "The Rapist in Frank Norris's *The Octopus*," *American Literature* 42.4 (January 1971): 567–69.

4. Don Graham compares Presley in this scene to the faun in Mallarmé's "L'Apres-midi d'un faune: eglogue" (1876). Presley, in other words, is depicted as a pastoral poet out of touch with his era. See Graham, *Aesthetic Context,* 69.

5. Pizer, *Novels of Frank Norris,* 148. Don Graham interprets this image as a symbolic destruction of Presley's pastoral vision, and the pastoral poetic form in general. The railroad, that multifaceted symbol of the late nineteenth century, massacres "those pastoral clichés: lambs and sheep." See Graham, *Aesthetic Context,* 72.

6. As Donald Pizer has pointed out, to Norris economic forces, represented here by the railroad, are natural forces. See Pizer, *Novels of Frank Norris,* 140.

7. Richard Allan Davison has observed that Vanamee's progression follows a Christian paradigm: "from that of knowledge of evil (Angéle's rape by the Other), to despair (his aimless wanderings and denial of God's goodness), to penance (his ascetic life and the long nights of contemplation in the Mission garden), to re-

birth and deepened spiritual insight first realized in the love of Angéle's grown daughter." Such a pattern seems to reinforce the characterization of Vandover as a modern prophet reinterpreting spiritualism for a new age. See Richard Allan Davison, "Frank Norris's *The Octopus:* Some Observations on Vanamee, Shelgrim, and St. Paul," in *Critical Essays on Frank Norris,* ed. Don Graham (Boston: G. K. Hall, 1980), 108.

8. Sir James George Frazer, *The Golden Bough: A Study in Magic and Religion* (1922; New York: Macmillan, 1963), 420ff.

9. LeConte, *Evolution,* 302.

10. Ibid., 356.

11. Ibid., 300.

12. Ibid., 356.

13. Donald Pizer was the first to note this fact. See Pizer, *Novels of Frank Norris,* 143–44.

14. See Frank Norris, "A Plea for Romantic Fiction," in *Literary Criticism,* 75–78.

15. Charles Duncan also identifies *The Octopus* as a *Künstlerroman* in an insightful recent essay, " 'If Your View Be Large Enough': Narrative Growth in *The Octopus,*" *American Literary Realism, 1870–1910* 25.2 (Winter 1993): 56–66. Duncan argues that Norris uses free indirect discourse—that is, the rhetorical device in which the voice of the narrator and a character merge—as a means of filtering several key events through Presley's consciousness, thereby placing Presley in the role of narrative artist who gives aesthetic cohesion to them. Duncan convincingly shows how Presley matures as an artist throughout the course of the novel, and how at the conclusion it is Presley, rather than an impersonal narrator, who is in control of the narrative.

16. See notes 4 and 5. As Don Graham also observes, Norris in "The Responsibilities of the Novelist" explicitly relegates the long poem (e.g., Presley's "Song of the West") to the past; to Norris, it is incapable of describing the modern world, is "no longer the right mode of expression." See Graham, *Aesthetic Context,* 100.

17. Norris, "A Plea," in *Literary Criticism,* 76–77.

18. Ibid., 76.

19. For an interesting yet different interpretation, see McElrath, "Norris's *The Octopus,*" 138–52. McElrath argues that the optimistic, LeContean conclusion is intended to be ironic, that Norris in fact asserts a pragmatic response to the social and economic problems dramatized in the novel. To McElrath, this pragmatism takes the form of Christian brotherhood—the transcendence of the self that is epitomized in Annixter's transformation.

20. Dewey, "Influence of Darwin on Philosophy," 400–401.

Chapter Five. *The Rise of Consciousness and Hemingway's Transformation of Literary Naturalism*

1. For a different reading of Hemingway's conception of the universe, see H. R. Stoneback, "In the Nominal Country of the Bogus: Hemingway's Catholicism and the Biographies," in *Hemingway: Essays of Reassessment,* ed. Frank Scafella (New York: Oxford University Press, 1991), 105–140; Stoneback, "From the rue Saint-Jacques to the Pass of Roland to the 'Unfinished Church on the Edge of the Cliff,'" *Hemingway Review* 6.1 (Fall 1986): 2–29; and Stoneback, "Lovers' Sonnets Turn'd to Holy Psalms: The Soul's Song of Providence, the Scandal of Suffering, and Love in *A Farewell to Arms,*" *Hemingway Review* 9.1 (Fall 1989): 33–76. Stoneback argues in each of these pieces that Hemingway possessed a Catholic vision and that that vision informs his work.

2. Carl Jung, "The Spiritual Problem of Modern Man," in *The Portable Jung,* ed. Joseph Campbell (New York: Penguin, 1971), 459–60.

3. Ibid., 460.

4. Ibid., 462.

5. Ibid., 467, 466.

6. Ibid., 466.

7. Jung, "Instinct and the Unconscious," in *The Portable Jung,* 54.

8. Zola, *The Experimental Novel and Other Essays,* 17.

9. Ibid., 54.

10. Jung, "On the Relation of Analytical Psychology to Poetry," in *The Portable Jung,* 302.

11. Jung, "Spiritual Problem," 473.

12. Only at the very end of *The Origin of Species* does Darwin venture the understatement: "Light will be thrown on the origin of man and his history" (458).

13. Carl N. Degler, *In Search of Human Nature: The Decline and Revival of Darwinism in American Social Thought* (New York: Oxford University Press, 1991), 15.

14. See Franz Boas, *The Mind of Primitive Man* (New York: Macmillan, 1911). For a clear exposition of Boas's ideas and influence, see Degler, *In Search of Human Nature.*

15. Alfred L. Kroeber, "The Superorganic," *American Anthropologist* 19.2 (April–June 1917): 203.

16. Ibid., 184.

17. Friedrich Nietzsche, *Thus Spoke Zarathustra,* trans. Walter Kaufmann (1892; New York: Penguin, 1954), 12.

18. Ibid.

19. Ibid., 23.

20. Ibid., 23, 24.

21. Ernest Hemingway, "A Clean, Well-Lighted Place," in *Winner Take Nothing* (New York: Scribners, 1933), 17.

22. Ernest Hemingway, *A Farewell to Arms* (New York: Scribners, 1929), 184–85.

23. Hemingway, *The Sun Also Rises*, 149.

24. Ezra Pound, "Hugh Selwyn Mauberley," in *Selected Poems of Ezra Pound* (New York: New Directions, 1957), 64.

25. Ernest Hemingway, *Death in the Afternoon* (New York: Scribners, 1932), 2.

26. Ibid.

27. Ernest Hemingway, "The Art of Fiction XXI: Ernest Hemingway," with George Plimpton, *Paris Review* 18 (1958): 84.

28. Jackson J. Benson, "Ernest Hemingway as Short Story Writer," in *The Short Stories of Ernest Hemingway*, ed. Jackson J. Benson (Durham, N.C.: Duke University Press, 1975), 285.

29. Robert Penn Warren, "Hemingway," *Kenyon Review* 9 (1947), 3–4.

Chapter Six. A Farewell to Arms: *Modern Response, Naturalistic Fate*

1. Carlos Baker, in *Hemingway: The Writer as Artist* (Princeton: Princeton University Press, 1963), was the first to note the symbolic division between the Abruzzi and the cafes of the cities—or what he termed "the Mountain and the Plain," or "the Home and Not-Home" (94–116). He astutely observed that the Mountain is associated with "the man of God and his homeland, with clear dry cold and snow, with polite and kindly people, with hospitality, and with natural beauty." The Plain, on the other hand, encompasses "the lowland obscenities of the priest-baiting captain, cheap cafés, one-night prostitutes, drunkenness, destruction, and the war" (103). Baker, however, views these symbolic associations only in general terms, not in naturalistic ones.

2. Hemingway, *A Farewell to Arms*, 71. Subsequent references to this edition are provided within the text.

3. Carlos Baker refers to Mt. Kilimanjaro as "a natural image of immortality." See Baker, *Writer as Artist*, 103.

4. For a very different interpretation of the significance of the Saint Anthony medallion, see Stoneback, "Lovers' Sonnets Turn'd to Holy Psalms," 49–51. Stoneback discusses the medallion in light of Catholic iconography, pointing out the ironic usage of Saint Anthony, a saint "chiefly invoked for the return of lost property, secondarily invoked for the protection of the pregnant, thirdly for protection of travellers" (50).

5. T. S. Eliot, "Sweeney Agonistes: Fragment of an Agon," in *Collected Poems: 1909–1962* (London: Faber and Faber, 1963), 130–36.

6. Carlos Baker refers to the rain as "a symbol of disaster." Malcolm Cowley calls it "a conscious symbol of disaster." And Robert Merrill views the rain as an omen that creates "tragic expectations." See Baker, *Writer as Artist*, 95; Cowley, "Introduction," in *The Portable Hemingway*, ed. Malcolm Cowley (New York: Viking, 1944), 16; Merrill, "Tragic Form in *A Farewell to Arms*," *American Literature* 45.4 (January 1974): 575.

7. Young comments: "This is really the old 'pathetic fallacy' put to new use, and—since there is no need to take it scientifically or philosophically, but simply as a subtle and unobtrusive device for unity—quite an acceptable one, too. Good and bad weather go along with good and bad moods and events. It is not just that, like everyone, the characters respond emotionally to conditions of atmosphere, light and so on, but that there is a correspondence between these things and their fate. They win when it's sunny, and lose in the rain." See Young, *Ernest Hemingway: A Reconsideration* (University Park: Pennsylvania State University Press, 1966), 92.

8. Richard Chase, *The American Novel and Its Tradition* (Garden City: Doubleday, 1957), 80.

9. Ray B. West, Jr., "The Unadulterated Sensibility," in *Twentieth Century Interpretations of "A Farewell to Arms,"* ed. Jay Gellens (Englewood Cliffs: Prentice-Hall, 1970), 23.

10. See Rene Girard, *Violence and the Sacred*, trans. Patrick Gregory (Baltimore: Johns Hopkins University Press, 1977), and Walter Burkert, *Homo Necans: The Anthropology of Ancient Greek Sacrificial Ritual and Myth*, trans. Peter Bing (Berkeley and Los Angeles: University of California Press, 1983).

11. James Nagel, in "Catherine Barkley and Retrospective Narration in *A Farewell to Arms*," in *Ernest Hemingway: Six Decades of Criticism*, ed. Linda W. Wagner (East Lansing: Michigan State University Press, 1987), 171–85, while focusing on what he calls the novel's "dual time scheme"—that is, the temporal division between the time of Frederic's narration and the events he is narrating (which Nagel places at approximately ten years)—also notes the obsession Frederic has with time, and how that obsession increases as his and Catherine's relationship progresses.

12. Robert E. Gajdusek, in "*A Farewell to Arms*: The Psychodynamics of Integrity," *Hemingway Review* 9.1 (Fall 1989): 26–32, notes the impossibility of an eternal "always": "Their 'always' must be accommodated to the rain and reality, and shown to be a fake absolute caught on a spinning wheel of season, time, and Fortune" (27).

13. Joyce Wexler, in "E.R.A. for Hemingway: A Feminist Defense of *A Farewell to Arms*," *Georgia Review* 35.1 (Spring 1981): 111–23, agrees that Catherine is Frederic's mentor, claiming that "Catherine is clearly presented as a forerunner of the

kind of person Frederic has become by the time he narrates the story of his wartime experiences. They are members of the same species, Hemingway heroes" (112–13). Wexler adds that Catherine "becomes Frederic's model of courage" (116), and that she teaches Frederic "how to be brave" (117). Sandra Whipple Spanier concurs, contending that Catherine is "the wiser, more experienced of the pair, whose role it is to educate Frederic Henry." Spanier also makes a strong argument for Catherine as the true "code hero" in the novel. Says Spanier: "Catherine Barkley not only is a strong and fully realized character, she is the one character in this novel who exemplifies in the widest range the controls of honor and courage, the 'grace under pressure' that have come to be known as the 'Hemingway code.' Her part is to teach Frederic Henry by example how to survive in a hostile and chaotic world in which an individual can gain at most a limited autonomy—through scrupulous adherence to roles and rituals of one's own devising. She is the code hero of this novel if anyone is." See Spanier, "Catherine Barkley and the Hemingway Code: Ritual and Survival in *A Farewell to Arms*," in *Modern Critical Interpretations: Ernest Hemingway's "A Farewell to Arms*," ed. Harold Bloom (New York: Chelsea House Publishers, 1987), 139, 132.

14. Carlos Baker calls Montreux "the closest approximation to the priest's fair homeland in the Abruzzi that they are ever to know." See Baker, *Writer as Artist*, 104.

15. Norman Friedman comes close to arguing that Catherine's death is "natural" by pointing to her "small hips" rather than the war as the primary cause. Robert Merrill, in his analysis of *A Farewell to Arms* as a modern tragedy, also argues that nature, or the universe, is the agent of destruction. He claims that "the assumption underlying this tragedy [*A Farewell to Arms*] is that the enemy is not only within— it is also out there, in the universe itself. In a sense, it *is* the universe, that dark and destructive context for all that happens in *A Farewell to Arms*." Judith Fetterley puts forth an opposing view. In her feminist critique, she makes the rather untenable argument that Catherine dies "because she is a woman"—that is, not so much a biological woman whose death is "natural," but a social/psychological woman who becomes the victim of male power. See Friedman, "Criticism and the Novel: Hardy, Hemingway, Crane, Woolf, Conrad," *Antioch Review* 18.3 (Fall 1958): 352–56; Merrill, "Tragic Form," 578; Fetterley, "*A Farewell to Arms*: Hemingway's 'Resentful Cryptogram,'" *Journal of Popular Culture* 10.1 (Summer 1976): 204.

16. It is interesting to note the irony of adding "The End" after the conclusion of the novel, something hackneyed in sentimental romances but quite pointed in this very unsentimental love story. Interestingly enough, Hemingway had also added it to the conclusion of *The Sun Also Rises*, another unsentimental love story, but left it out of *For Whom the Bell Tolls*—a very different novel in which the protagonist tells his lover just before they part, "I go always with thee wherever thou goest. . . . As

long as there is one of us there is both of us." See Hemingway, *For Whom the Bell Tolls* (New York: Scribners, 1940), 463.

Chapter Seven. The Sun Also Rises: *Learning to Live in a Naturalistic World*

1. Hemingway, *The Sun Also Rises*, 97. Subsequent references to this edition are provided within the text.

2. For a thorough discussion of the economic/financial metaphor that runs throughout the novel, see Scott Donaldson, "Hemingway's Morality of Compensation," *American Literature* 43.3 (November 1971): 399-420.

3. Mark Spilka has noted that in this scene fishing is "given an edge over religion." See Mark Spilka, "The Death of Love in *The Sun Also Rises*," in *Modern Critical Interpretations: Hemingway's "The Sun Also Rises*," ed. Harold Bloom (New York: Chelsea House Publishers, 1987), 31.

4. Ernest Hemingway, *Ernest Hemingway: Selected Letters, 1917–1961*, ed. Carlos Baker (New York: Scribners, 1981), 229.

5. Richard Lehan, *A Dangerous Crossing: French Literary Existentialism and the Modern American Novel* (Carbondale: Southern Illinois University Press, 1973), 47.

6. For a different view of Brett and her behavior, see Wendy Martin, "Brett Ashley as New Woman in *The Sun Also Rises*," in *New Essays on "The Sun Also Rises*," ed. Linda Wagner-Martin (Cambridge: Cambridge University Press, 1987), 65–82. Martin examines Brett in a social and cultural, rather than naturalistic, context, making the case for her as a "self-reliant modern woman" (71).

7. Allen Josephs, in *"Toreo:* The Moral Axis of *The Sun Also Rises*," *Hemingway Review* 6.1 (Fall 1986): 88–99, argues that the fiesta embodies a primitive spiritualism that is closely connected to natural process.

8. Mark Spilka calls Cohn "the last chivalric hero, the last defender of an outworn faith [romance], and his function is to illustrate its present folly—to show us, through the absurdity of his behavior, that romantic love is dead, that one of the great guiding codes of the past no longer operates." See Spilka, "Death of Love," 27.

9. Mark Spilka was the first to note this connection; he refers to Jake as "a restrained romantic, a man who carries himself well in the face of love's impossibilities, but who seems to share with Cohn a common (if hidden) weakness." See Spilka, "Death of Love," 28.

10. Hemingway, *Death in the Afternoon*, 259. For discussions of the spiritual aspect of bullfighting—its connection to pagan and Christian ritual—see Josephs, *"Toreo"*; Stoneback, "From the rue Saint-Jacques," 2–29; Peter L. Hays, "Hunting Ritual in *The Sun Also Rises*," *Hemingway Review* 8.2 (Spring 1989): 46–48.

11. Allen Josephs makes this important distinction between the bullfighter and

the bullfight, Romero and his *metier:* "It is *toreo* itself, the *art* of *toreo* [as opposed to Romero himself], that is at the core of *The Sun Also Rises.*" See Josephs, *"Toreo,"* 92.

12. Hemingway, *Death in the Afternoon,* 54.

13. Hemingway, "The Art of Fiction XXI," 66.

14. Hemingway, *Death in the Afternoon,* 213.

15. Hemingway, "Art of Fiction," 84.

16. Wayne C. Booth, *The Rhetoric of Fiction* (Chicago: University of Chicago Press, 1961), 299.

17. Carlos Baker quotes Maxwell Perkins on *The Sun Also Rises* and its satire of romantic novels. Perkins called *The Sun Also Rises* "a healthy book, with marked satirical implications upon novels which are not—sentimentalized, subjective novels, marked by sloppy hazy thought." See Baker, Writer as Artist, 86.

Chapter Eight. *Fields, Systems, and DeLillo's Postmodern Transformation of Literary Naturalism*

1. Zola, *The Experimental Novel and Other Essays,* 17.

2. Ibid., 26.

3. LeConte, *Evolution,* 354.

4. Ibid., 356.

5. N. Katherine Hayles, *The Cosmic Web: Scientific Field Models and Literary Strategies in the Twentieth Century* (Ithaca: Cornell University Press, 1984).

6. Ibid., 9–10.

7. Ibid., 24.

8. Ibid., 20.

9. Werner Heisenberg, *Physics and Philosophy: The Revolution in Modern Science* (New York: Harper, 1958), 29. Subsequent references to this edition are provided within the text.

10. Hayles, *Cosmic Web,* 39.

11. Ludwig von Bertalanffy, *General System Theory: Foundations, Developments, Applications* (New York: Braziller, 1968), 5. Subsequent references to this edition are provided within the text.

12. Tom LeClair, *In the Loop: Don DeLillo and the Systems Novel* (Urbana: University of Illinois Press, 1987), 3.

13. Ibid., 6.

14. Quoted in *Anything Can Happen,* ed. Tom LeClair (Urbana: University of Illinois Press, 1983), 80.

Chapter Nine. End Zone: *The End of the Old Order*

1. Robert Nadeau notes that, in *End Zone*, DeLillo draws "extensive parallels between the game [i.e., football] as exemplar of all closed systems used in the construction of human reality, and the nuclear defense system." See Nadeau, *Readings from the New Book on Nature: Physics and Metaphysics in the Modern Novel* (Amherst: University of Massachusetts Press, 1981), 165.

2. Don DeLillo, *End Zone* (New York: Penguin, 1972), 7. Subsequent references to this edition are provided within the text.

3. Quoted in *Anything Can Happen*, 81.

4. Ibid.

5. Hayles, *Cosmic Web*, 20.

6. LeClair, *In the Loop*, 3.

Chapter Ten. Libra: *Undoing the Naturalistic Novel*

1. Don DeLillo, *Libra* (New York: Viking, 1988), 14. Subsequent references to this edition are provided within the text.

2. Hayles, *Cosmic Web*, 24.

3. Don DeLillo, "'An Outsider in This Society': An Interview with Don DeLillo," with Anthony DeCurtis, *South Atlantic Quarterly* 89 (1990): 294.

4. See Frank Lentricchia, "The American Writer as Bad Citizen — Introducing Don DeLillo," *South Atlantic Quarterly* 89.2 (Spring 1990): 239-44. Lentricchia cites Will, Jonathan Yardley, and "a *New Criterion* puppet" (242) among the many reviewers of *Libra* who attacked DeLillo for his unpatriotic social irresponsibility.

5. Lentricchia notes in "*Libra* as Postmodern Critique," *South Atlantic Quarterly* 89.2 (Spring 1990): 431-53, that *Libra*, among other things, is a "transformation of naturalism's traditional social scene of determination" (437). Lentricchia, however, contends that the naturalistic determinants of heredity and environment have been replaced in *Libra*, and in the postmodern world, by "the charismatic environment of the image" (436) — that is, by the various forms of media representation. Oswald, for example, is determined by "Hollywood's image factories" (437), which create and reinforce his desire to be someone else — to move, in Lentricchia's words, from the first to the third person. While the media image is certainly an important force in Oswald's life and goes a long way toward shaping his identity, I do not think DeLillo is merely replacing one set of determining factors with another. Rather, he is demonstrating that there are a plethora of factors, none of which can be isolated.

6. Zola, *L'Assommoir*, 21.

7. DeLillo, "Outsider in This Society," 299.

8. Ibid., 286.

9. Indeed, such a science has been discovered: the new science of "chaos" or "chaos theory." For background, see James Gleick, *Chaos: Making a New Science* (New York: Penguin, 1987). For a study of the relationship between chaos theory and contemporary literature, see N. Katherine Hayles, *Chaos Bound: Orderly Disorder in Contemporary Literature and Science* (Ithaca: Cornell University Press, 1990); and Hayles, ed., *Chaos and Order: Complex Dynamics in Literature and Science* (Chicago: University of Chicago Press, 1991).

10. DeLillo, "Outsider in This Society," 294.

11. Hayles, *Cosmic Web*, 22.

12. DeLillo, "Outsider in This Society," 286–87.

13. Ibid., 295.

14. Ibid., 289.

15. Bertalanffy, *General System Theory*, 116.

WORKS CITED

Ahnebrink, Lars. *The Beginnings of Naturalism in American Fiction.* Cambridge, Mass.: Harvard University Press, 1950.

———. *The Influence of Emile Zola on Frank Norris.* 1947. Cambridge, Mass.: Harvard University Press, 1976.

Baker, Carlos. *Hemingway: The Writer as Artist.* Princeton, N.J.: Princeton University Press, 1963.

Benson, Jackson J. "Ernest Hemingway as Short Story Writer." In *The Short Stories of Ernest Hemingway: Critical Essays,* edited by Jackson J. Benson, 272–310. Durham, N.C.: Duke University Press, 1975.

Bertalanffy, Ludwig von. *General System Theory: Foundations, Developments, Applications.* New York: Braziller, 1968.

Boas, Franz. *The Mind of Primitive Man.* New York: Macmillan, 1911.

Booth, Wayne C. *The Rhetoric of Fiction.* Chicago, Ill.: University of Chicago Press, 1961.

Brace, Charles Loring. *The Dangerous Classes of New York, and Twenty Years' Work Among Them.* 1872. Montclair, N.J.: Patterson Smith, 1967.

Burkert, Walter. *Homo Necans: The Anthropology of Ancient Greek Sacrificial Ritual and Myth.* Translated by Peter Bing. Berkeley and Los Angeles: University of California Press, 1983.

Burkhardt, Richard W., Jr. *The Spirit of System: Lamarck and Evolutionary Biology.* Cambridge, Mass.: Harvard University Press, 1977.

Burns, Stuart L. "The Rapist in Frank Norris's *The Octopus.*" *American Literature* 42.4 (January 1971): 567–69.

Cady, Edwin H. *The Light of Common Day: Realism in American Fiction.* Bloomington: Indiana University Press, 1971.

Chase, Richard. *The American Novel and Its Tradition.* Garden City, N.Y.: Doubleday, 1957.

Conder, John J. *Naturalism in American Fiction: The Classic Phase.* Lexington: University of Kentucky Press, 1984.

Cowley, Malcolm. Introduction to *The Portable Hemingway*, edited by Malcolm Cowley. New York: Viking, 1944.

Crow, Charles L. "Gnawing the File: Recent Trends in *McTeague* Scholarship." *Frank Norris Studies* 13 (Spring 1992): 1–5.

Darwin, Charles. *The Descent of Man, and Selection in Relation to Sex*. 1871. London: John Murray, 1875.

———. *The Origin of Species*. 1859. New York: Penguin, 1968.

Davison, Richard Allan. "Frank Norris's *The Octopus:* Some Observations on Vanamee, Shelgrim, and St. Paul." In *Critical Essays on Frank Norris*, edited by Don Graham, 99–115. Boston, Mass.: G. K. Hall, 1980.

Degler, Carl N. *In Search of Human Nature: The Decline and Revival of Darwinism in American Social Thought*. New York: Oxford University Press, 1991.

DeLillo, Don. *End Zone*. New York: Penguin, 1972.

———. *Libra*. New York: Viking, 1988.

———. "'An Outsider in This Society': An Interview with Don DeLillo." With Anthony DeCurtis. *South Atlantic Quarterly* 89 (1990): 281–304.

———. *White Noise*. New York: Viking, 1985.

de Vries, Hugo. *The Mutation Theory: Experiments and Observations on the Origin of Species in the Vegetable Kingdom*. Translated by A. D. Darbishire and J. B. Farmer. Chicago, Ill.: Open Court Publishing Company, 1909.

Dewey, John. "The Influence of Darwin on Philosophy." *The Influence of Darwin on Philosophy, and Other Essays in Contemporary Thought*. New York: Holt, 1910. Reprinted in *Darwin*, edited by Philip Appleman, 393–402. New York: Norton, 1970.

Donaldson, Scott. "Hemingway's Morality of Compensation." *American Literature* 43.3 (November 1971): 399–420.

Duncan, Charles. "'If Your View Be Large Enough': Narrative Growth in *The Octopus*." *American Literary Realism, 1870–1910* 25.2 (Winter 1993): 56–66.

Dunn, L. C. *A Short History of Genetics: The Development of Some of the Main Lines of Thought, 1864–1939*. New York: McGraw-Hill, 1965.

Eliot, T. S. "Sweeney Agonistes: Fragment of an Agon." In *Collected Poems: 1909–1962*, 130–36. London: Faber and Faber, 1963.

Elliot, Hugh Samuel Roger. *Herbert Spencer*. 1917. Freeport, N.Y.: Books for Libraries Press, 1970.

Fetterley, Judith. "*A Farewell to Arms:* Hemingway's 'Resentful Cryptogram.'" *Journal of Popular Culture* 10.1 (Summer 1976): 203–14.

Frazer, Sir James George. *The Golden Bough: A Study in Magic and Religion*. 1922. New York: Macmillan, 1963.

Friedman, Norman. "Criticism and the Novel: Hardy, Hemingway, Crane, Woolf, Conrad." *Antioch Review* 18.3 (Fall 1958): 343–70.

Gajdusek, Robert E. "*A Farewell to Arms:* The Psychodynamics of Integrity." *Hemingway Review* 9.1 (Fall 1989): 26–32.

Girard, Rene. *Violence and the Sacred.* Translated by Patrick Gregory. Baltimore, Md.: Johns Hopkins University Press, 1977.

Gleick, James. *Chaos: Making a New Science.* New York: Penguin, 1987.

Graham, Don. *The Fiction of Frank Norris: The Aesthetic Context.* Columbia: University of Missouri Press, 1978.

Gray, Asa. *Darwiniana: Essays and Reviews Pertaining to Darwinism.* Edited by A. Hunter Dupree. Cambridge, Mass.: Harvard University Press, 1963.

Hayles, N. Katherine. *Chaos Bound: Orderly Disorder in Contemporary Literature and Science.* Ithaca, N.Y.: Cornell University Press, 1990.

———. *The Cosmic Web: Scientific Field Models and Literary Strategies in the Twentieth Century.* Ithaca, N.Y.: Cornell University Press, 1984.

Hayles, N. Katherine, ed. *Chaos and Order: Complex Dynamics in Literature and Science.* Chicago, Ill.: University of Chicago Press, 1991.

Hays, Peter L. "Hunting Ritual in *The Sun Also Rises.*" *Hemingway Review* 8.2 (Spring 1989): 46–48.

Heisenberg, Werner. *Physics and Philosophy: The Revolution in Modern Science.* New York: Harper, 1958.

Hemingway, Ernest. "The Art of Fiction XXI: Ernest Hemingway." With George Plimpton. *Paris Review* 18 (1958): 61–89.

———. "A Clean, Well-Lighted Place." In *Winner Take Nothing.* New York: Scribners, 1933. 13–17.

———. *Death in the Afternoon.* New York: Scribners, 1932.

———. *Ernest Hemingway: Selected Letters, 1917–1961.* Edited by Carlos Baker. New York: Scribners, 1981.

———. *A Farewell to Arms.* New York: Scribners, 1929.

———. *For Whom the Bell Tolls.* New York: Scribners, 1940.

———. *The Sun Also Rises.* New York: Scribners, 1926.

Hochman, Barbara. *The Art of Frank Norris, Storyteller.* Columbia: University of Missouri Press, 1988.

Howard, June. *Form and History in American Literary Naturalism.* Chapel Hill: University of North Carolina Press, 1985.

Josephs, Allen. "*Toreo:* The Moral Axis of *The Sun Also Rises.*" *Hemingway Review* 6.1 (Fall 1986): 88–99.

Jung, Carl. *The Portable Jung.* Edited by Joseph Campbell. New York: Penguin, 1971.

Kaplan, Harold. *Power and Order: Henry Adams and the Naturalist Tradition in American Fiction*. Chicago, Ill.: University of Chicago Press, 1981.

Kroeber, Alfred L. "The Superorganic." *American Anthropologist* 19.2 (April–June 1917): 163–213.

Lamarck, Jean-Baptiste. *Zoological Philosophy*. Translated by Hugh Elliot. Chicago, Ill.: University of Chicago Press, 1984.

LeClair, Tom. *Anything Can Happen*. Urbana: University of Illinois Press, 1983.

——— . *In the Loop: Don DeLillo and the Systems Novel*. Urbana: University of Illinois Press, 1987.

LeConte, Joseph. *Evolution: Its Nature, Its Evidences, and Its Relation to Religious Thought*. 1888. New York: D. Appleton and Co., 1908.

Lehan, Richard. "American Literary Naturalism: The French Connection." *Nineteenth Century Fiction* 38.4 (1984): 529–57.

——— . *A Dangerous Crossing: French Literary Existentialism and the Modern American Novel*. Carbondale: Southern Illinois University Press, 1973.

——— . *Theodore Dreiser: His World and His Novels*. Carbondale: Southern Illinois University Press, 1969.

——— . "The Theoretical Limits of the New Historicism." *New Literary History* 21.3 (Spring 1990): 533–53.

Lentricchia, Frank. "The American Writer as Bad Citizen—Introducing Don DeLillo." *South Atlantic Quarterly* 89.2 (Spring 1990): 239–44.

——— . "*Libra* as Postmodern Critique." *South Atlantic Quarterly* 89.2 (Spring 1990): 431–53.

Lyell, Charles. *Principles of Geology; or, The Modern Changes of the Earth and Its Inhabitants*. 9th ed. New York: D. Appleton and Co., 1853.

McElrath, Joseph R., Jr. "Frank Norris: A Biographical Essay." *American Literary Realism, 1870–1910* 11.2 (Autumn 1978): 219–34.

——— . *Frank Norris Revisited*. New York: Twayne Publishers, 1992.

——— . "Frank Norris's *The Octopus:* The Christian Ethic as Pragmatic Response." In *Critical Essays on Frank Norris*, edited by Don Graham, 138–52. Boston, Mass.: G. K. Hall, 1980.

——— . "Frank Norris's *Vandover and the Brute:* Narrative Technique and the Socio-Critical Viewpoint." *Studies in American Fiction* 4.1 (Spring 1976): 27–43.

Malthus, Thomas Robert. *An Essay on the Principle of Population*. 1798. Edited by Philip Appleman. New York: Norton, 1976.

Martin, Ronald E. *American Literature and the Universe of Force*. Durham, N.C.: Duke University Press, 1981.

Martin, Wendy. "Brett Ashley as New Woman in *The Sun Also Rises.*" In *New Essays on "The Sun Also Rises,"* edited by Linda Wagner-Martin, 65–82. Cambridge, Eng.: Cambridge University Press, 1987.

Mendel, Gregor. *Experiments in Plant Hybridisation.* Translated by the Royal Horticultural Society of London. Cambridge, Mass.: Harvard University Press, 1965.

Merrill, Robert. "Tragic Form in *A Farewell to Arms.*" *American Literature* 45.4 (January 1974): 571–79.

Michaels, Walter Benn. *The Gold Standard and the Logic of Naturalism.* Berkeley and Los Angeles: University of California Press, 1987.

Mitchell, Lee Clark. *Determined Fictions: American Literary Naturalism.* New York: Columbia University Press, 1989.

Nadeau, Robert. *Readings from the New Book on Nature: Physics and Metaphysics in the Modern Novel.* Amherst: University of Massachusetts Press, 1981.

Nagel, James. "Catherine Barkley and Retrospective Narration in *A Farewell to Arms.* In *Ernest Hemingway: Six Decades of Criticism,* edited by Linda W. Wagner, 171–85. East Lansing: Michigan State University Press, 1987.

Nietzsche, Friedrich. *Ecce Homo.* 1888. Translated by R. J. Hollingdale. New York: Penguin, 1979.

———. *Thus Spoke Zarathustra.* 1892. Translated by Walter Kaufmann. New York: Penguin, 1954.

Norris, Frank. *The Literary Criticism of Frank Norris.* Edited by Donald Pizer. Austin: University of Texas Press, 1964.

———. *The Octopus.* 1901. New York: Penguin, 1986.

———. *The Pit.* New York: Doubleday, Page, 1903.

———. *Vandover and the Brute.* 1914. Garden City, N.Y.: Doubleday, Page, 1928.

Peckham, Morse. "Darwinism and Darwinisticism." *Victorian Studies* 3.1 (September 1959): 19–40.

Pizer, Donald. *The Novels of Frank Norris.* Bloomington: Indiana University Press, 1966.

———. *Realism and Naturalism in Nineteenth-Century American Literature.* Carbondale: Southern Illinois University Press, 1966.

———. *Twentieth-Century American Literary Naturalism: An Interpretation.* Carbondale: Southern Illinois University Press, 1982.

Pound, Ezra. "Hugh Selwyn Mauberley." In *Selected Poems of Ezra Pound,* 61–64. New York: New Directions, 1957.

Russett, Cynthia Eagle. *Darwin in America: The Intellectual Response, 1865–1912.* San Francisco, Calif.: W. H. Freeman, 1976.

Seltzer, Mark. "The Naturalist Machine." In *Sex, Politics, and Science in the Nineteenth-Century Novel*, edited by Ruth Bernard Yeazell, 116–47. Baltimore, Md.: Johns Hopkins University Press, 1986.

Spanier, Sandra Whipple. "Catherine Barkley and the Hemingway Code: Ritual and Survival in *A Farewell to Arms.*" In *Modern Critical Interpretations: Ernest Hemingway's "A Farewell to Arms,"* edited by Harold Bloom, 131–48. New York: Chelsea House Publishers, 1987.

Spencer, Herbert. *First Principles.* 1862. New York: D. Appleton and Co., 1864.

Spilka, Mark. "The Death of Love in *The Sun Also Rises.*" In *Modern Critical Interpretations: Hemingway's "The Sun Also Rises,"* edited by Harold Bloom, 25–37. New York: Chelsea House Publishers, 1987.

Stoneback, H. R. "From the rue Saint-Jacques to the Pass of Roland to the 'Unfinished Church on the Edge of the Cliff.'" *Hemingway Review* 6.1 (Fall 1986): 2–29.

———. "In the Nominal Country of the Bogus: Hemingway's Catholicism and the Biographies." In *Hemingway: Essays of Reassessment*, edited by Frank Scafella, 105–40. New York: Oxford University Press, 1991.

———. "Lovers' Sonnets Turn'd to Holy Psalms: The Soul's Song of Providence, the Scandal of Suffering, and Love in *A Farewell to Arms.*" *Hemingway Review* 9.1 (Fall 1989): 33–76.

Walcutt, Charles Child. *American Literary Naturalism: A Divided Stream.* Minneapolis: University of Minnesota Press, 1956. Reprint. Westport, Conn: Greenwood, 1973.

Warren, Robert Penn. "Hemingway." *Kenyon Review* 9 (1947): 1–28.

West, Ray B., Jr. "The Unadulterated Sensibility." In *Twentieth Century Interpretations of "A Farewell to Arms,"* edited by Jay Gellens, 15–27. Englewood Cliffs, N.J.: Prentice-Hall, 1970.

Wexler, Joyce. "E.R.A. for Hemingway: A Feminist Defense of *A Farewell to Arms.*" *Georgia Review* 35.1 (Spring 1981): 111–23.

Young, Philip. *Ernest Hemingway: A Reconsideration.* University Park: Pennsylvania State University Press, 1966.

Ziff, Larzer. *The American 1890s: Life and Times of a Lost Generation.* New York: Viking Press, 1966.

Zola, Emile. *L'Assommoir.* 1876. Translated by Leonard Tancock. New York: Penguin, 1970.

———. *The Experimental Novel and Other Essays.* Translated by Belle M. Sherman. New York: Haskell House, 1964.

INDEX